Praise for *Race Against Time*

"In *Race Against Time: The Politics of a Darkening America*, Keith Boykin provides us with the insights of someone who is an eyewitness to history. This is history we have made together and lessons Boykin recommends to help shape the future."

— Donna Brazile, former chair of the Democratic
National Committee

"In evocative fashion, and through the depth of his personal experiences at the highest levels of American politics, Keith Boykin traces the parameters of America's 'never-ending civil war,' from the shock of Clinton's Black-voter-driven presidency though Bush and Obama and the white nationalist nightmare of Donald Trump. *Race Against Time* is essential reading at a calamitous time."

— Joy Reid, host of MSNBC's *The ReidOut*

"With clear insights and provocative analysis, Keith Boykin showcases why he is one of the country's foremost experts on race and politics in America. This book is timely, relevant, and important."

— Leah Wright Rigueur, associate research professor at
Johns Hopkins University

"*Race Against Time* is Keith Boykin's best book yet in a long list of books and anthologies that have helped define what cultural criticism is. This book is also an account of what it means to be overlooked in a capitalist landscape that denies the existence and contribution of Black queer citizens. What floors me is that Boykin's genius— from all the political and racial history from Reconstruction onward, to his well-wrought recounting of the antics of US presidents from Reagan to Trump—still allows him to remain a man of hope and a writer that affirms the spirit in essays that speak to us as a comforting brother would."

— Jericho Brown, author of *The Tradition*

RACE AGAINST TIME

RACE AGAINST TIME

THE POLITICS OF A DARKENING AMERICA

KEITH BOYKIN

BOLD TYPE BOOKS

New York

Bold Type Books
116 East 16th Street, 8th Floor, New York, NY 10003
www.boldtypebooks.org
@BoldTypeBooks

Printed in the United States of America

First Edition: September 2021

Published by Bold Type Books, an imprint of Perseus Books, LLC, a subsidiary of Hachette Book Group, Inc. Bold Type Books is a co-publishing venture of the Type Media Center and Perseus Books.

The Hachette Speakers Bureau provides a wide range of authors for speaking events. To find out more, go to www.hachettespeakersbureau.com or call (866) 376-6591.

The publisher is not responsible for websites (or their content) that are not owned by the publisher.

Print book interior design by Trish Wilkinson

Library of Congress Cataloging-in-Publication Data
Names: Boykin, Keith, author.
Title: Race against time : the politics of a darkening America / Keith Boykin.
Description: First edition. | New York, NY : PublicAffairs ; New York, NY : Bold Type Books, 2021.
Identifiers: LCCN 2021006571 | ISBN 9781645037262 (hardcover) | ISBN 9781645037293 (ebook)
Subjects: LCSH: Racism—United States—History. | African Americans—Politics and government—21st century. | African Americans—Social conditions—21st century. | United States—Race relations—21st century. | United States—Politics and government—21st century.
Classification: LCC E184.A1 B695 2021 | DDC 305.800973—dc23
LC record available at https://lccn.loc.gov/2021006571

ISBNs: 978-1-64503-726-2 (hardcover), 978-1-64503-729-3 (ebook)

LSC-C

Printing 1, 2021

CONTENTS

Introduction

OUR WEARY YEAR

The year began in a cold, dreary vestibule of a former women's prison in Mexico City. A few minutes past midnight in the first hour of 2020, I walked through an open cage, past a row of locked jail cells and into the unusual venue of the New Year's Eve party to which I had been invited. I watched young people in jeans and T-shirts dancing to house music and nonbinary stage performers gyrating their bodies on pedestals. This was not the Mexico of the American-tourist stereotypes of mariachi bands and wide-brimmed sombreros. Nor was it the Mexico that America's current president had described when he first launched his campaign. It was a country that was evolving with modern times, much like ours, and it reminded me just how much that change frightened so many people in my own country.

I had not expected to start the new year in this space, but like so much of what would happen in 2020, things did not work out as planned. Twelve months of covering an unwieldy Democratic presidential campaign and a pre-Christmas presidential impeachment left me racing to catch my breath in the final days of December 2019. As a reward to myself, I booked a trip to Mexico to relax and prepare

1

for the year to come. I was eager to try a nontraditional celebration venue as a symbol of my openness to the possibilities of a new year, and as I walked from one dark caged room to another, I interpreted my New Year's Eve adventure as a sign that the year ahead might also be filled with exhilarating new experiences. But, perhaps, I considered later, it was actually an omen that I would soon find myself in jail.

Some time after I woke up from my hangover on New Year's Day, my travel partners convinced me to take an Uber to the Lindavista neighborhood for yet another unusual activity. This involved a Mexican shaman who cleansed my body with burning sage and instructed me to kneel in front of an igloo-shaped heat lodge and ask Ōmeteōtl, the god of duality, for permission to enter the temazcal. I had never heard of any of these things before, but I gamely went along, crawling shirtless into the cramped space of the igloo until the tiny doors were closed, and I found myself suffocating from the hot, stifling steam of the volcanic rock in the pitch-black chamber.

A few minutes into the ceremony, I panicked and demanded to leave. The shaman tried to calm my nerves, but I was too frightened to relax. I clumsily stepped over the four other people in the temazcal, crawled my way out the door, and exhaled when I finally stood alone in the daylight. When the shaman came out to check on me later, I explained that I have claustrophobia and could not return for the remainder of the forty-minute ceremony. We had a brief discussion and negotiated a compromise. I agreed to return, but only if I could sit closest to the exit with my hand on the door. That simple technique allowed me to relax and survive the remainder of the ordeal. I had no idea at the time, but this experience would also serve as a valuable lesson for the calm I would need to call upon to face the challenges of 2020.

Two days later, I loaded my bags into a car to the airport, as the trip came to an end. I knew I was returning to political drama in the United States that I had successfully avoided for seven days, but I did not know that I, along with everyone else on the planet, would soon find myself unable to travel to international destinations. As the car drove past Parque México, I said goodbye to my peaceful week in our rental apartment in the quiet neighborhood of La Condesa, and I braced myself for the year to come.

Shortly after I arrived home in New York, I started feeling the effects of a strange illness so serious that it left me contemplating my own mortality. For several days, I left the door of my Harlem apartment locked but unlatched in case a friend with a key needed to rescue and transport me to the hospital. With the aid of the Internet, I self-diagnosed my condition as everything from cancer to Montezuma's Revenge, but I stubbornly refused to see a doctor because I had forgotten to renew my health insurance on the Affordable Care Act exchange. I would be without coverage until February 1.

I blamed myself for becoming so distracted with the impeachment coverage that I forgot to take care of my own needs. Surely, my self-indulgent vacation was the root cause of my sickness, I thought, and I hoped a quick detox and convalescence would cure me. It took two weeks for my condition to improve, but it would take another two months before I would suspect a more alarming explanation for what had happened—that I might have been afflicted with a strange new virus that the world would soon come to know intimately.

During those days of rest and recovery, I also dreaded the exhaustion the next twelve months would bring. I expected that 2020 would be dominated by two stories—an impeachment trial in January and a presidential election in November—and I knew how demanding both of those experiences could be. Only three US presidents had been impeached in history. I had lived through two of those impeachments, and I remembered how the previous Senate trial consumed the nation for five weeks in the winter of 1999. I also remembered that even the most routine election is a monumental undertaking. Having worked on half a dozen political campaigns as an activist and covered six presidential campaigns as a journalist, I thought I knew exactly what to expect—the caucuses, the primaries, the rallies, the conventions, the debates, and the campaign ads, all conducted at the lightning-fast speed of an unrelenting news cycle. What I did not know was that the country was about to experience a dramatic convulsion.

Four cataclysmic crises were about to converge at once. First, we would be thrust into a deadly public health emergency worse than any outbreak since the Flu Epidemic of 1918. At the same time, we would plunge into an economic crisis more disruptive than any recession since the Great Depression began in 1929. Third, a racial justice movement would emerge larger than any since the protests after Dr. Martin Luther King Jr. was assassinated in 1968. And, finally, we would end the year in a crisis of democracy unlike anything seen in America since the disputed presidential election of 1876. This was not just a once-in-a-century confluence of events; it was a unique moment in our history. Four gigantic tectonic plates would shift at the same time in America, putting into grave doubt the health of our people, the stability of our economy, the safety of our most vulnerable citizens, and the survival of our democracy. The result would shake the foundation of our nation.

Of course, these crises were not simply the fallout of one epic year. They were the outgrowth of a longer national history of a broken health care system, an unfair economic structure, the failure to remedy centuries-old constitutional flaws, and, most threatening of all, the perpetuation of white supremacy. Yet, at some level, they all had to do with race.

This book examines the politics of our darkening America in three parts. In part one, I discuss the four crises of 2020 and how they led to the capitol insurrection of 2021. In part two, I go back in time to explore America's racist political history and the realignment of the two dominant political parties from the Reconstruction era to the present. And in part three, I propose ideas to move forward.

I argue that the problem of racism in American politics transcends specific political parties and leaders. From the end of Reconstruction in 1877 until the Civil Rights Act of 1964, both major political parties failed Black people. The Republican Party of Abraham Lincoln reneged on its promise to protect African Americans, while the racist Democratic Party of Andrew Jackson didn't even bother to try. But as the Democrats slowly began to evolve in the 1960s, one could draw a straight line in the Republican Party from Goldwater's opposition to civil rights in 1964 to Nixon's "Law and Order" and "War on Drugs" campaigns in 1968 and 1971 to Reagan's "Welfare Queen" and "States' Rights" campaigns in 1976 and 1980 to George H. W. Bush's "Willie Horton" attacks in 1988 to Pat Buchanan's "Culture War" speech in 1992 to George W. Bush's response to Hurricane Katrina in 2005 to Donald Trump's birther campaign against President Barack Obama in 2011 and his politics of overt white nationalism through 2021. At the heart of the racism of the old Democratic Party and the devolution of the Republican Party was the same concern—the fear of a changing America and the end of white supremacy.

"This world is white no longer, and it will never be white again," James Baldwin wrote in 1955. Those prescient words from *Notes of a Native Son* ring truer today than ever before. As America has become blacker and browner, influential forces have tried to turn back the clock to stop the inevitable diversification and potential transformation of the country. From the eighteenth-century founding of the republic to the nineteenth-century Reconstruction era to the twentieth-century civil rights movement, the fear of the collapse of the white state has animated what historian Carol Anderson has appropriately called "white rage." Throughout a long history of racial upheaval, the trigger for this rage, she wrote, has inevitably been Black advancement. By the time America entered the twenty-first century, each new election cycle and census report left many white citizens so threatened by the nation's changing demographics that they were willing to enact new restrictive policies to stop the rise of an emerging new majority.

The white rage grew more urgent in 2008 with the election of the first Black president. Although nothing in his proposed platform or his executed policies threatened to restructure race in America, his mere presence signaled a new American future. Those who worried about that future found comfort in his successor, aptly described by author Ta-Nehisi Coates as "America's first white president."

In March 2015, three months before Donald Trump announced his presidential campaign, the US Census Bureau projected that America would become a "majority-minority" nation in 2044. And even though white Americans had engineered systems to maintain disproportionate power in the new multiracial democracy, many were still determined to stop this symbolic loss of status. For four years, Donald Trump gave them what they wanted. He governed with the most overt brand of white identity politics of any president in my lifetime, engaging an energetic minority of fearful whites in a last-ditch race against time to stop the progress of newly empowered "minorities" and their allies.

By the end of his final year in office, a cold civil war was well underway.

Fueled by their commander-in-chief, citizen soldiers enlisted in a relentless series of daily skirmishes of microaggressions, racial profiling, shouting matches, and hate crimes, often broadcast on social media and television, and all foreshadowing a larger and more perilous battle looming beyond the horizon.

These are dangerous times.

Despite some signs of progress, America's story has always been a complicated one, with years of despair and disappointment punctuated by moments of hope and optimism. The same country that enabled state-sanctioned slavery and segregation would one day adopt constitutional amendments and civil rights laws to end those evil institutions. And the same republic that was forged for white men would one day elect a Black man as president and a Black woman as vice president. Nonetheless, each step forward for African Americans threatened to undermine a delicate social order established centuries ago.

When white indentured servants partnered with enslaved Black people in colonial America to resist the socioeconomic hierarchy, planters responded by "luring whiteness away from blackness," Ibram X. Kendi writes in his book, *Stamped from the Beginning: The Definitive History of Racist Ideas in America.* By the time Nathaniel Bacon led a rebellion against the ruling elite of Jamestown, Virginia, in 1675, the planter class was so alarmed by his multiracial coalition of rebels that it developed a scheme to co-opt lower-income whites by separating them from African Americans.

Michelle Alexander, in her book, *The New Jim Crow: Mass Incarceration in the Age of Colorblindness*, has called this scheme a "racial bribe," which provided "special privileges to poor whites in an effort to drive a wedge between them and Black slaves." These privileges would eventually give white Americans what legal scholar Derrick Bell has called a "property right in their 'whiteness.'" As Bell explains, "Even those whites who lack wealth and power are sustained in their sense of racial superiority and thus rendered more willing to accept their lesser share."

Over time, this "racial bribe" would expand into a broader strategy to invite other racial and ethnic groups to advance "by becoming 'white,'" Lani Guinier and Gerald Torres write in *The Miner's Canary: Enlisting Race, Resisting Power, and Transforming Democracy.* But there was a catch. To do so, Guinier and Torres explain, they would have to maintain their "social distance from blackness."

Guinier and Torres published their book in 2002, but the words "social distance" ring differently in the postpandemic world after the coronavirus. For the majority of 2020 and a significant period of 2021, many of us would remain socially isolated, quarantined in our homes, hidden behind masks, and sheltered from normal human contact. This necessary but unnatural social distancing, no doubt, impeded our ability to connect with one another and literally prevented us from seeing each other as human beings.

At the very moment our divided union desperately needed leadership, with four concurrent crises threatening to tear apart the social fabric, we instead got opportunism and demagoguery. Instead of solutions for the health care crisis, we got racist virus blaming, unproven treatments, and antimask messages. Instead of monthly assistance for those struggling through the economic crisis, we got antilockdown protests and attacks on mayors and governors who tried to protect their citizens. Instead of dealing with the racial justice crisis, we got "law and order" tweets, rants about left-wing "terrorist organizations," and a cynical photo op outside a church near the White House. And instead of dealing with the crisis of democracy, we got a slowdown of mail service, a refusal to accept the election results, and an insurrection at the US Capitol.

Rather than bring us together, America's president and his enablers used the crises of the moment to exploit the long-standing fears of their majority-white base of voters. Even after Donald Trump had left office, they continued directing their energy to frivolous complaints about "cancel culture" instead of providing serious policy solutions to the crises facing the country. And in one rushed flurry of desperation, they tried to change the rules to stop the new emerging majority. By March 24, 2021, just two months after Donald Trump had skipped town on his successor's inauguration, 361 bills had been introduced to restrict voting access in forty-seven states, according to the Brennan Center for Justice.

When an existing social order begins to unravel, it inevitably creates friction for those who most depended on it for stability. Political scientists like Diana Mutz describe this tension as "dominant group status threat," and author Isabel Wilkerson has connected it to research showing an unusual rise in death rates for middle-aged white Americans starting in the late 1990s and continuing into the Obama administration. "The people dying of despair could be said to be dying of the end of an illusion," Wilkerson writes in her book, *Caste: The Origins of Our Discontents*. "They had relied on this illusion, perhaps beyond the realm of consciousness and perhaps needed it more than any other group," she writes.

It was precisely because of that illusion of perpetual white dominance that far too many working-class white Americans had been conditioned throughout history to position themselves as the bulwark in defense of an inequitable economic system and an unjust social order. Because of that illusion, they would rather allow hundreds of thousands of their fellow citizens to die of a deadly disease than to wear a mask or provide health care for all Americans. Because of that illusion, they would rather enable an imbalanced plutocratic economy than protect fundamental labor rights for ordinary workers like themselves. Because of that illusion, they would rather empower a racially biased police state than resolve the nation's deep-seated socioeconomic challenges. And because of that illusion, they would rather suspend democracy itself than share their political power with a new emerging majority.

It's important to understand that the fear of a darkening America did not begin with the presidency of Donald Trump. These trends have been growing in our country for decades. The sad reality is that America has never reconciled its racial history with its lofty founding promises, and until it does, we are destined to repeat our patterns of crisis and division. In the decades since the civil rights era, our stunning racial progress has yet to eliminate the most staggering racial disparities. Under Democratic and Republican presidents, Black Americans have seen no major structural changes since the 1960s. A few Blacks may have become billionaires, but millions more have no jobs at all. Some have soared to the heights of elected office, while millions of others have been disenfranchised. Two have become attorney general, while hundreds of thousands remain incarcerated. As Black Americans progressed over the decades, white America's progress offset any potential gains, seemingly freezing the status quo in perpetuity. These disparities contribute to festering resentments among African Americans at the same time that Black advancement generates backlash and rage among white Americans. The result is to create the conditions for dangerous and explosive outbursts of energy from both communities.

Every approach we have tried in the past has failed to stop these periodic racial crises, and the most common current proposals under discussion will likely fail as well. That's because most of the approaches are not designed to resolve America's fundamental race problem. They are designed only to avoid conflict and respond to the crisis of the moment rather than resolve the structural injustice of the system. But any society that consistently prioritizes peace over justice will soon find itself with neither. Which is why I believe there is still a way out.

If we've learned anything from American history, it is that no simple panacea can remedy hundreds of years of oppression. The way forward will require a long-term national commitment beyond the lifetime of any of us alive today. It will require Americans of all races to work both separately and together. And it will require a reaffirmation of the founding principles of our nation.

Moving beyond our unrelenting race crisis will involve, at least, three distinct and difficult interventions by the white community, the Black community, and the nation at large. First, white America must atone for a legacy of slavery and racism that still persists today. This cannot be accomplished with mere apologies; it requires compensatory action. Second, Black America must hold the dominant political parties and our leaders accountable. This does not mean shifting the burden to Black people to solve white racism; it means we must unapologetically demand that all of our elected leaders, public officials, and those in positions of responsibility serve our needs. Third, America, as a country, must embrace a goal of equality that is race-based, historically informed, and results-oriented. This does not mean everyone should be treated equally without regard to historical inequities; it means our goal must be equal outcomes, not just equal access or opportunities.

After four hundred years of racial oppression, after nearly 250 years of slavery, after a century of Jim Crow segregation, and after six decades of white resistance to modern civil rights laws, we should know better than to perpetuate the fantasy that equal opportunity, alone, will lead to racial equality. It will not.

"If you stick a knife in my back nine inches and pull it out six inches, there's no progress," Malcolm X once explained. "If you pull it all the way out, that's not progress," he added. "The progress is healing the wound that the blow made," but as Malcolm X reminded us, many white Americans "haven't even begun to pull the knife out, much less try to heal the wound. They won't even admit that the knife is there."

To make African Americans whole in the country that enslaved and segregated us—that robbed us of our history, our land, our families, our bodies, and our names—the nation can't just pull the knife out that stabbed us and expect to move on in a newly professed spirit of unity. Instead, we must find a way not just to make Black lives matter, but to make them equal.

PART ONE

THE HOPE THAT THE PRESENT HAS BROUGHT US

"Sing a song full of the hope that the present has brought us."

—James Weldon Johnson,
Lift Every Voice and Sing

1

FROM TRAYVON MARTIN
TO GEORGE FLOYD

Three years after I signed up, I still hadn't figured out how to make good use of an app called Twitter. Although I used it regularly, I felt like I was talking to myself, and nobody was really listening to what I had to say. I was starting to question the utility of this social media outlet until I discovered that it could actually serve as a valuable platform to learn about news that had been unreported or underreported in the mainstream media.

All this first dawned on me in the early days of March 2012, when I kept seeing the same name mentioned by several people I followed on Twitter. An unarmed Black teenager was killed in Sanford, Florida, by a man who had stalked and chased him. The police knew the identity of the killer, but he had not been arrested.

The gravity of the story did not register for me at first, but by the time I saw it again, I had become more curious. I wondered why I had not seen this story in the press. There's no way a man on the street could shoot and kill an unarmed teenager, admit to the shooting, and not be arrested, I thought to myself. That would be a huge scandal. It would be all over the news. A teenager covering his head with a hoodie to protect himself from the rain in his own gated community being gunned down by a vigilante while walking home from a convenience store holding nothing but a can of Arizona Iced

Tea and a bag of Skittles? How could that be true and not provoke national outrage?

Not long afterward, I heard the name again from several other Black people I trusted and followed on Twitter. At this point, the story became impossible to ignore, even if the national news media chose to do so. I started seeing more Twitter posts about the case, and although I wasn't quite sure what impact it would have, I began liking and retweeting them on my feed.

One day, a Twitter user I followed posted the exact number of days it had been since the shooting, and yet the killer had not been arrested. The next day, the same user posted the information again with the updated number of days. At that point, I had no special knowledge of the case or new information, so I had no idea what I could add to the conversation. But on March 15, I posted my first tweet about the tragedy. It simply read: "Trayvon Martin Shooter Still Not Arrested." Only four people retweeted my post. The next day I posted again. "I'm still outraged that the publicly known killer of 17-year-old Trayvon Martin has not been arrested," I wrote. This time nine people retweeted the post.

I wasn't having much of an impact, but I decided I would continue tweeting about Trayvon Martin every day until his killer was arrested. Almost everyone else seemed to have the same idea at the same time. An unprecedented national pressure campaign developed overnight. The story blew up, and on March 23, even President Barack Obama weighed in. "If I had a son, he'd look like Trayvon," he said. The same day, NBA star LeBron James tweeted a photo of his Miami Heat teammates wearing hoodies in honor of Trayvon. Finally, on April 11, 2012, George Zimmerman was arrested for the murder of Trayvon Martin, forty-six days after he killed him. A jury that included five white women and one mixed-race woman acquitted Zimmerman the following year, and three Black women—Patrisse Cullors, Alicia Garza, and Opal Tometi—responded by forming Black Lives Matter.

A year after Zimmerman's trial, I read an interview with NBA star Kobe Bryant in *The New Yorker*. It turned out that Bryant was uncomfortable with the hoodie photograph the Miami Heat released in honor of Trayvon Martin. "I won't react to something just because I'm supposed to because I'm an African-American," Bryant explained. I was disturbed and disappointed, and I immediately wrote a column for BET.com critiquing Bryant's comments. "Kobe, you should sit and listen to the facts before you speak about controversial topics," I wrote. "But the facts in this case have been known for quite some time, and I can't find a single public statement you've made about it until now." Not surprisingly, my column met with mixed reactions. Some applauded it, while others attacked me for bringing down one of our Black heroes.

That same day, Bryant posted a statement on Twitter. "Trayvon Martin was wronged," he wrote. "The system did not work." The next morning, he sent me a direct message. He told me that he had posted a comment on Instagram on July 15, 2013, two days after Zimmerman was acquitted. I checked. What he actually posted was an oblique quotation about justice from abolitionist Frederick Douglass, but he never mentioned Trayvon Martin or George Zimmerman by name. I tweeted a copy of his Instagram post and let it go. I had made my point, and I had no desire to spark a public battle with him.

That was the one and only time I ever had any direct contact with Kobe Bryant, and it was not an entirely pleasant experience for either of us, I'm sure. Which is why I was a bit surprised by the dramatic clutch of emotions I felt when I received a message one Sunday afternoon, six years later.

It was late January 2020, and I had finally recovered from my mysterious illness. I had just finished texting a close friend about a small party he was hosting for the Grammys that night. I stepped away from the phone for a few minutes, and when I returned, I could not believe what I saw on my screen. He had sent me a news article from TMZ.com with the shocking headline: "Kobe Bryant Dead, Dies in Helicopter Crash."

I didn't believe it at first, but TMZ had a reputation for breaking the news of celebrity deaths. I quickly read the article, then looked on Twitter for more information. The story was already trending, and everyone seemed to be either in shock or denial. I turned on the TV and saw the Breaking News banner. Despite all the information before me, the story did not compute. Kobe Bryant was younger than me. He was not supposed to die. He had so much life ahead of him, I thought.

I remembered the sadness I had felt when Michael Jackson, Whitney Houston, and Prince had died, but, for some reason, those deaths did not surprise me as much as Kobe Bryant's did. As I sat on the edge of the sofa watching the news and scrolling through my Twitter feed, it finally hit me that this was real, and in that moment, I took off my glasses and cried.

This was not the way 2020 was supposed to begin. This was supposed to be a good year, when we finally rid ourselves of the menace in the White House, either by impeachment or electoral defeat. If a prominent life had to be sacrificed for the good fortune that 2020 would inevitably bring, why did it have to be a Black prince? And why his young daughter, too? Later that night, as I sat at the Grammy party, I quickly realized the promised escapism of the ceremony would not provide answers to my questions or refuge from my sadness. Alicia Keys, the host for the evening, began the program with a special a cappella musical tribute to Kobe, joined by the R&B group Boyz II Men. "It's so hard to say goodbye to yesterday," they sang.

At that moment, I wondered if I might have been wrong about the year to come. From its very first week, 2020 was no ordinary year. Just three days into the new year, the United States brazenly assassinated an Iranian military general, raising the specter of war. By mid-January, Donald Trump's Senate impeachment trial showed no signs of persuading Republicans, who were determined to prevent even a single witness from testifying.

February defied expectations in a host of different ways, as the impeachment trial concluded with an unwarranted acquittal, an openly gay man won the Democrats' Iowa caucuses, a self-described socialist won the New Hampshire primary, and a New York billionaire seemed poised to buy his way to the Democratic nomination. All the while, the mainstream establishment candidate for president seemed to be losing everywhere. It was not until the very last day of the month that African American voters in South Carolina rescued the former vice president's campaign and put him on the path to the presidency. On that very same date of February 29, Leap Year Day, the United States reported its first death from the novel coronavirus.

The sobering prospect of an impending pandemic seemed to support Senator Bernie Sanders's argument for universal health care, and I expected the story would become an issue in what was shaping up to be a hard-fought, months-long campaign with former vice president Joe Biden. My assumptions would prove completely wrong. Within a matter of days, the entire presidential primary season would come to an abrupt halt, and within a month, it would become an afterthought.

It had been fourteen months since Elizabeth Warren launched the 2020 presidential campaign in the midst of a federal government shutdown with a video announcing her candidacy on New Year's Eve in 2018. Since that time, dozens of people had been killed and injured in a Walmart in El Paso, Texas; Jeffrey Epstein had reportedly died by suicide in his cell; the Mueller Report had been released and downplayed; Donald Trump had tried to pressure a foreign government to manufacture dirt on his chief rival; Britain's prime minister had resigned; and our own president had been impeached.

The primary campaign had begun way too early—more than a year before the first ballots were cast in the first caucus—and the seemingly endless procession of unwieldy debates did not inspire confidence. What made 2020 different from past campaign seasons, however, was its diversity of talent. Six women, four African Americans, three Asian Americans, one Latino, and one openly gay man competed for the Democratic Party's presidential nomination. Yet, despite the growing diversity of the party, two of the whitest states in the country—Iowa and New Hampshire—continued to exercise disproportionate influence as the first to judge the candidates. The overemphasis on these two unrepresentative states forced candidates of color to drop out of the race and misrepresented the political sentiment of a party that had become increasingly dependent on Black voters.

South Carolina was the first contest in which Black voters made up more than half of the electorate, but by the time voters in that state went to the polls on the last Saturday in February, all four Black candidates had already withdrawn from the race. The candidate who emerged victorious was the man who had served as vice president to the nation's first Black president. After two prior failed presidential campaigns spanning more than three decades and three consecutive primary losses in his new campaign, Joe Biden finally won the first presidential primary of his life on the last day of Black History Month in 2020 thanks to African American voters in the South.

When the sun rose on the first day of March, few people could have predicted how dramatically the nation was about to change. While the political world turned its attention to the upcoming Super Tuesday primaries, the World Health Organization was on the verge of declaring a pandemic and a reluctant American president was about to declare a national emergency and shut down the country. On March 1, only a few dozen isolated coronavirus cases had been reported across the nation. By the end of the month, nearly two hundred thousand Americans had been infected. By the end of the year, the number had grown to twenty million.

The shutdown changed everything. The presidential campaign ground to a halt, and the candidate who lost the first three contests swept to victory on Super Tuesday, suddenly emerging as the de facto nominee. Within days, the public health crisis swelled into an economic catastrophe. Tens of millions of workers lost their jobs. Thousands of businesses shut down. Stock markets crashed. Entire cities emptied out. And the president of the United States, who refused to follow the directives of his own public health officials to wear a mask, took no responsibility for any of it, even as he continued to spread false hope and misinformation from the official podium of the White House.

By the end of May, as a number of states gradually began to reopen, more than one hundred thousand Americans had already perished over a period of three months, and a weary nation cautiously looked forward to Memorial Day. Yet even as the country hoped the coming summer would turn the page to a better chapter, a new crisis was about to emerge.

I observed Memorial Day by visiting the Houston National Cemetery with my mom to place flowers on my stepfather's grave. It was just a plot of dirt the last time I visited, but now it was covered with lush spring grass. As we opened the doors of the car, a maskless middle-aged woman called out to us. My instinct was to dismiss her interruption of our pilgrimage, but my mother carelessly walked over to talk to her, and I followed with a small bottle of hand sanitizer for protection. The woman offered my mom an American flag to place on her husband's grave and a pair of scissors to cut the flowers we had brought with us. It was an act of generosity I had not expected from a white woman at a military cemetery in Texas, and it forced me to question if I had been too judgmental of other white people in the South.

Years earlier, when I was still a student in college, I spent a summer working at a clothing store in a predominantly white area of Georgia. It was just two decades removed from the era of segregated water fountains, and every time I had to serve an old white person, I felt a sense of rage in my body as I wondered if they were the same people who had called my parents and grandparents "niggers." Over time, my animosity toward old white Southerners evolved into mere annoyance, but in recent years it had developed into something new. I instinctively assumed that the white woman in the Texas cemetery was one of the 47 to 52 percent of white women who had willingly elected a bankrupt, blustering game show host over an accomplished woman with decades of knowledge and experience.

My visceral reaction and suspicion grew out of a long history of psychological priming. For centuries, white women had repeatedly scapegoated, threatened, and endangered Black lives in service of the white supremacist fantasy that depicted Black males as sexual deviants in lustful pursuit of the white female body. It was two white women, Victoria Price and Ruby Bates, who lied and helped to wrongfully convict a group of Black teenagers who would come to be known as the Scottsboro Boys in Alabama in 1931. And it was a white woman named Carolyn Bryant whose lie about a fourteen-year-old Black boy named Emmett Till caused him to be brutally lynched in Mississippi in 1955.

The intuition I felt in the graveyard was not locked in the Jim Crow era. In my lifetime, I remembered how a white woman named Susan Smith had murdered her own children in South Carolina in 1994 and then blamed a Black carjacker for killing them. And in May of 2020, a white woman named Patricia Ripley drowned her autistic nine-year-old son in a canal in Miami and blamed Black men for her crime.

After years of living in the North, I also knew that this type of racism was not limited to the South. In "progressive" New York City, Linda Fairstein and Elizabeth Lederer prosecuted Black and brown teenagers in the infamous 1989 "Central Park Five" case despite the absence of any witnesses or physical evidence connecting the teens to a rape that they clearly did not commit. The notoriety of that case helps explain why it was so easy for a white man named Charles Stuart to blame a Black carjacker after he killed his own wife in Boston later that same year. Even white men had learned to weaponize white women's pain.

On the very same day I encountered the woman in the cemetery, yet another white woman in New York was blaming a Black man for a crime he did not commit. When Amy Cooper went for a morning walk with her cocker spaniel in Central Park, she came across a fifty-seven-year-old Black man who was bird-watching. He asked her to leash her dog. Instead of complying with his request and the park rules, she called the police and filed a false report of "an African American man threatening my life." Moments later, the 911 dispatcher called back, and the woman elevated the threat level by falsely claiming that the bird-watcher tried to "assault" her. The seemingly casual ease with which Amy Cooper quickly and instinctively lied about Christian Cooper and endangered his life dredged up all that painful history for African Americans of white women scapegoating us for their own transgressions.

When I realized that many white women have historically identified with their race over their gender, it also helped explain why Hillary Clinton had not been elected president and why no woman had broken that glass ceiling in the century that passed since the ratification of the Nineteenth Amendment in a country where women constitute a majority of the population. Although women and Blacks both remain oppressed in America, white women could escape some of that oppression by aligning with their oppressor in maintaining white patriarchal hegemony. For white women to elect even one of their own to high office would require them to "make common cause" with other outsiders in society, as feminist and civil rights activist Audre Lorde suggested in her book *Sister Outsider*. "The master's tools will never dismantle the master's house," Lorde wrote. "And this fact is only threatening to those women who still define the master's house as their only source of support."

My mom had never been one of those women who depended on "the master's house" as her source of support. In her twenties and thirties, she had been a student of the work of Black activist Angela Davis, and eventually she fled her hometown of St. Louis to seek a new life in California. As time passed, I inherited her rebellious instincts and distrust of white Americans and moved to Harlem, while she married a military man and settled into a slower life in the conservative and predominantly white suburbs of Texas.

Throughout these various chapters in her life, one thing remained consistent—my mom loved to cook for me. She hadn't cooked as much since she retired, but when she did, it was an expression of her love for those around her. That day was no exception. After the cemetery, we drove back to her house to eat a traditional Memorial Day feast of barbecue, baked beans, and corn on the cob that she had been asking me about for several days. "Do you prefer beef ribs or pork ribs?" she queried. I was never the type to plan my meals days in advance, but I indulged her in the conversation anyway. It was the first indicator in months that normalcy might one day return to our lives. Easter had come and gone with no celebration, and I had not been to a gym, on a plane, or in the studio at the network where I worked since March.

After three months off the air, I was hopeful that I would be able to work again once I returned to New York. But on the same day I was enjoying the last few hours of downtime with my mom, the nation's president was posting a gratuitous and racially inflammatory tweet about what he called the "China Virus," and a set of racial encounters in different parts of the country were about to change the course of the year.

At the exact same moment that I was scrubbing the barbecue sauce off my plate in Texas, a former Houston resident was sitting in the driver's seat of a blue Mercedes-Benz SUV at the intersection of Chicago Avenue and East 38th Street in Minneapolis. Employees at a nearby convenience store had just called police to report that the forty-six-year-old Black man had allegedly used a counterfeit twenty-dollar bill to buy cigarettes. Yet the man continued peacefully sitting in his car across the street from the store. Minutes later, the police arrived, and Officer Thomas Lane yanked the man out of his car and handcuffed him. Officer Alex Kueng then walked the man to a nearby wall and asked him a preliminary question. "All right, what's your name?" he said. His name was George Floyd.

Two more police cars arrived. Officers Derek Chauvin and Tou Thao approached the scene. Minutes later, George Floyd lay face down on the ground virtually motionless. Officer Derek Chauvin brazenly pressed his knee on Floyd's neck while Officers Lane and Kueng sat on his back and legs. "I can't breathe," Floyd pleaded, again and again, at least sixteen times in five minutes. In Floyd's desperate appeal we could hear the same words spoken by Eric Garner, the Staten Island man who had been choked to death by New York police officers in 2014. George Floyd and Eric Garner were two Black men, both fathers, both in their forties, both killed by white police officers for minor infractions involving cigarettes, and both uttered the same last words—"I can't breathe." No three words in the English language could better articulate the suffocation of African Americans living under the burden of white supremacy, and for many of us, Floyd's death symbolized the ways in which America had repeatedly avoided and ignored our appeals for justice.

With blood dripping from his mouth, Floyd finally called out to the first person he had ever known. "Mama!" he cried. Moments later, his eyes closed. Then, his body stopped moving. Bystanders who filmed the video of Floyd on the ground urged police to "check his pulse," but Officer Chauvin relentlessly continued to press his knee into Floyd's immobilized neck. That knee remained on George Floyd's neck for nine minutes and twenty-nine seconds, and the disturbing video that circulated on television and social media sent shockwaves across the country and far beyond the shores of the nation.

Protests erupted almost immediately. The weight of five long months of conflict, controversy, scandal, impeachment, shutdowns, layoffs, masks, isolation, and social distancing had already crushed the American spirit. For African Americans, it felt like ancient magma deep in the core of the republic was once again bubbling to the surface to erupt. The knees of the Minneapolis police officers represented the cumulative impact of four centuries of pressure applied to the necks of our Black ancestors, and in a season of unparalleled trauma, years of unreleased energy finally burst into the atmosphere. We had lived through the tragic death of forty-one-year-old Kobe Bryant in California and the murder of twenty-five-year-old Ahmaud Arbery in Georgia. And we had experienced the horror of the police shooting in Louisville, Kentucky, of twenty-six-year-old Breonna Taylor, whose death was woefully underreported in March of 2020. And through it all, we watched a deadly virus kill thousands of our sisters and brothers. And now we watched the slow-motion murder of yet another unarmed Black man at the hands of the very people who were sworn to protect us.

We had already seen a hint of what lay ahead in 2020, when armed white protesters stormed the Michigan State Capitol in late April. Almost every Black person I know immediately understood that the protesters' act of white defiance was about race, yet a number of well-respected observers in the media seemed reluctant to draw that conclusion.

The George Floyd story was different. The nine minutes of excruciating video made state-sanctioned torture of Black bodies visible for Americans of all races. This was exactly what Black Lives Matter activists had been protesting since Trayvon Martin was killed. George Floyd's death was a turning point.

A few days after he was killed, an autopsy from the Hennepin County Medical Examiner's office revealed that George Floyd had tested positive for coronavirus. We also learned that he had recently lost his job as a bouncer in a restaurant after the pandemic forced businesses to close in Minnesota. This was the moment when the four tectonic plates of 2020 would all collide. George Floyd had been a victim of the nation's health crisis, its economic crisis, and its racial justice crisis, and in death he would provide the pretext for the president to instigate a new crisis of democracy. In each crisis, the victims were disproportionately Black. And in each case, the common thread was race.

2

RECKONING

The day after George Floyd was killed, I boarded an aircraft for the first time in three months. I wore a cloth mask, a plastic face shield, and disposable gloves on my flight from Houston to Newark Liberty International Airport. I sanitized my seat and tray table with alcohol wipes. I washed my hands repeatedly with soap and water. I kept my distance from other passengers on the plane.

Despite the steps I took to protect myself from the new threat that plagued us, I knew that at any given time I could still be stopped, accosted, and killed with impunity from the old threat that had never been eradicated. I knew that the federal government's failure to prevent the deaths of thousands of Black and brown people from coronavirus would not prompt eight congressional investigations, as had the deaths of four white Americans who died in an attack in Benghazi. I knew that the lives of thousands of Black people who had been criminalized during the crack cocaine epidemic in the Reagan-Bush era were more disposable than the lives of white people who were sympathetically eulogized during the opioid crisis in the Trump era. And I knew that no matter how successful I became, no matter how many degrees I obtained, at any given moment, America could remind me that my Black life did not matter.

Once I arrived, I hesitantly boarded a commuter train from Newark into the city that had become the epicenter of the public health crisis. Anxious to return to my apartment and my normal routine,

I soon discovered that my old way of life was impossible. Unlike my mom's community in Texas that had already begun to reopen, nearly everything remained closed in Manhattan. At first, I was not concerned because I needed time to catch up on work I had been neglecting. But by Saturday, I could hear the voices of outraged protesters chanting outside my window, and I knew I could no longer remain quarantined, sitting behind a keyboard or watching the revolution on a television screen. I left my apartment, ran into the streets, and began documenting the demonstration that spread through Harlem like wildfire.

The peaceful protesters quickly took control of the main thoroughfares of the neighborhood and marched down 125th Street to the West Side Highway. Because there are only two major highways in all of Manhattan, the protesters' movement onto that roadway would effectively shut down half of the borough's high-speed traffic. Undeterred by the prospect of placing their bodies in front of four thousand-pound vehicles racing downtown at sixty miles an hour, hundreds of people proceeded up a ramp onto the southbound highway and forced traffic to a halt. I recorded the event as it happened and posted it online. The demonstrators expanded to the northbound lanes of the highway and shut down all vehicular movement in both directions. I continued recording, posting video and interviewing participants as they proceeded past the celebrated tomb of Civil War general Ulysses S. Grant, past the iconic steeple of the Riverside Church where Dr. King delivered his famous speech against the Vietnam War, and away from the historically Black community of Harlem into the mostly white Upper West Side. That's when the police arrived.

The show of force came swiftly. City of New York Police Department (NYPD) vehicles blocked traffic at the 95th Street exit while an intimidating phalanx of officers advanced toward the protesters. I stood near the side of the road in between the police and the protesters to film the inevitable confrontation. When the police approached me, I told them I was with the press. They moved past me but then turned around in a group and advanced on me again. "You're under arrest," an officer announced. "I'm with the press," I repeated. "Doesn't matter," an officer said. "You're going to jail."

The police took my cell phone and cuffed me with tight plastic zip ties that bruised my wrists. I learned later that they were actually called "nylon tactical restraints." Two officers carried me backward to the police blockade, where they removed my mask, photographed me, and stuck me in a sweltering van. I have had several dangerous encounters with the police in the past, but none had ever escalated this quickly. As an editor for my school newspaper, I had once embedded with Black student protesters when they took over the administration building at Dartmouth College in 1986, and as a freelancer, I had been tear-gassed covering protests in Ferguson, Missouri, in 2014, but 2020 was the first time in my life I had ever being handcuffed or arrested. My arrest took place just one day after a Black CNN colleague, Omar Jimenez, had been arrested while reporting live on the air from the protests in Minneapolis. He was arrested even though a white CNN reporter, Josh Campbell, was not arrested near the same area. Campbell publicly acknowledged that he had been "treated much differently" than Jimenez, and the televised arrest, along with the disparity in treatment, served as yet another reminder of why the protesters were marching in the first place.

For some Black men, being arrested had become a grim rite of passage. For me, it was a possibility that I had dreaded for years and a ritual that I had been fortunate to bypass. Since childhood, I have lived with claustrophobia and syncope, and the thought of being locked up and handcuffed has always been particularly terrifying. I did not realize it at the time I was arrested, but George Floyd was also claustrophobic, and he told the police officers about his condition as they tried to lock his handcuffed body in the back of a police car minutes before he was killed. I can easily imagine his horror. I have passed out many times in my life—at my grandfather's burial, in a crowded Black church with President Clinton, in the middle seat on a transcontinental flight, and in my own home—under less stressful circumstances. As I sat alone in the back of the police van, my mind immediately started to worry about my physical health. I made a point to tell the officers that I could faint at any moment. And when they finally closed the thick metal door, I thought about Freddie Gray, the twenty-five-year-old Black man in Baltimore who died in suspicious circumstances in the back of a police van in 2015.

A few minutes later, another unmasked prisoner, a twenty-one-year-old Hispanic man, joined me. We sat only a few feet apart, sweating in the back of the vehicle. No other passengers boarded. The police drove us to East 39th Street, where we were moved to an un-air-conditioned prisoner transport bus and waited for an hour with our hands tied behind our backs as new prisoners were loaded onto the vehicle. Next, the bus drove us to police headquarters downtown, where I was processed, photographed again, and stuck in a jail cell with thirty-four other inmates. After spending time in Texas carefully social distancing and avoiding public spaces, I was now locked up with dozens of unmasked prisoners in the very city that had been hardest hit by the pandemic. I remained in police custody for six hours, uncertain when I would be released or allowed to speak to someone. I was given no food, no phone call, nor any opportunity to contact a lawyer or a loved one throughout the ordeal.

It was not until 9:30 that evening that my arresting officer finally returned to release me. He gave me two pink sheets of paper—a summons to appear in court for the charge of "disorderly conduct" and another for blocking a highway. The officer escorted me to the door and handed me a property tag to reclaim my bicycle. When I finally stepped outside and took my first breath of freedom, the warm air of the city enveloped me. It had been five months since I had emerged from the confinement of the temazcal in Mexico, and the lesson of serenity I learned from the shaman had served me well. I took my bike and cautiously turned away from the door. Like a newly emancipated slave stepping off the plantation for the first time at his master's direction, I felt a bit uncertain as I walked to the edge of the station. Only when I exited the gate into the glare of a bright police light and heard the applause of a small crowd of legal observers across the street did I finally relax. I gave my name and contact information to the legal representatives. Then I climbed onto my bike and rode nine miles uptown to Harlem.

The hour-long ride home through New York City traffic gave me plenty of time to reflect on what had happened. It made no sense. My arrest, incarceration, and potential exposure to a deadly virus—it was all for nothing more than a simple civil ticket. But I guarded those pink documents in my pocket like a free Black man in the antebellum South who needed his papers to prove that he had a right to be on the white man's roads after sunset. If the police stopped me again, I hoped the ticket would explain why I was riding at night on a bike with no headlights.

When I passed another group of protesters in the streets on my way home, I stopped for a few minutes to watch their confrontation with the police from a safe distance, but I knew I could not remain and cover it. I had very little battery charge left on my phone and even less in my soul. After just being released from jail, I was tired and hungry and did not want to risk going back. I felt like a fugitive, and maybe that was the point. "When you control a man's thinking you do not have to worry about his actions," the historian Carter G. Woodson once warned. He was right. They had successfully controlled my thoughts that night, and I was too defeated to continue fighting. It soon occurred to me that this was precisely the point. This was exactly why white America had historically and repeatedly chosen to respond to Black outrage as a criminal justice issue rather than a social justice concern. Instead of addressing our needs, the nation had always responded by policing and criminalizing our conduct, and by doing so, they could try to make us feel like criminals just for existing, just for demanding our dignity.

It had been this way since the founding of the republic. Whenever a threatening moment of Black empowerment arose, white backlash followed. The pattern repeated itself during abolitionism and Reconstruction in the nineteenth century to the demonstrations of the civil rights movement in the twentieth century and the election of a Black president in the twenty-first century.

Since that historic election, the existential threat to white patriarchal hegemony has only grown stronger. White Christians, who accounted for eight out of ten Americans at the nation's bicentennial, have now become a minority in this country. White birth rates have declined. Nonwhite immigrant communities have swelled. The population of native Spanish speakers has quadrupled in four decades. The Asian American population has grown more rapidly than any other demographic group in the nation. And gays and lesbians have won the freedom to marry in all fifty states. The long-standing institutions that maintained social hierarchy are slowly crumbling. And America's changing demographics appear to be placing the nation on a seemingly irreversible path toward a blacker and browner future. After an unbroken string, two centuries long, of white men in charge of our government, the line of succession was ruptured by a Black president, then challenged by a white woman who received more votes than her white male opponent, and then threatened by the election of a Black woman of Jamaican and Indian descent. But most threatening of all is the report from the census bureau that more than half of all children in America are now Black or brown, and the projection that by 2044, white Americans will no longer be the majority of the US population.

By the time in late May that demonstrators began to assemble in the streets beyond Minneapolis to protest the killing of George Floyd, it was already too late to hold back the tide. The vanguard of a new emerging majority was marching through cities, shutting down traffic, taking over buildings, and demanding disruptive, revolutionary change to overturn the status quo. Conservatives disparaged them as "shock troops" preparing to initiate an assault on traditional America, but they were not "outside agitators" from some foreign land. They were real Americans, no less so than the venerated white farmers of the heartland. In some protests, you could find the mainstream party activists who helped Democrats win the popular vote in all but one of the presidential elections of the previous three decades. In other protests, you could find radical insurgents who abhorred the dominant political parties and wanted to dismantle the entire corrupt system. In many protests, you could find both groups represented. They were Black and brown and white; young and old; rich and poor; Democrat, independent, socialist; and yes, some Republicans; and they were more multicultural than any previous movement for racial justice in American history. But much like the ancient shield and spear paradox, the irresistible force of inevitable change was about to confront the immovable object of determined resistance.

This is a story about the second half of 2020—a time when many of our nation's leaders and our media confidently assured us that America was experiencing a long-overdue racial reckoning that would force the nation and its people to reexamine their behavior. But in 2020, as before, with every step toward racial progress, it became abundantly clear that a significant percentage of white America was deeply concerned about the changing complexion of the country.

White America's concern was not new. Decades earlier, James Baldwin described it as a "panic-stricken apprehension on the part of those who have maligned and subjugated others for so long that the tables have been turned." This apprehension created an opportunity for cynical political leaders to exploit those fears for personal political gain. For years, these leaders had developed racist, sexist, homophobic, transphobic, and xenophobic laws and policies, often hidden behind ostensibly neutral language, to slow down the inexorable rise of the emerging majority. Suddenly, in 2020, the threat they had long anticipated was beginning to materialize right in front of them, on their living room television screens.

Some responded with predictable and hypocritical demagoguery about law and order. "When the looting starts, the shooting starts," President Donald Trump tweeted the day before I was arrested. His words were stolen from racist Miami Police Chief Walter Headley, who threatened Negroes with dogs and shotguns during the height of the civil rights protests in 1967. Others, like a seventeen-year-old Trump supporter from a small town in northern Illinois, would respond by crossing state lines with an illegal firearm and killing two protesters. An age-old tradition of white rage found a volatile accelerant in the toxic, symbiotic relationship between president and his devotees. A leader, desperate for reelection, needed a new enemy to fight, and his most fanatical supporters, desperate for validation of their beliefs, were all too willing to help.

Over the course of the election year, the president took unprecedented steps to divide the country, engaging a powerful minority of fearful whites in a last-ditch race against time to stop the progress of newly empowered people of color and their allies. Eight years of white resentment to President Obama and nearly four years of white backlash under President Trump had already immersed America in a cold civil war. Daily skirmishes were broadcast on social media and television, from the Black bird-watcher in New York's Central Park to a Black barbecue in Oakland, California's Lakeside Park. But through it all, many of us suspected that a larger and more dangerous battle loomed beyond the horizon.

The summer months of 2020 would usher in the most racially divided period in America since the spring and summer of 1968. On the very first day of June, the president, already angered by reports that he had hidden in a bunker during recent protests, was determined to project a sense of strength. By the end of the day, Black Lives Matter protesters across the street from the White House in Lafayette Park were violently removed. In a stunning display of reckless judgment, US forces tear-gassed hundreds of peaceful protesters live on national television. Minutes later, the president and his top advisers walked out of the White House, across the street, and through a now empty park to stand in front of St. John's Episcopal Church, where the president posed for a photo opportunity with a copy of the Holy Bible.

Of course, there was nothing sacred about the spectacle of a famously irreligious president gassing innocent civilians to stage a photo op holding a Bible he did not read at a church he did not attend, but the president's white evangelical supporters remained faithful to their leader. They had already stood by their leader as he told more than twenty thousand documented lies in office. They were not about to abandon him just for attacking a group of Black Lives Matter protesters.

In the meantime, the ordinary functioning of daily life in America continued to be disrupted. Despite the hasty effort by some governors to reopen their states, the ongoing coronavirus pandemic worsened in the summer and forced the cancellation of events all across the country. For the first time in memory, both the Democratic National Convention and the Republican National Convention were effectively canceled and held online. And throughout the summer, I covered several more racial justice protests and lamented the loss of more Black people to COVID.

As the pandemic proceeded, the racial inequities driving the overlapping crises grew more apparent. On the first Friday in June, the Labor Department reported a significant disparity in the jobless rate as Black unemployment reached a record high for May while the white unemployment rate dropped. That same afternoon, the president denied the existence of systemic racism while also claiming he had a plan to fix it. "Our country is so strong, and that's what my plan is," he said. Despite the glaring racial inequality in unemployment, access to health care, coronavirus deaths, and police profiling, top administration officials confirmed this view. The president's national security adviser and economic adviser both flatly claimed that they did not believe in systemic racism, and the president's only Black cabinet member, Secretary of Housing and Urban Development Ben Carson, dismissed the question by saying, "I grew up in a time when there was real systemic racism."

Dodging the question would not quell the uprising. One day after the president denied the existence of systemic racism, half a million protesters, according to the *New York Times*, turned out in nearly 550 venues throughout the United States. By July, a survey from the Kaiser Family Foundation suggested that twenty-six million people had participated in demonstrations across the country. Friends and family members I had known for years who had no political inclinations and had never walked a picket line were suddenly marching through streets, holding up signs, and chanting the names of Rayshard Brooks, Sandra Bland, and Elijah McClain. Social media pages turned black in solidarity with the cause. And even white people were walking through the streets of New York with "Black Lives Matter" face masks and T-shirts. It was the largest movement in American history, the *Times* reported, but as quickly as it generated new supporters, it also inflamed old opponents.

Throughout the summer, the president continued to fan the flames of racial resentment. He borrowed the problematic language of white grievance from Richard Nixon to tweet about a "SILENT MAJORITY." He condemned bipartisan efforts to rename military bases that honored Confederate generals. He retweeted a video of a supporter chanting "White power" at a Florida retirement community. He tried to scare white voters with warnings that Democrats would "totally destroy the beautiful suburbs." He resurrected the birther campaign that originally propelled his war on Barack Obama with a baseless new attack on Senator Kamala Harris, arguing she "doesn't meet the requirements" to be vice president. And he invited a St. Louis couple who had previously threatened Black Lives Matter protesters at gunpoint to deliver a prime-time speech at his Republican National Convention.

Despite all the insults and attacks, the president still had the audacity to brag in October that "nobody has done more for the Black community than Donald Trump." The remarks came in the same debate where he told a Black moderator, "I am the least racist person in this room." But, sadly, his words were consistent with his previous boastful exaggerations about his relationship with the community. Earlier in the year, he claimed that "I made Juneteenth very famous" and that "nobody had ever heard of it" before he came along, even though African Americans in Texas had been celebrating the day when slavery ended for 155 years. Given Trump's record, it was easy to see why he fell short of his wildly unrealistic goals for Black votes. During the 2016 campaign, he had promised his supporters that "at the end of four years, I guarantee you that I will get over 95 percent of the African American vote." Instead, in 2020 he received only 8 to 12 percent of the Black vote, according to exit polls and voter surveys.

Trump's failure to connect with Black voters was not a surprise. Donald Trump never made any serious effort to reach Black voters. He was the first president since Warren Harding not to speak to the National Association for the Advancement of Colored People (NAACP). And throughout four years in office, he never visited a Black community for an open Black event. Even in the final stretch of the 2020 campaign, he refused to condemn the white extremist group that called itself the Proud Boys, and he issued an executive order banning diversity trainers from even discussing racial bias. In reality, his campaign was almost entirely geared toward motivating his base of predominantly white voters. Still, he did attempt a last-minute, transparently perfunctory effort to appeal to African Americans by soliciting and exploiting the support of a handful of Black male rappers who had no political experience. This ploy was destined to fail. Despite the overhyped claims from a small but vocal group of Black Trump supporters, the Democratic ticket was never in danger of losing a significant percentage of the Black vote in 2020. In fact, the real purpose of Trump's outreach was to depress Black turnout for Democrats in a few targeted cities in swing states and to provide political cover for white voters anxious about casting their ballot for a man who was almost universally despised by African Americans.

As summer turned into fall, the general election campaign turned out to be relatively brief and anticlimactic. Considering the rescheduled party conventions and a canceled presidential debate, the most dramatic moments took place away from the campaign trial. This first occurred when the president who spent the entire year denying the seriousness of the pandemic suddenly found himself stricken by coronavirus. In a bizarre sequence of events that illustrated his privilege and isolation from ordinary Americans, the president was airlifted by helicopter from the White House to Walter Reed National Military Medical Center and given access to the nation's top doctors and latest therapies. Once he had begun to recover, he flew back to the executive mansion on Marine One and ripped off his mask for a photo op on the South Portico of the White House. It was exactly the wrong message to communicate to the American public, and it would set the tone for a breathtaking surge in COVID cases in the coming months.

The second and final dramatic moment of the campaign took place in the Senate, when Republicans, who refused even to hold a hearing on President Obama's Supreme Court nominee in 2016 because it was nine months too close to an election, voted to confirm Trump's nominee, Amy Coney Barrett, to the same court with just eight days left in the presidential election. The hypocrisy was stunning even for Republicans. "I want you to use my words against me," Senator Lindsey Graham said during a March 2016 discussion on Merrick Garland, when Republicans were still pretending that they had a consistent approach to government. "If there's a Republican president in 2016 and a vacancy occurs in the last year of the first term, you can say 'Lindsey Graham said let's let the next president, whoever it might be, make that nomination.'" A Republican president was elected in 2016. And a vacancy occurred in the last year of his first term. And the Lindsey Graham of 2020 refused to listen to the Lindsey Graham of 2016.

What changed during those four years was the presidency of Donald Trump and his party's realization that there would be few or no consequences for antidemocratic efforts to perpetuate white supremacy. Elected without a majority of the popular vote, Trump governed by discrediting any institution of democracy that stood in his way. He became the avatar of whiteness in America, and only he could legitimately represent its people. "*L'état, c'est moi,*" French king Louis XIV is attributed to have said. "I have the right to do whatever I want as president," said Trump.

Republicans published a hundred-page autopsy in the wake of their 2012 election loss and vowed to "modernize" the party with outreach efforts to Blacks and Latinos and young people, but after Trump's victory in 2016, they discovered they didn't have to bother. Instead of building a more diverse and inclusive party, they could redirect their focus to the party's base of angry white voters. And since many Republicans believed themselves to be ordained by God, any challenge to their rule was inherently illegitimate and would be crushed by the good (white) people of America. Asked if he was concerned about the prospect of impeachment in early December 2018, Trump responded, "I think that the people would revolt if that happened."

When the 2020 presidential campaign finally came to an end on November 3, the country was about to see just how true that was. The real drama—a crisis of democracy—was about to begin.

Triggered by safety concerns around the coronavirus pandemic, and given the opportunity to vote by mail, Americans cast their ballots in record numbers for the fall election, but there was no clear victor when I went to bed at five in the morning on Wednesday, November 4. The country waited for several sleepless nights until the major news outlets projected a winner four days after the polls closed. Many in the nation breathed a sigh of relief, but it would take much longer to convince the outgoing president that he had lost. Four states—Michigan, Georgia, Pennsylvania, and Wisconsin— received the bulk of his attention and criticism. Within those states, he focused on four cities where he claimed, without evidence, that votes were "fraudulently or illegally obtained," and he demanded that millions of votes in those places be thrown out. Those cities, not surprisingly, were Detroit, Atlanta, Philadelphia, and Milwaukee, each with a Black population significantly larger by percentage than the proportion of the nation's overall Black population.

It took three difficult and draining weeks for the administration simply to allow the ordinary transition process for a new president to begin. It would take three additional weeks and dozens of fruitless lawsuits before the Republican Senate majority leader would finally recognize the election of the new president. All the while, members of the outgoing president's party conspired with him to perpetuate his farcical conspiracy theories that the election had been stolen. For those who had thought the election would put an end to the long national nightmare of Donald Trump, they were mistaken. His ego would not permit him to be chastened or humbled in failure.

Trump, the man, had been temporarily defeated, but Trumpism, itself, was far from vanquished. He received more than seventy-four million votes, and he won the majority of votes in half the states of the union. Prior to 2020, no other candidate in history had received even seventy million votes. Yet after four years of chaos, crisis, controversy, scandal, resignations, indictments, arrests, impeachment, bigotry, and division, and after eight months of gross negligence and mismanagement of a pandemic that cost the lives of hundreds of thousands of Americans, seventy-four million people still felt comfortable voting for him. That, in and of itself, was an indictment of Trump's America, even in his opponent's historic moment of victory.

In the same way I knew in my bones as a college student that the old white Southerners I served at the clothing store in Georgia did not miraculously abandon their racist beliefs when legal segregation ended, I also knew that seventy-four million Americans who voted for Donald Trump in 2020 would not experience some transformative epiphany when Joe Biden, or any other Democrat, took office. If they weren't all racists, they were at least racist-adjacent in their willingness to prioritize some other alleged political objective above the offense of Trump's racism. Those voters and their children and grandchildren would remain a troubling presence in America for decades to come.

Despite the gracious calls for unity and talk of "reaching across the aisle," there was never a serious possibility to do this so long as tens of millions of Americans continued to support one man's delusional narcissism and hundreds of lawmakers in his party continued to enable him. That perspective helped me clarify why the overused term "reckoning" felt so woefully inappropriate to describe the drama of America's racial crisis in 2020. A true reckoning involves a settling of accounts and an obligation to repay the debts of the past. Yet nothing in the behavior of the conquered or the conqueror in American politics indicated that the country was ready to do this. And nothing in the outcomes of the four major crises of 2020 suggested that the nation appreciated the gravity of the challenge before it. At the end of the year, America remained just as divided as it was at the beginning, and the fundamental fault line that separated us was still the same issue that had torn us apart since 1776—the issue of race.

A month after the election, the vast majority of Republicans still refused to recognize that Trump lost the race by an overwhelming seven million votes and lost the electoral college by a decisive 306–232 margin. As the lame-duck president defiantly telephoned Republican government officials in Michigan, Georgia, and Pennsylvania to solicit their help in overturning the will of the people, one of his former primary opponents—hoping to position himself as the heir to the legacy of Trumpism—even volunteered to represent the president by arguing his case in the US Supreme Court. Senator Ted Cruz of Texas was willing to defend the very bully who once called his wife ugly and insinuated that his father had been an accomplice in the assassination of President John F. Kennedy. It demonstrated a grotesque perversion of masculinity that these tough-talking, self-professed patriots would more willingly fight to disenfranchise vulnerable Black and brown voters in America's cities than to fight against a white supremacist bully in their own midst.

The Republican-dominated Supreme Court, with three Trump appointees on its bench, rejected the case Cruz would have argued. Trump's own attorney general was forced to admit that there was no evidence of fraud that would change the outcome of the election. And the Republican governor and secretary of state in Georgia both defended the integrity of their state's election that their Republican president had lost. But, in an indication of how Black progress has always fueled white backlash, Republicans in Georgia immediately announced a new scheme to change the state's voting laws to reduce turnout in future elections. The party that once fought to open up the franchise to Black voters after the Civil War now manufactured baseless claims of Black voter fraud to justify voter suppression laws.

As the year ended, ten million Americans who had lost their jobs at the beginning of the pandemic were still unemployed and nearly twelve million were soon expected to be behind on their rent and utility bills, yet the leaders of the president's party refused to ac-knowledge the incoming president who would inherit these crises in just a matter of weeks. Then, just when it seemed the troubling year had produced all the drama it could, two new stories emerged in the criminal justice system. An Ohio sheriff's deputy, who was search-ing for someone else, shot and killed a law-abiding twenty-three-year-old Black man in his front door as he returned to his home in Columbus with Subway sandwiches after a dentist's appointment. Casey Goodson's grandmother and two toddlers witnessed his grisly shooting near the door. And, in another part of the country, the Chicago Police Department fought to prevent the release of body camera footage showing officers raiding the wrong house and forcing a Black woman to stand naked in her living room while they searched. Anjanette Young had to sue the city to force the release of the evidence. It was as if the nation's law enforcement officers had learned nothing from the year of protests after the deaths of George Floyd and Breonna Taylor.

On December 31, 2020, none of the four crises that defined the year had been resolved. Black people remained hardest hit by all of them. We were still disproportionately hospitalized and killed by coronavirus. We were still more likely to be unemployed from the lingering recession. We were still far more likely to be shot and killed by police or racially profiled by ordinary citizens. And we were still the primary target of an ongoing political effort to disenfranchise voters and throw away legally cast ballots.

There had been no reckoning.

Despite the groundbreaking election of the nation's first Black vice president in November 2020, there had been no fundamental or structural change to improve the lives of Black people in the course of the long, historic, and exhausting year. There had been no effort to eliminate the persistent racial disparities in economic conditions, health outcomes, policing, or voting. And, as some leaders called for yet another return to normalcy, I knew there would be a steep price to pay. I knew that we would one day soon find ourselves in yet another crisis of racial upheaval that would prove far more violent and divisive than the last. I knew that the actual day of reckoning was yet to come. I knew that the fragile truce that kept the peace would not last forever. And I knew that America could never fully embrace the richness of the diversity of the twenty-first century until it revisited its dark history and finally came to terms with the unresolved battles of a conflict that many thought had ended in the nineteenth century.

PART TWO

THE FAITH THAT THE
DARK PAST HAS TAUGHT US

"Sing a song full of the faith that the dark past has taught us."

—James Weldon Johnson,
"Lift Every Voice and Sing"

3

THE NEVER-ENDING CIVIL WAR

Aside from good barbecue, the Gateway Arch, and the Cardinals, there were few things in my youth that gave Black St. Louisans as much pride as Homer G. Phillips Hospital, Sumner High School, and the annual Annie Malone May Day Parade. I was born in the hospital exactly two months before the Gateway Arch was completed and would have attended the high school had my family not moved. I also participated in the parade for several years performing motorcycle stunts with the Black Shriners youth group on a Harley Davidson built for kids. But despite my personal connection, I spent the first fifteen years of my life in St. Louis never fully understanding why these Black institutions were so revered.

I grew up never being told that the hospital name on my birth certificate belonged to a Black lawyer born in post-Reconstruction Missouri in 1880. Even in my twenties and thirties when I lived in Washington, DC, I had no idea that Homer G. Phillips had lived just a mile away from me when he attended Howard University Law School nearly a century earlier. He lived in the home of poet Paul Laurence Dunbar. "We wear the mask that grins and lies," Dunbar wrote in a famous poem that I had often quoted. After graduating from law school, Phillips returned to Missouri to practice in St. Louis, joining thousands of other Blacks who had moved to the city during the Great Migration.

One summer night in 1917, across the Mississippi River from the St. Louis courthouse, where Dred Scott had sued for his freedom from slavery seventy years earlier, howling screams and piercing gunshots could be heard. White men, already angry at what the *St. Louis Post-Dispatch* called "an influx of Negro laborers from the South, taking jobs in industrial plants," began attacking Black people. "Get a nigger!" a reporter from the paper heard them yell. Black residents were "pulled from streetcars, burned out of their homes, stoned in the streets and hanged in broad daylight," the paper reported later.

As one Black man emerged from a burning building, the mob yelled, "Get him!" A man in the crowd "clubbed his revolver and struck the Negro in the face with it," according to Hugh L. Wood's account in the *St. Louis Republic.* "Another dashed an iron bolt between the Negro's eyes. Still another stood near and battered him with a rock." After the man fell to the ground, "a girl stepped up and struck the bleeding man with her foot," Wood reported. "The blood spurted onto her stockings and men laughed and grunted."

In another moment of violence, three white men came upon a Black man lying in a gutter after dark on Fourth Street near Broadway. They flashed a lamp in his face and discovered he was still breathing, the *Post-Dispatch* reported. "Look at that," one man exclaimed. "Not dead yet." Each of the three men then "fired a bullet into the dying man's head, put their revolvers back in their pockets and went on," the paper reported.

Throughout the massacre, the local police appeared absent or complicit. "The only thing that I saw policemen do was to keep the fire line," *Post-Dispatch* journalist Carlos F. Hurd reported from the scene. Officers who tried to check on Black people lying on the pavement received a sharp rebuke from their sergeant, Hurd reported. "They were not supposed to bother themselves about dead Negroes."

When the massacre ended after three days, more than six thousand Black residents of East St. Louis had been forced to leave their homes, at least one hundred were killed, and numerous others were wounded or injured, according to a report in the September 1917 issue of *The Crisis*, the official magazine of the NAACP. Outraged African Americans protested as far away as New York City, and W. E. B. DuBois and James Weldon Johnson marched with hundreds of other Blacks in a silent demonstration down Manhattan's Fifth Avenue.

More than 140 people, mostly white, were charged for their role in the race massacre, including East St. Louis mayor Fred Mollman, although the charges against him were later dropped. A few Blacks were also charged, and it was attorney Homer G. Phillips who defended some of them.

Phillips was a prominent member of the Republican Party, like most politically active African Americans at the time, and he went on to run for Congress after the East St. Louis cases. He also cofounded the Mound City Bar Association, the first Black bar association west of the Mississippi River, and was elected president of the National Bar Association, the oldest and largest national network of predominantly Black attorneys and judges. Then one morning in 1931, while he read a newspaper and waited for a streetcar to take him to work, Phillips was shot and killed. He died before he could see the results of a major development project that he worked on with other African American leaders—a hospital for Black St. Louisans. A generation later, I was born in that hospital, which had been named in his honor.

The Annie Malone May Day Parade was another venerable institution that I knew little about. It had already been going on for sixty-five years when I put on my bright red jumpsuit and my shiny red helmet and rode my kid-sized red motorcycle in the parade in the late 1970s. At the time, I did not know that Annie Minerva Turnbo Malone was an African American entrepreneur who became a millionaire by selling Black hair care products in the early 1900s.

Like Homer G. Phillips, Malone was born in the Reconstruction-era Midwest and moved to St. Louis in the early 1900s. She hired sales agents across the country, and her most famous protégé was a woman ten years her senior named Sarah Breedlove Davis, who would later become known to students of Black history as Madam C. J. Walker. At the same time that Phillips was trying to raise financing to build a Black hospital in 1922, Malone bought a new building for the St. Louis Colored Orphans Home, and eventually it was renamed in her honor. Unbeknownst to me, the parade that I had participated in all those years in St. Louis was the biggest annual fundraiser for the Annie Malone Children's Home.

The other famous Black institution was my mom's high school. Over the years, I listened in disbelief as my mom told stories about the school's famous graduates. The first name I remember was Julius Hunter, the local Black TV news anchor in St. Louis. He graduated from Sumner High School in 1961, along with tennis star Arthur Ashe. There was also a young woman named Anna Mae Bullock, who graduated from the school in 1958. She would later become known as the singer Tina Turner. The long list of the school's alumni included rock star Chuck Berry, opera singer Grace Bumbry, Congressman Bill Clay, and comedian Dick Gregory. I heard a lot of names over the years, but the one name that no one explained to me was Sumner. Who was Sumner? And why was this person connected to this school?

I learned years later that Charles Sumner was a US senator from Massachusetts who served from 1851 until his death in 1874. Unlike Homer G. Phillips and Annie Malone, he was white. That surprised me. Why was this famous Black school named after a white man? I knew a family member who graduated from Jefferson Davis High School in Montgomery, Alabama, but that Confederate name was adopted in 1968 as a racist response to Black empowerment. Naming a Black school in St. Louis after a white man in Massachusetts was different.

What I realized after I left St. Louis and grew older was that all three of these famous institutions were, directly or indirectly, the products of the Reconstruction period in America. Historians define

Reconstruction as the time from the end of the Civil War in 1865 to the withdrawal of federal troops that protected African Americans in the South in 1877. But the needs of African Americans after the Civil War did not end when the troops withdrew.

The Homer G. Phillips Hospital was necessary in St. Louis, Missouri, because the city remained racially segregated throughout most of the twentieth century, and African Americans needed access to health care in their own community. Were it not for another institution of Reconstruction, Howard University Law School, Homer G. Phillips might not have received the law degree that enabled him to help the people of his community.

The children's home that bore Annie Malone's name was also a testament to Reconstruction. It had originally opened in 1888 as a refuge for African American orphans. It, too, reflected a reality in which Black St. Louisans were separate but never equal—a reality that worsened with the collapse of Reconstruction after 1877.

Sumner High School also had a history connected to Reconstruction. Opened in 1875, just ten years after the Civil War ended, it was the first Black high school west of the Mississippi River. The school's name was a tribute to the famed Northern abolitionist and prominent white Republican senator who fought against slavery and supported the thirteenth, fourteenth, and fifteenth amendments, giving freedom, citizenship, and voting rights to African Americans. It was a compelling story that seemed to merit recognition by a Black public school in Missouri. But the deeper story of Sumner, like the story of America itself, was a story of disappointing racial compromise and willingness to sacrifice the needs of African Americans for partisan political expediency.

From the very first day Black Americans were freed from slavery, fearful white Americans began a race against time to stop the people they had once enslaved from becoming too powerful. It would not take long before the Republican Party of Abraham Lincoln would eventually retreat from its commitment to Black people, but it would take nearly a century before Black people would finally abandon the Grand Old Party (GOP). During that ninety-nine-year span from 1865 to 1964, the racist Democratic Party of the nineteenth century slowly evolved into the party of civil rights, while Lincoln's Republican Party very gradually began to transition into the party against those rights. Not surprisingly, the realignment of the two major political parties focused on the one core issue that had divided the nation from its founding in 1776 to the Civil War in 1861 to the civil rights movement of the 1960s—race.

The story begins in 1856 in a bitterly divided young country. With sixteen free states and fifteen slave states, the nation's leaders struggle to strike an agreement to admit new states to the union. A small but bloody civil war breaks out between abolitionists and slave supporters in Kansas, and an uncivil battle erupts in Washington as Representative Preston Brooks of South Carolina ambushes Massachusetts senator Charles Sumner on the floor of the United States Senate and bashes his head with a cane. It is in this contentious climate that the new Republican Party adopts a platform urging Congress to prohibit slavery in the territories, and Democrats respond with a dire warning that efforts to interfere with slavery could lead to "the most alarming and dangerous consequences."

By the time Lincoln wins the 1860 election, the nation is on the brink of civil war. South Carolina, Mississippi, Florida, Alabama, Georgia, Louisiana, and Texas quickly secede from the union in the four-month period between Lincoln's election in November and his first day in office in March. South Carolina's declaration of secession in December 1860 complains that Northern states have "united in the election of a man to the high office of President of the United States, whose opinions and purposes are hostile to slavery." Then, just a month after Lincoln's inauguration, Confederate forces fire on federal troops at Fort Sumter, South Carolina, and America's deadliest war is launched.

Abraham Lincoln would prove to be more complicated than his Southern detractors suggested. "I have no purpose, directly or indirectly, to interfere with the institution of slavery in the States where it exists," he maintained in his first inaugural address. Even as seven Southern states had already withdrawn from the union, he appealed to the "bonds of affection," the "mystic chords of memory," and the "better angels of our nature" to convince the departed to return. They did not, and Lincoln prosecuted the war against them while still maintaining white supremacist views. "There must be a position of superior and inferior, and I as much as any other man am in favor of having the superior position assigned to the white race," he wrote. Even as he commanded soldiers into battle, he expressed his "paramount object" was to save the Union, not to save or destroy slavery. "If I could save the Union without freeing any slave I would do it, and if I could save it by freeing all the slaves I would do it; and if I could save it by freeing some and leaving others alone I would also do that," he wrote to *New-York Tribune* newspaper editor Horace Greeley in August 1862.

Lincoln's successor, Southern Democrat Andrew Johnson, raised troubling new concerns for Black people. He vetoed civil rights legislation to protect African Americans and became the first president in American history to be impeached—avoiding Senate conviction and removal from office by only one vote. In his last months as president, three years after the Civil War ended, Johnson announced "a full pardon and amnesty" for Confederate soldiers and gave them "restoration of all rights, privileges, and immunities" under the law. Echoing a theme that white politicians of various parties would repeat for centuries, Johnson described his Christmas Day amnesty proclamation as a step to "secure permanent peace" and "restore confidence and fraternal feeling." It was one of many examples in American history in which the country would choose peace for white people over justice for Black people.

Despite Johnson's resistance, Reconstruction-era Republicans pushed through sweeping new federal civil rights laws, including the

Civil Rights Act of 1866 (giving Blacks citizenship), the Ku Klux Klan Acts of 1870 and 1871 (placing elections under federal control), and the Civil Rights Act of 1875 (banning discrimination in public places). In a dramatic update of the nation's founding documents, Republicans also pushed through three new historic civil rights amendments between 1865 and 1870, the first changes to the US Constitution in more than sixty years. The Thirteenth Amendment, abolishing slavery, passed the House by a vote of 119–56, with Republicans voting 86–0 in favor and Democrats voting overwhelmingly against it.

Black voters flocked to the Grand Old Party as soon as they were allowed to vote. Millions of Black men registered as Republicans, thousands were elected to public office, dozens were elected to state legislatures, a few made their way to the United States Congress, two were elected US senators, and one became the nation's first Black governor. In a stunning reversal of fortune, voters in South Carolina—the first state that had seceded from the union—elected a Black majority to the state legislature just three years after the conclusion of the Civil War.

It was a moment when even white Republicans boldly demanded racial equality, no matter the consequences. "From the beginning of our history, the country has been afflicted with compromise," Charles Sumner complained to his Senate colleagues in 1866. "It is by compromise that human rights have been abandoned," he argued. "I insist that this shall cease."

Sumner was right. Since the founding of the republic, America had repeatedly chosen compromise over conscience. As the new nation formed in 1776, the founders deleted a paragraph from Thomas Jefferson's Declaration of Independence that described slavery as an "execrable commerce" and condemned Great Britain for its determination "to keep open a market where men should be bought and sold." Jefferson knew very well that the institution of slavery was evil. "I tremble for my country when I reflect that God is just, that His justice cannot sleep forever," he wrote. "Commerce between master and slave is despotism," he said. "Nothing is more certainly written in the book of fate than that these people are to be free," Jefferson predicted. Yet Jefferson maintained the ownership of Black human beings as slaves and compromised his personal business affairs and the nation's. It was compromise that caused the language of freedom to be removed from the document that would serve as the nation's own birth certificate.

A decade after declaring the nation's independence, the framers expunged any mention of the word "slave" or "slavery" from the Constitution that they approved in 1787, even as they brokered a compromise to reduce slaves to three-fifths of a person for the purpose of counting residents of the various states. They also approved another compromise that expressly prohibited Congress from outlawing the slave trade until 1808. After debating the issue of slavery at the Constitutional Convention, many of the attendees knew the institution was indefensible, but they allowed the slave trade to continue for another two decades.

In order to preserve the fragile coalition of Northern and Southern states that formed the union, America's leaders made more compromises to appease the various factions. The Compromise of 1790—the famous "room where it happened" deal chronicled in the musical *Hamilton*—sought to bridge the chasm between North and South by locating the nation's capital on the Potomac River in exchange for allowing the federal government to assume states' debt.

The Missouri Compromise of 1820 sought to maintain the balance between North and South by admitting Missouri as a slave state and Maine as a free state and prohibiting slavery in the northern parts of the new Louisiana Territory.

The Compromise of 1850 also sought to avoid the inevitable conflict. In return for admitting California as a free state and abolishing the slave trade in Washington, DC, Congress passed the Fugitive Slave Act, which required former slaves to be returned back to the brutality of bondage, even if they had escaped into free territory.

Next, the Kansas-Nebraska Act of 1854 repealed the boundaries of the 1820 Missouri Compromise and allowed new territories to determine the question of slavery based on popular sovereignty.

Time after time, the white men in power continued to prioritize peace between the states over justice for Black people, and by 1861, when the union finally collapsed under the weight of these untenable compromises, the nation had neither.

It would take the deaths of more than six hundred thousand Americans to settle the issue of slavery, but the country would never attempt to eliminate the systemic racism and white supremacy that undergirded the institution. Those dangerous ideologies would remain. Even after the nation's bloodiest war, a number of lawmakers returned to the language of compromise, insisting on unity to heal the wounds and bring the republic back together. Sumner called the nation to equality instead. "It is not enough to show me that a measure is expedient," the Massachusetts senator said. "You must show me also that it is right."

Sumner was correct, and his passionate critique of compromise in the face of injustice is the core argument of this book. Yet Sumner, too, would become a perpetrator of the very evil he condemned. Despite his lofty language, he backtracked over time, along with several other white Republicans who had been champions of the cause of abolition.

Just seven years after the Civil War, Sumner bolted from Lincoln's Republican Party to join the newly created Liberal Republican Party. Despite the new party's name and its progressive government reform agenda, there was nothing liberal for Black people in its call for reconciliation with the former Confederate states. Instead, it was another example of how allegedly supportive politicians would betray Black people when doing so served their political agenda.

Among those aligned with Sumner in the new breakaway political party was a prominent St. Louisan named Carl Schurz, an abolitionist and former Civil War general who served as a US senator from

Missouri from 1869 to 1875. I had never heard of Schurz during the years I lived in St. Louis and first came across his name while on a bike ride in New York City. There, along the East River, I found a fifteen-acre park named after him, sitting next to Gracie Mansion, the mayor's residence. I hadn't given much thought to Schurz until I started teaching at Columbia University and took a stroll one day to the faculty house across from Morningside Park. A huge bronze statue of Schurz stood guard over the park. The adjoining inscription declared him "a defender of liberty and a friend of human rights." This time, I googled him and quickly found an article in *The New Yorker* by Columbia professor Nicholas Lemann.

Schurz had joined the Liberal Republican Party and argued for the withdrawal of federal troops from the South in an 1875 speech to the US Senate. "I declare I shall hail the day as a most auspicious one for the colored race in the South," Schurz told the Senate, "when they begin to see the identity of their own true interests with the interests of the white people among whom they have to live."

Despite the widespread documentation of white violence and intimidation that Black citizens faced in the South, Schurz told the Senate that "the only act of terrorism and intimidation" he had ever witnessed "was the cruel clubbing and stoning of a colored man" in North Carolina "by men of his own race." It was a stunningly disingenuous argument, made just ten years after the abolition of slavery in America, that shifted the blame of racial division away from the white people who had owned Black human beings as property from 1619 to 1865—that is, 246 of the preceding 256 years in American history.

Why, I asked myself, did Schurz deserve this statue high above a park that overlooked the Black community of Harlem? And why, for that matter, had Charles Sumner's shift not disqualified him from hero worship, as well? When Sumner passed away in March of 1874, Carl Schurz was asked to deliver a eulogy in the Boston Music Hall the following month. Schurz told the audience: "He belongs to all of us in the North and in the South—to the Blacks he helped to make free, and to the whites he strove to make brothers again." This was precisely the problem. After belatedly but appropriately abolishing slavery, far too many white elected officials became more concerned with repairing the friendships between white people in North and South than repairing the breach between Black and white.

Step by step, compromise by compromise, the promise of Reconstruction began to wither away before it could even bloom. Soon, it would vanish altogether. In 1877, Republicans abandoned their commitment to Black Southerners as part of a deal to resolve a disputed presidential election. Although New York Democrat Samuel Tilden defeated Ohio Republican Rutherford B. Hayes in the popular vote in 1876, Democrats allowed Hayes, the Republican, to become president in exchange for the withdrawal of federal troops from the South and the return of control over the former Confederate states to the very white Southerners who had led the rebellion against the union. It was barely a dozen years since the end of the Civil War, and the old South had already won back the right to resume its oppression of its Black residents. Final details of the notorious 1877 deal, which effectively ended Reconstruction, were determined at Washington's Wormley's Hotel, owned by a Black businessman named James Wormley.

Over the next several decades, the federal government lurched away from Black concerns. Violent voter suppression campaigns diminished Black political power and drove Black elected officials out of office, leaving the two main political parties free to realign themselves to compete for white voters. Democrats largely ignored the concerns of Black voters, while Republicans continued to send mixed signals to them. Republican president James Garfield spoke of racial inclusion and appointed several African Americans to government posts, including former US senator Blanche K. Bruce of Mississippi as Register of the Treasury, a position that made him the first Black man whose signature appeared on US currency. (Ironically, Bruce's signature appeared next to an image of Charles Sumner on the five hundred-dollar bill.) But the dream died when the forty-nine-year-old president was struck by an assassin's bullet in a Washington, DC, train station.

Two years later, the Republican-controlled Supreme Court struck down the Civil Rights Act of 1875, in a blatantly racist decision written by Justice Joseph Bradley. "When a man has emerged from slavery," Bradley wrote, "there must be some stage in the progress of his elevation when he takes the rank of a mere citizen and ceases to be the special favorite of the laws." The *special favorite* of the laws? Eight of the nine Supreme Court justices—all appointed by Republican presidents—struck down a law that protected former slaves from discrimination because they thought it gave Black people special rights. The sitting Republican president, Chester Arthur, asked lawmakers to correct the Supreme Court's error in the *Civil Rights Cases*, but Congress never did. It would take another eighty years of waiting and a virtual role reversal of the political parties before the federal government finally passed another civil rights bill commensurate to the law that the Supreme Court struck down in 1883.

As racist Democrats took back control of the post-Reconstruction South, anti-Black violence soared, and yet the federal government, under the leadership of ten different Republican presidents from 1877 to 1933, failed to enact any new major civil rights laws to protect Black citizens from lynching or discrimination. After years of white Southern voter intimidation, literacy tests, poll taxes, grandfather clauses, ballot-box stuffing, violent threats and reprisals, the number of Black elected officials dwindled. In contrast to the popular and inaccurate narrative of steady racial progress, post-Reconstruction America set Black people backward. In 1877, in the waning days of Reconstruction, there were eight Black members of the United States Congress. By 1901, when Republican George Henry White of North Carolina left office, there were none. After Representative White, no Black person would serve in Congress for another twenty-eight years.

The same was true in state legislatures. In the 1870s, there were more than three hundred Black state legislators in office in the South, according to data from the US Department of Justice Civil Rights Division, but by the turn of the century, there were none. They had become victims of the politics of a darkening America. Three decades of Southern Democratic resistance, and the failure of the Republican Party to respond to the threat, took its toll. The hope that was constructed in the 1870s for a new Black political power was almost completely demolished by the early twentieth century.

Though Republicans continued to win Black votes around the turn of the century, Black voters grew increasingly disappointed by the party's failure to stop white violence against African Americans. After Republican president William McKinley appointed a Black man named Frazier Baker as the postmaster for the predominantly white town of Lake City, South Carolina, an angry lynch mob set fire to Baker's home office in February 1898 and shot and killed him and his two-year-old daughter as they tried to flee the burning building.

That same year, just 150 miles away, an angry mob of hundreds of white people in Wilmington, North Carolina, destroyed the offices of the local newspaper, burned Black businesses, and lynched Black residents just two days after a biracial fusion government had been elected. The violent mob deposed the elected government and installed their own white supremacist leaders to replace them. "It was the only *coup d'état* ever to take place on American soil," Adrienne LaFrance and Vann R. Newkirk II wrote in *The Atlantic* in 2017. It also set a precedent for what angry white Americans would attempt again 123 years later at the United States Capitol.

In response to the violence, journalist and civil rights leader Ida B. Wells-Barnett wrote to President McKinley, "During the past fifteen years, more than 2500 men, women and children have been put to death through lynchings, hanging, shooting, drowning and burning alive." She continued, "Our government has not taken the first step to stop the slaughter."

Wells-Barnett met with McKinley, and he assured her that the federal government would "prosecute the lynchers of the Black postmaster," she wrote in her autobiography. But when a trial was held in federal court, an all-white jury in Charleston, South Carolina, refused to convict any of the eleven defendants accused of murdering a federal employee and burning down a federal building. As archivist Trichita Chestnut wrote for the US Archives, the jury deadlocked on charges for eight of the defendants, and the Justice Department did not seek further prosecution.

Just a few years later, when a white bartender was killed in Brownsville, Texas, local residents blamed Black soldiers stationed in the city for the murder. Without even holding a military trial, Republican President Teddy Roosevelt dishonorably discharged 167 Black soldiers of the Twenty-Fifth Infantry in Brownsville. It would take another six decades, after the 1970 publication of *The Brownsville Raid* by John D. Weaver, before the army investigated and disproved the charges and the federal government finally reversed Roosevelt's 1906 order.

By the mid 1920s, African Americans had been voting Republican for nearly sixty years, and although the GOP membership included many champions of Black civil rights, the party had failed to enact any new major civil rights legislation in five decades. It had failed to renew the civil rights law struck down by the high court. It had failed to enact an elections bill to protect Black voters. And it had failed to enact an antilynching bill to protect Black bodies. The inability to protect Black lives from white terrorism, along with the rise of the "lily-white movement" within the Republican Party and the collapse of the economy with the Great Depression, would create an unexpected opening for Democrats to win Black voters for the first time in that party's history. A few weeks before the 1928 election, *The Chicago Defender*, one of the most influential Black newspapers in the country, endorsed Democratic presidential nominee Al Smith over Republican nominee Herbert Hoover, according to an account by Ethan Michaeli in his book, *The Defender: How the Legendary Black Newspaper Changed America*. As cited in the book, an editorial in *The Defender* read: "If 50 years of support to the Republican Party doesn't get us justice, then we must of necessity shift our allegiance to new quarters."

Finally, in 1935, after decades of Republican domination, Arthur Wergs Mitchell of Illinois became the first African American to serve in Congress as a Democrat. The floodgates opened, and African Americans left the Republican Party in droves. Franklin Roosevelt received 71 percent of African American votes in the 1936 election, the first time in history a Democratic presidential candidate won the Black vote. His successor, Harry Truman, won an even higher percentage of Black voters in his 1948 campaign. But the Black vote remained competitive, and Dwight Eisenhower, the only Republican to serve between Herbert Hoover and Richard Nixon, earned a respectable 24 percent of the Black vote in 1952 and then increased his share to an impressive 39 percent in 1956.

As president, Eisenhower signed the Civil Rights Act of 1957 and sent federal troops to Little Rock, Arkansas, to integrate Central High School, but he also appeared to discourage the 1954 *Brown v. Board of Education* decision. At a dinner with Chief Justice Earl Warren during the time the court was still considering the famous integration case, Eisenhower reportedly defended white segregationists: "These are not bad people," he told the chief justice. "All they are concerned about is that their sweet little girls are not required to sit in school beside some big, overgrown Negroes."

At the dawn of the 1960s, both Democrats and Republicans had given Black voters decades of disappointment and broken promises. "I must make it palpably clear that the dearth of positive leadership from Washington is not confined to one political party," Dr. King announced in a September 1960 speech to the National Urban League. "The fact is that both major parties have been hypocritical on the question of civil rights. Each of them has been willing to follow the long pattern of using the Negro as a political football."

A month later, not long before the presidential election, King was sitting in a Georgia jail cell, after being arrested for participating in a civil rights protest. While his pregnant wife, Coretta, worried about her husband's well-being, the two major presidential nominees— John Kennedy and Richard Nixon—struggled to develop a response to the news. Neither wanted to offend white Southerners by speaking out publicly in King's defense, but Kennedy was persuaded to place a quick private phone call to Mrs. King to convey his concern. After that call, Dr. King's influential preacher father, Martin Luther King Sr., announced his support for the Democratic candidate, and Kennedy narrowly won one of the closest races in American presidential history with 68 percent of the Black vote, improving on the 61 percent won by the party's 1956 nominee, Adlai Stevenson.

Eight months after Kennedy's assassination, Democrat Lyndon B. Johnson (LBJ) signed the Civil Rights Act of 1964 with bipartisan support in the House and Senate. For many white Southern Democrats, it would be seen as a betrayal of the party's white supremacist roots. As a Texas Democrat who had voted against civil rights bills early in his career and was widely known to use offensive racial slurs, LBJ was an unlikely champion for African Americans. Yet, with the stroke of a pen, a racist white Southern Democratic president named Johnson finally allowed the party to begin moving beyond the legacy of the last racist white Southern Democratic president named Johnson.

Among the twenty-seven Senate "nay" votes on the Civil Rights Act of 1964 was Republican Barry Goldwater. Goldwater's opposition to civil rights did not doom his campaign. Instead, just a few weeks after he cast that vote, his party nominated him to be its presidential nominee. Outside the party's convention in San Francisco, Black baseball legend and longtime Republican Jackie Robinson joined fifty thousand demonstrators against Goldwater. Meanwhile, one of the few Black Republican delegates inside the building was barred from participating "solely because of their race," author Leah Wright Rigueur explains in her book, *The Loneliness of the Black*

Republican: Pragmatic Politics and the Pursuit of Power. One Pennsylvania delegate, William Young, even had his suit set on fire and was told to "keep in your own place." Another delegate, George Fleming of New Jersey, briefly walked out of the convention "sobbing that he was tired of being mistreated by 'Goldwater people,'" the *New York Times* reported. Fleming told the *Times* that the Republican convention delegates called him "nigger," pushed him, and stepped on his feet. "I had to leave to keep my self-respect," he said.

These protests did not change the outcome of the convention. On July 16, 1964, Barry Goldwater accepted the Republican Party's nomination for president, urging the country to be "proud of its past," and did not back down on his rhetoric. "I would remind you that extremism in the defense of liberty is no vice," Goldwater thundered to the crowd. "And let me remind you also that moderation in the pursuit of justice is no virtue." As the delegates cheered, the old Republican Party perished. The party that once freed the slaves, amended the Constitution, enacted progressive civil rights legislation, and dispatched federal troops to protect African Americans from racism in the 1860s had become a new party that nominated a right-wing standard-bearer in the 1960s. The Grand Old Party was dead.

As the party of Lincoln died, a new Republican Party was slowly birthed. The 1960s GOP planted its seeds deep in the poisonous soil of white racial resentment. But when the roots strengthened and the sapling grew to maturity, the ripened fruit from that forbidden tree would tempt the party back toward the sin that had repeatedly torn the nation asunder. The modern racial conflicts we face today trace their roots to that tainted ground.

After signing the Civil Rights Act, President Johnson reportedly predicted, "We just lost the south for a generation." He was, at least, partly correct. The Democrats' unexpected embrace of civil rights slowly wiped out the party in the South. After Johnson signed the bill, Georgia—a state the Democrats had carried in every presidential election from 1868 to 1960—voted Republican for the first time in its history. Louisiana, Mississippi, Alabama, and South Carolina joined in, voting Republican for the first time since the Reconstruction era. The pattern continued for decades. In six of the next fourteen presidential elections after 1964, Democrats failed to carry even a single state in the South.

The post–civil rights political realignment of white Southerners from Democrat to Republican allowed some ticket splitting for a few Democratic congressional candidates over the years, but when Louisiana Democrat Mary Landrieu lost her Senate reelection race to a Republican in 2014, it marked the end of an era. It had been a remarkable fifty-year transition. On the day President Johnson signed the Civil Rights Act of 1964, there were twenty-one Southern Democrats in the Senate, but by January 3, 2015, with a Black Democratic president in office, there were no Democrats from the Deep South left in the chamber. After a century of political dominance in the South, the Democratic dynasty had come to an end.

The root cause of this dramatic political realignment was race, America's original fault line. As the two major parties swapped their identities, the two largest racial groups in America correspondingly switched their party affiliation. In 1964, 94 percent of Black voters cast their ballots for Democrat Lyndon Johnson, the highest percentage of Black voter support of any year on record at that time. In contrast, white voters started moving in the opposite direction. The post-1964 racial dynamics taught Democrats that they needed to assemble multiracial coalitions to win presidential elections and taught Republicans that they no longer needed a significant percentage of Black votes to win those same elections. Democrats tried repeatedly to win back white voters by nominating white Southern men like Jimmy Carter of Georgia, Bill Clinton of Arkansas, and Al Gore of Tennessee, or by selecting running mates like Lloyd Bentsen of Texas, John Edwards of North Carolina, and Tim Kaine of Virginia, but this would not fundamentally alter the trajectory of the two parties. Despite numerous outreach efforts, no Democratic presidential nominee has won the white vote since 1964. Even the two white Southern Democrats who did capture the presidency—Carter and Clinton—failed to win the white vote.

The new political reality did not happen by accident. "Political success goes to the party that can cohesively hold together the largest number of ethnic prejudices." That was the theory put forward by Republican operative and Nixon campaign veteran Kevin Phillips in a 1970 *New York Times* article entitled "Nixon's Southern Strategy." Phillips laid out a cynical argument for why Republicans should essentially ignore Black voters. "Republicans are never going to get more than 10 to 20 percent of the Negro vote and they don't need any more than that," Phillips argued.

Other Republicans, while not disputing the math, understood there was danger in speaking so publicly about these intentions. When Nixon nominated two segregation-supporting Southerners— Clement Haynsworth and G. Harrold Carswell—to the US Supreme Court, the Senate rejected both of them—the first time a president had been denied two of his Supreme Court nominees since Grover Cleveland. "We flat out invited the kind of political battle that ultimately erupted," grumbled a young Nixon aide named Lamar Alexander. "This confirmed the southern strategy just at a time when it was being nationally debated," he wrote in a White House memo. Years later, in a 2007 interview with the Richard Nixon Presidential Library and Museum, by which time Alexander had become a Republican senator, he confirmed that "the Southern strategy of John Mitchell [Nixon's campaign manager] and Kevin Phillips was so important in the '68 campaign."

Other postmortem confessions also confirmed what was happening. In a 1981 interview, Republican strategist Lee Atwater described how the changing status of Black people forced the language of white racial resentment to evolve from the explicit opposition to integration of the 1950s to a more subtle racism of the Reagan-Bush era of the 1980s:

You start out in 1954 by saying, "Nigger, nigger, nigger." By 1968 you can't say "nigger"—that hurts you, backfires. So you say stuff like, uh, forced busing, states' rights, and all that stuff, and you're getting so abstract. Now, you're talking about cutting taxes, and all these things you're talking about are totally economic things and a byproduct of them is, Blacks get hurt worse than whites. . . . "We want to cut this," is much more abstract than even the busing thing . . . and a hell of a lot more abstract than "Nigger, nigger."

Politicians rarely leave smoking guns behind, but this was as close as one could come to finding one. The forty-two-minute recorded Atwater interview was not released until November 2012, when it was finally published in *The Nation*. By that time, Atwater had already tried to atone for his 1988 campaign tactics in a widely reported deathbed confession, where he specifically apologized for calling Mike Dukakis a "little bastard" and for saying he would make Willie Horton his running mate. "I am sorry for both statements: the first for its naked cruelty, the second because it makes me sound racist, which I am not," Atwater said. The apology interview appeared in January 1991, when Atwater was fighting a brain tumor that he knew would soon take his life. Two months later, the forty-year-old adviser to Presidents Ronald Reagan and George H. W. Bush was dead.

In yet another confession, former Nixon domestic policy adviser, John Ehrlichman, explained the rationale behind the "War on Drugs" in a 1994 interview published in *Harper's Magazine* in 2016.

The Nixon campaign in 1968, and the Nixon White House after that, had two enemies: the antiwar left and Black people. . . . We knew we couldn't make it illegal to be either against the war or Black, but by getting the public to associate the hippies with marijuana and Blacks with heroin, and then criminalizing both heavily, we could disrupt those communities. We could arrest their leaders, raid their homes, break up their meetings, and vilify them night after night on the evening news. Did we know we were lying about the drugs? Of course we did.

Nixon's campaign against Blacks and hippies was a fitting strategy for the Archie Bunker era, a time when Americans sat down every week to watch a racist white man from Queens, New York, pine for the good old days when non-college-educated, working-class white men could still earn a decent living and settle down in a safe, nonthreatening white neighborhood. But the values of racial resentment that led those white voters to political conservatism were also being used to justify the eradication of government policies and institutions that protected working-class whites. By weakening labor unions, depressing wages, deregulating corporate activity, canceling pension funds, cutting taxes, and dismantling the social safety net, conservatives were not only hurting Black and brown people, they were also reconditioning an entire generation of white people to expect less from the government than what it had offered their parents. As job security disappeared, health care benefits vanished, and college education costs skyrocketed, working-class whites were encouraged to direct their anger at low-income "minorities" alleged to be on welfare, rather than at a corporate-driven economic system that primarily served the interests of, and skewed its resources toward, big businesses and the wealthy.

By using racially coded words and dog whistles, Nixon gave Republicans and conservative Democrats a seemingly neutral language they could use to speak to white voters without making them feel racist. Instead of calling for segregation, they complained about "forced busing." Instead of calling Blacks criminals, they talked about "law and order." Instead of labeling Blacks as lazy, they talked about "welfare." At the same time, they created a caricature image of blackness that was wholly dependent on government largesse for survival. Although white welfare recipients vastly outnumbered Black and brown ones, welfare was portrayed as a government device to help minorities.

Thus, by attacking the federal government, conservatives could simultaneously appeal to hard-core white racists who believed the government was forcing them to live with Black people, and, at the same time, reach soft-core racists who did not necessarily object to the *theory* of equality but felt their hard-earned tax dollars were being wasted to feed and house lazy Black people. Antigovernment rhetoric also allowed Republicans to merge two important wings of their party— the country club Republicans who wanted tax cuts and the racial resentment Republicans who felt they were losing out to Black people because of government programs and affirmative action. Reducing the size of government was a stroke of evil political genius. It limited the amount of help given to Black people, and it limited the number of tax dollars given to the government, thereby appeasing both the country club Republicans and the racial resentment Republicans.

Post-Nixon Republicans expanded on the strategy. "There's a woman in Chicago," Ronald Reagan told a white New Hampshire audience in 1976. "She has 80 names, 30 addresses, 12 Social Security cards and is collecting veterans' benefits on four non-existing deceased husbands." Reagan told the audience the woman was collecting Social Security, Medicaid, food stamps, and other welfare benefits under her multiple aliases. "Her tax-free cash income alone is over $150,000," he claimed. Without ever mentioning the woman by name or race, Reagan's use of the words "Chicago" and "welfare" conjured up a powerful image of a Black inner-city "welfare queen" who was abusing the system to enrich herself at the expense of the good, white taxpaying citizens. It did not matter to Reagan that the story was an elaborate exaggeration about a forty-seven-year-old woman named Linda Taylor who did not have eighty aliases and did not make $150,000 a year. "The story does not quite check out," the *New York Times* reported after Reagan's speech, but at that point, the damage was done.

When Reagan secured the Republican presidential nomination in 1980, he turned to another racist dog whistle. "I believe in states' rights," he told a white Southern audience at the Neshoba County Fair in Mississippi. Republicans from Lincoln to Eisenhower had publicly rejected states' rights arguments that racist Southern Democrats used to justify slavery and the segregation of Black Americans, but here was Reagan in 1980 sounding just like a 1950s Southern Democrat as his campaign traveled to the same community where three civil rights workers—James Chaney, Andrew Goodman, and Michael Schwerner—were notoriously kidnapped and killed in 1964.

This was not the party of Lincoln that had deployed the United States military to wage war against rebellious slave states. Nor was this the party that ratified three historic constitutional amendments to prevent states from blocking the rights of African Americans. This was a new party that had nominated a self-described "extremist" presidential nominee in 1964 and learned from that experience of bitter loss how to communicate to Southern racists without offending Northern moderates. Nothing, from slavery to segregation, had bothered Southern racists more than federal government intrusion in the affairs of their states, and Reagan's message of states' rights communicated a clear sense of solidarity with that cause.

Reagan followed through on those commitments as president. Just a few weeks before the 1982 midterm elections, he launched his controversial War on Drugs. "Most people assume the War on Drugs was launched in response to the crisis caused by crack cocaine in inner-city neighborhoods," Michelle Alexander wrote in *The New Jim Crow*. The truth, she explained, is that Reagan launched the war *before* crack became an issue and "hired staff to publicize the emergence of crack cocaine in 1985" to build support for the war. This explains why Reagan never mentioned "crack" or "cocaine" anywhere in his October 1982 speech. He did mention that "millions of dollars will be allocated for prison and jail facilities." That was the hidden agenda, and African Americans would soon become the direct targets of mass incarceration.

Even aside from the War on Drugs, Reagan governed with shameless indifference toward the concerns of Black Americans. His administration reversed long-standing policy at the Internal Revenue Service when it tried to give tax exemptions to racially segregated private schools like Bob Jones University in South Carolina. His Justice Department waged a war on affirmative action and minority contracting requirements. He fired all three Democratic members of the US Commission on Civil Rights, including distinguished Howard University professor Mary Frances Berry, and replaced them with Blacks who were hostile to civil rights. And in 1986, while Nelson Mandela remained imprisoned in South Africa, Reagan vetoed a bill that authorized economic sanctions against the racist apartheid government of that country. In an extraordinary rebuke, Congress overrode Reagan's veto. It was, according to Politico, "the first time since enactment of the War Powers Resolution in 1973 that Congress had overridden a presidential foreign policy veto."

History would soon vindicate Nelson Mandela and the Black South Africans for whom he fought, yet the broader success of Ronald Reagan as a political figure gave him mythological status among Republicans. In Reagan, the GOP found a smooth-talking, union-busting, tax-cutting, defense-spending, welfare-hating spokesman who could articulate the party's values and appeal to white racial resentment more effectively than any Republican in modern history. His landslide victories in 1980 and 1984 paved the way for future candidates and convinced a generation of young Republicans that they were the proper heirs to a new "permanent majority" that would rule the nation for a century. Reagan's legacy of antigovernment rhetoric would shape American political debate for decades, but it was his party's racial rhetoric that would eventually expose the most glaring paradox.

America had entered a new stage in its never-ending civil war, and just like the conflicts of the 1860s and 1960s, it was never just a battle about the federal government; it was a battle about race. As the country would learn in the decades that followed, a significant percentage of white Americans were never as antigovernment as Republicans suggested they were. They were anti-Black.

Looking back now from the vantage point of the post-Trump era, it's clear how the Reagan brand of politics altered the trajectory of both the country and the Republican Party for generations to come. Reagan provided Republicans a suburban-friendly script for future elected officials to disguise an unpopular procorporate, antiworker agenda behind a veil of telegenic demagoguery and plausibly deniable racism. After Reagan, it would only get worse.

4

GEORGE H. W. BUSH'S KINDER, GENTLER RACISM

I was twenty-three years old, working in my first job out of college, when I heard the name "Willie Horton." It lingered like a cloud in the air for long stretches of time, casting a shadow over the work I was doing. He was the star of a new television commercial in which he played the role of a super villain—a menacing, bearded Black man who raped, kidnapped, and murdered his victims. But Horton was a real person, and he had been plucked from obscurity to be featured in an advertisement for George H. W. Bush's 1988 presidential campaign. The message to white America was unmistakable, and the lesson for politicians was unambiguous. If Goldwater, Nixon, and Reagan had created the conditions for elected officials to manipulate white racial resentment, it was George H. W. Bush who first showed Republicans how to weaponize that resentment.

I stood on the other side of the fence, watching my dream job in politics slowly turn into a nightmare. I had never imagined when I graduated from college and took a job working for the Dukakis campaign that my candidate would become the Democratic nominee for president a year later and I would land a position traveling with him every day on the campaign trail. Unfortunately, after surviving the primary, the campaign was faltering under the strain of the general election, and I felt like I was a cornerman for a boxer who was being beaten up in the ring and refused to fight back.

In the wake of two terms of Ronald Reagan, the election pitted Republican Vice President George Bush against Democratic Massachusetts Governor Michael Dukakis. Always a gentleman, Dukakis had vowed to run a clean campaign. But when Bush accused Dukakis of being a soft-on-crime, unpatriotic, out-of-touch, elitist "Massachusetts liberal," Dukakis refused to engage Bush forcefully until it was too late to make a difference. The great irony of Bush's campaign of attacks was that he—the wealthy patrician scion of a political dynasty who summered at a seaside mansion in Kennebunkport, Maine—convinced America that Dukakis—the thrifty son of immigrants who shopped at Filene's Basement for discounted suits and lived in a modest two-family duplex—was the elitist. It was maddening that people believed Bush's attacks, but it was difficult to fight Bush's scorched earth campaign while Dukakis hemmed his staff in with a public pledge of positivity.

Run by Lee Atwater, Bush's campaign seemed to understand the larger societal forces in play that ours did not. During a trip to Washington, DC, early in the general election season, I remember a group of protesters, dressed in old-fashioned-looking black-and-white prison uniforms, greeted our motorcade and distributed "Get Out of Jail Free" cards to the traveling press and onlookers. The cards described Dukakis as "the prisoner's best friend." The protest group claimed to be college Republicans, but at one point during the demonstration I recognized the face of a runner jogging down the street and right through the protesters. It was Lee Atwater, the man *CBS Evening News* anchor Dan Rather had described as "George Bush's negative campaign specialist," and the "college Republicans" cheered when he passed through.

By late October 1988, the campaign had devolved into a frustrating slog of exhausting travel, missed debate opportunities, sinking poll numbers, and bad news stories. We had spent most of the general election playing defense, and I had lost confidence in the campaign's ability to win. By this point, everyone on the campaign staff and the traveling press crew knew the routine of Dukakis's appearances and could recite his stump speech by heart. He would arrive to Neil Diamond's "America," smile, wave, and then deliver the same speech over and over again about "good jobs at good wages." But one day in New Haven, Connecticut, Dukakis ventured off the routine.

He interrupted the usual stump speech to mark the fifteenth anniversary of an infamous moment in American history, in which Richard Nixon ordered Attorney General Elliot Richardson to fire Watergate Special Prosecutor Archibald Cox. Richardson refused and resigned, forcing Nixon to turn to his deputy attorney general, William Ruckelshaus, who also refused and resigned. The third in line at the Justice Department, Robert Bork, then carried out Nixon's unscrupulous order. Nixon's elimination of three high-ranking Justice Department officials became known as the "Saturday Night Massacre." That day in New Haven was a year after President Reagan nominated Bork to the US Supreme Court, and the Senate rejected him. Bush had praised Bork as an "excellent" choice, and Dukakis took this anniversary as an opportunity to pounce. "Truth was the first casualty in the Nixon White House, and it has been the first casualty in the Bush campaign," Dukakis said. After the speech, we stopped at an Italian restaurant near Wooster Street so the press could file their stories, and I called the Boston headquarters to check in. By the time I got off the phone, the campaign was in chaos.

As the motorcade continued moving to the airport so we could travel to the next location, to a white-tie event in Manhattan, the staff and reporters couldn't stop talking about one person: Donna Brazile. When I first met Donna in Iowa, I was intimidated by her imposing stature and her reputation. At only twenty-eight years old, she was a political prodigy who had already worked in senior staff positions in three presidential campaigns. When I got to know her on the Dukakis campaign, I discovered that she was a very candid, hardworking, fun-loving person, and I enjoyed being around her. She also talked to white people in power the way I wanted to, and the way I someday would, but not yet.

As the national field director of the Dukakis campaign, Donna did not always travel with the candidate, but on this day, she was with us and she had a lot to say. While talking to reporters earlier in the day, she accused Bush of two things that no one on the campaign had ever said publicly. First, she said that Bush was running a racist campaign. He was "using the oldest racial symbol imaginable," Donna explained: "a Black man raping a white woman." Second, she told reporters that Bush needed to come clean about rumors of his alleged marital infidelity. The criticism about Bush's racist campaign barely registered at first. The swift reaction that day centered on the other charge, and the story that would appear in the *New York Times* focused on Donna's resignation after she had told reporters to investigate rumors about Bush's personal life. "Donna was not speaking on behalf of the campaign in any way whatsoever," press secretary Dayton Duncan told reporters.

Later that day in the staff room of the Waldorf Astoria in New York, I relayed a message to Donna that the campaign manager, Susan Estrich, was on the phone. "Would you like to talk to Susan?" I asked. She did. After that conversation, I saw Donna for the last time during the campaign. She sat in a dark corner of the back room of the staff suite, staring wistfully into the air. Her body language and facial expression were so lifeless that she looked as if someone had sapped the energy from her. It was a defeated look that I had never seen in her before. When it was all over, she released a statement of regret. "Because the time is short, and the issues are so important, I have decided to leave the campaign," she told the press. I was very disappointed to see her go, but I also recognized something powerful in her inner peace, and I wrote about it in my journal that day. "Donna is a tough woman," I wrote. "She'll be back."

Lost in the initial controversy of the campaign's palace intrigue was that Donna actually initiated a critically important conversation on race in the 1988 presidential campaign. Her comments triggered weeks of discussion and news articles about the racist origin of the Willie Horton ad and about the racist campaign that Bush and his surrogates were waging. That debate was too little, too late to save the struggling Dukakis campaign, but it forever framed how the 1988 Bush campaign would be perceived in victory. Even today, some remember George H. W. Bush with fondness because of his perceived moderation in comparison to other Republican presidents, but he was all too willing to embrace the racist elements of his party to achieve his political ambitions.

George Bush was not the first candidate to run a racist national campaign or to govern with racist policies. America had a long history of racism in presidential politics. At least a dozen American presidents had owned slaves, and neither major party was immune to the disease of racism, but it was the Democrats who had been most problematic in the nineteenth century and early twentieth century. Even as the nation entered the 1960s, the Democratic Party still had a stunningly intolerant record on civil rights. Democrat Woodrow Wilson racially segregated the federal government and purged Black civil servants from management jobs in federal government. He also held a screening of the racist film *The Birth of a Nation* in 1915, but when Black civil rights leader William Monroe Trotter complained about Wilson's policies, Wilson had him thrown out of the White House. The next Democrat, Franklin Roosevelt, locked up Japanese Americans in internment camps, refused to support antilynching legislation to protect Blacks, and excluded gold medalist Jesse Owens and other Black athletes from a White House victory ceremony following the 1936 Olympic games in Adolf Hitler's Berlin. When Democratic President Harry Truman desegregated the armed forces in 1948, his fellow Democrat Strom Thurmond temporarily bolted from the party and ran against him on a segregationist platform as a Dixiecrat. Democrat George Wallace followed suit with his own third-party segregationist campaign two decades later in 1968.

The Democratic Party of the nineteenth century and throughout much of the twentieth century was steeped in racism. But for Republicans, the full-throated embrace of racist appeals to white voters reflected a dramatic shift from where their party began. Sensitive to the concerns of appearing heartless, modern Republicans learned to couch their language in flowery words and gauzy poll-tested rhetoric. It was an approach that began decades before Bush's 1988 campaign.

When George Bush ran in his first race for public office in 1964, the forty-year-old oil company executive knew that his party had a branding problem. The campaign to reelect Democratic president Lyndon Johnson had framed the Republican nominee, Arizona senator Barry Goldwater, as a trigger-happy maniac who might blow up the world. In a famous Johnson TV commercial that ran only once, in September 1964, a little white girl was shown miscounting daisy petals as she pulled them from a flower in an empty field. "Six, eight, nine, nine," the girl says slowly. Suddenly, she's interrupted by the booming male voice of a mission control countdown announcer. "Ten, nine, eight, seven, six, five, four, three, two, one." She stops counting and looks up from the daisy as the camera zooms in on her face and into the pupil of her right eye. An image of a huge explosion and a mushroom cloud of debris fills the screen. It's followed by the voice of President Johnson. "These are the stakes—to make a world in which all of God's children can live, or to go into the dark," Johnson said. "We must either love each other," he added, "or we must die."

Bush, the son of a US senator from Connecticut, understood the need for better Republican messaging to respond to Johnson's criticism, and he found a way to distinguish his brand of politics from the unsympathetic reputation of his party's standard-bearer. "His conservatism is 'compassionate,'" *The Texas Observer* quoted him. However, the magazine didn't buy it. It reminded readers that Bush had "so little sensitivity" that he explained his opposition to Medicare, which provides medical care for the aged, by comparing it to a federal program to put air-conditioning on cargo ships for

African apes and baboons, which Bush jokingly called "medical air for the caged."

Nevertheless, Bush had articulated what would one day become the basis of a new messaging campaign for Republicans. "I don't believe that we conservatives should be placed in the position of being opposed to compassion for our fellow men," Bush said in 1964. His philosophy was compassionate conservatism, a phrase that would, years later, be associated not with the candidate, but with his then eighteen-year-old son, George W. Bush. As the 1964 Republican Party was moving toward the politics of white anxiety, Bush still continued outreach efforts to people of color. He attended a fundraiser for a group called "Negroes for Bush," although thirty of the eighty people who showed up were white, according to *The Texas Observer*. And he visited an "Amigos for Bush" event to reach Hispanic voters, but the only Latino person in the audience was the manager of the restaurant where it was held, the *Observer* noted.

For the next fifty years, this would be the political strategy and stagecraft of the Bush family and, by extension, of the Republican Party, at times. It was a strategy that often emphasized a compassionate tone and symbolic gestures of inclusion rather than compassionate policy. Thus, Bush was able to oppose the federal Medicare program to provide health care for the elderly because, he claimed, it unfairly forced the working class to subsidize the wealthy. "I would not say to this fella working with his hands, 'Look, you've got to pay for medical care for this rich fella over here,'" Bush explained. Similarly, Bush opposed the Civil Rights Act of 1964, not because he was racist, he claimed, but because he wanted, once again, to help the little guy. "I'm not opposed to equal rights for all," Bush said, "but I want to see we don't violate the rights of 86 percent to try to correct the grievances—and legitimate ones, often—of the other 14 percent."

Bush's argument against civil rights might have won him that Senate seat in other Southern states, but in 1964 he was running not only against incumbent Texas Democratic senator Ralph Yarborough, he was running against a popular incumbent president who was the first Texan to hold the office. Yarborough was the only Southern Democrat in the United States Senate to vote for the 1964 Civil Rights Act, and Bush slammed him for this. "I opposed the recently passed Civil Rights Bill," Bush proudly reported in a 1964 print ad. Yarborough, on the other hand, voted for what Bush called a "so-called Civil Rights Bill."

Yarborough was also vulnerable because of an embarrassing encounter he had recently had with South Carolina Senator Strom Thurmond. After President Johnson signed the 1964 Civil Rights Act, Thurmond, a devout segregationist, was determined to block the confirmation of one of Johnson's nominees to run the Community Relations Service, an agency created by the act. Thurmond positioned himself outside the committee room to prevent senators from entering to vote. When Yarborough arrived, Thurmond challenged him. "If I can keep you out, you won't go in, and if you can drag me in, I'll stay there," Thurmond said. The two sixty-one-year-old senators then tussled, removing their suit jackets and wrestling to the ground. Thurmond pinned the out-of-shape Yarborough to the ground and demanded his submission. Only when the committee chairman, Senator Warren Magnuson, broke up the contest, was the hearing able to commence. Although Thurmond won the wrestling match, he lost the vote, sixteen to one. And despite the embarrassment of his physical defeat, Yarborough won the political matchup later that year against George Bush, 56 percent to 44 percent.

Two years later, Bush found a different path into politics. He ran for Congress and won. From there he moved through a series of high-profile jobs that led him to the presidency. He was US ambassador to the United Nations and then chair of the Republican National Committee under President Nixon. In the Ford administration, Bush served as chief of the US Liaison Office in Beijing following the US normalization of relations with China and as director of the Central Intelligence Agency. And when Republicans swept back into power in 1981, Bush became Reagan's vice president for eight years.

By the time he stood at the podium of the 1988 Republican National Convention in the New Orleans Superdome, Bush sounded almost nothing like the 1964 version of himself who had campaigned against the civil rights bill. "I'll try to be fair to the other side," he said. He promised to help "urban children" who live and play amidst "shattered glass and shattered lives" and assured Americans that he would be guided by the tradition that "we must be good to one another." Bush spoke of an America with a "brilliant diversity spread like stars, like a thousand points of light in a broad and peaceful sky." And, coming after the Reagan administration had been caught trading arms for hostages in the Iran-Contra affair, his speech tried to distance the candidate from scandal by reminding his convention audience that night that he still believed that "public service is honorable" and that it broke his heart whenever there was a breach of the public trust. He even acknowledged that America had lived through "a sin called slavery" and cautioned against materialism and blind ambition. "Prosperity has a purpose," he declared. "Prosperity with a purpose means taking your idealism and making it concrete by certain acts of goodness." In words and phrases that seemed uncommon for a Republican in the Reagan era, Bush spoke in broad, poetic language that many Democrats could easily embrace, as well. "I want a kinder and gentler nation," he told the convention.

Yet sandwiched between various points of light in Bush's lofty rhetoric was the familiar right-wing agenda of the modern Republican Party—fear and loathing of a changing America. Bush contrasted his American family values as a transplanted Texan against what he framed as the unorthodox values of his Greek American opponent from Massachusetts. The Republicans represented "old fashioned common sense" and "tradition," Bush said repeatedly in his speech. On the other hand, "the liberal Democrats"—another phrase he used repeatedly—would undermine the existing social order. And

Bush—who was born in Massachusetts, raised in Connecticut, and summered in Maine—would spend much of the campaign denouncing Dukakis as being a "Massachusetts liberal" whose Northern values didn't match those of the rest of America. He rattled off a list of examples in his speech to prove his point.

"Should public school teachers be required to lead our children in the pledge of allegiance? My opponent says no—but I say yes," Bush said. This was an attack on Dukakis for vetoing an unconstitutional 1977 bill that would have required teachers to lead schoolchildren in reciting the pledge of allegiance.

"Should society be allowed to impose the death penalty on those who commit crimes of extraordinary cruelty and violence? My opponent says no—but I say yes." This was a response to Dukakis's well-publicized opposition to capital punishment, a principled opinion that did not poll well but also had little practical impact in a federal government that in 1988 had not executed anyone in a quarter of a century.

"Should our children have the right to say a voluntary prayer, or even observe a moment of silence in the schools? My opponent says no—but I say yes." This was an absurd distortion of Dukakis's views. No prominent Democratic elected official had ever advocated the abolition of the first amendment right to prayer. Any student in America's public schools has the right to pray voluntarily. The question was always whether those public schools and their employees of various faiths should be required to lead such prayers and whether students should be coerced into participating in them.

Bush continued, sometimes fairly and sometimes otherwise, in contrasting his views with his opponent on gun control, abortion, and taxes. That's when he made an infamous promise. "My opponent won't rule out raising taxes," he said. "But I will. And the Congress will push me to raise taxes, and I'll say no, and they'll push, and I'll say no, and they'll push again, and I'll say to them, 'Read my lips: No new taxes.'" It was the sound bite of the evening, receiving thunderous applause and replayed on television news broadcasts for days. Then, just two years later, Bush would break his promise and sign a bill raising taxes. He would eventually pay a steep price for his reversal, but in the meantime, it bolstered his argument that his opponent was out of step with America—and under the surface, many of us knew his argument was rooted in race.

For most voters, school prayer, the pledge of allegiance, the death penalty, gun control, and taxes did not appear to be racial issues. Tax cuts and "values" issues had become standard Republican talking points in the 1980s. But the debate over "traditional values" had itself been racialized in a country where Black Americans and people of color were often depicted as un-American for challenging the existing order. The absence of school prayer, for example, posed no real threat to white America, but it represented something that did. It represented a withering away of old traditions that had long served the dominant class. It represented the disappearance of an established but antiquated social order, where people knew their place. School prayer, the pledge of allegiance, and standing for the national anthem had all become symbols of a deeper struggle, serving as battle flags to be carried into a theater of war, just as the "Make America Great Again" slogan would come to symbolize that struggle decades later. The details of the issues mattered less than the lines of demarcation they represented. It was our team versus the other team, us versus them, the past versus the future.

By 1988, Bush was able to reap the political benefits of poisonous seeds that had been sown decades earlier by his own party. One had been planted firmly by Richard Nixon. When Nixon ran for reelection in 1972, he resurrected his "law and order" theme to win by the largest electoral vote margin of any president since Franklin Roosevelt in his first election. Nixon carried every state except Massachusetts. At the same time, the Republican governor of Massachusetts, Francis Sargent, was moving in what appeared to be a different direction from Nixon and his party. In 1972, Sargent signed into law a weekend furlough program allowing inmates a brief and temporary respite from prison for good behavior and time served. Such programs were adopted in other states as well, and they became particularly popular during holiday seasons. By Christmas of 1974, New Jersey's furlough program reported a success rate of nearly 99 percent, according to the Associated Press (AP). "The state feels that the furloughs reduce tensions in the prisons by giving inmates hope for freedom," AP reported.

While the furlough programs grew, Nixon's fortunes diminished. In August 1974, the embattled president boarded Marine One helicopter on the South Lawn of the White House and waved his final farewell to his staff. But less than three months later, the failed leader became "popular" again, the *Dallas Morning News* reported, as trick or treaters dressed up in Nixon masks. A few days before Halloween, a tragic incident had taken place that would reverberate for years. A seventeen-year-old gas station attendant was robbed and stabbed to death in Lawrence, Massachusetts. The suspects were convicted and sentenced to prison. No one had any idea at the time that the fate of one of those suspects would determine who would become the president of the United States fourteen years later.

William Robert Horton, one of the men convicted in the 1974 gas station murder, was released from the Northeast Correctional Center in a rural stretch of Concord, Massachusetts, on a weekend furlough on June 6, 1986. It was his tenth furlough since being incarcerated. He had dutifully returned to prison nine times before. But this time, Horton never returned. Instead, he remained at large for ten months, finally surfacing more than four hundred miles away in Maryland on April 3, 1987, when he reportedly terrorized a couple, assaulting a man in his home and then raping the man's fiancée when she returned home hours later. The couple managed to escape and called the police. Horton fled, but he was caught, arrested, tried, convicted, and imprisoned in Maryland.

Senator Al Gore of Tennessee was one of the first national political figures to raise concerns about the case during the 1988 Democratic presidential primary campaign. The critique barely registered, and Massachusetts Governor Michael Dukakis went on to beat Gore and his other Democratic opponents on his way to his party's presidential nomination. Republicans were not as forgiving. They took the Horton story, slapped it into a campaign commercial, and attacked Dukakis relentlessly. In the skilled hands of the Republican attack machine, William Robert Horton suddenly became "Willie Horton," and the grainy mug shot image of the menacing Black man with a beard was indelibly attached to the Democratic candidate.

"The fact is, my name is not 'Willie,'" Horton told *The Nation* in 1993. He argued that the fictitious name was part of "the myth of the case" that "was created to play on racial stereotypes: big, ugly, dumb, violent, Black—'Willie.'" As a Black man convicted of raping a white woman, Horton admitted he provided "the perfect scapegoat" for the Bush campaign. Along with a Bush campaign television ad that compared the Massachusetts furlough program to a "revolving door prison policy," the message of fear was clearly communicated. If you vote for Dukakis, a scary Black man will come to your home, attack you, and rape your partner.

The dog whistle political messages of the Republican Party in the post–civil rights era were inaudible only to those who chose to pretend they did not exist. In 1972, the Nixon campaign ran a television ad depicting a white construction worker in a hard hat taking a lunch break while perched on an elevated steel beam. The offscreen announcer critiques a litany of Democrat George McGovern's welfare proposals as the worker watches the crowd below. "And who's going to pay for this?" the announcer asks. "Well, if you're not the one out of two people on welfare, you do."

By 1990, in the middle of the Bush administration, North Carolina's notorious Republican senator Jesse Helms used a pair of white hands in a television ad to convince voters that his Black Democratic opponent, Harvey Gantt, would give jobs to unqualified Blacks instead of hiring qualified whites. "You needed that job," the announcer says. "And you were the best qualified. But they had to give it to a minority because of a racial quota." As the announcer concludes his message, the white hands are shown crumpling up the rejection letter. It was the ultimate culmination of the reassignment of victimhood, allowing Republican politicians to appeal directly to white resentment by embracing a duplicitous notion of racial neutrality. But no one needed a political science degree to understand the message. George Bush's "kinder, gentler" Republican Party left plenty of room for family-friendly racism.

By the summer of 1990, the country was suffering through a recession that would eventually cost Bush his own job. American jobs were moving overseas. Labor unions were being attacked and weakened. Long-promised corporate pensions began to evaporate. And through it all, the Reagan-Bush economic policies exacerbated the nation's rising income inequality, transferring billions of dollars of wealth from government programs for the poor and the middle class to programs giving tax cuts for the wealthy. The social contract that had governed the nation for decades after World War II was quickly being dismantled. Working-class Americans of all races felt the suffering, but it was easier for demagogic politicians to demonize working-class Black and brown Americans than to hold wealthy white America and corporate America responsible. It was a divide-and-conquer strategy as old as time. Yet Black Americans were suffering even more. As unemployment spiked, unemployment among Blacks rose even more sharply than in the white community. By June 1992, five months before the presidential election, the white unemployment rate topped out at 6.9 percent. That same month, the Black unemployment rate reached 14.6 percent.

During Bush's term in office, the world changed rapidly in both domestic and international affairs, but many of these dramatic changes made existing powers uncomfortable. In China, courageous young protesters defied their government in Beijing's Tiananmen Square. In Germany, the Berlin Wall fell and reunited East and West for the first time in decades. In South Africa, Nelson Mandela was released from prison after twenty-seven years of incarceration. And in Russia, the Soviet flag was finally lowered from the Kremlin in Moscow. Meanwhile, back at home, Black Americans celebrated as David Dinkins was elected the first African American mayor of New York City and Virginia elected Doug Wilder the first Black governor of the state that had once been the capital of the Confederacy. It was not quite the "new world order" that Bush spoke of in his address to a Joint Session of Congress on September 11, 1990, but for a brief moment in time, it felt like anything was possible.

Each time someone strikes out against injustice, they send forth "a tiny ripple of hope," Robert F. Kennedy once told a college audience in apartheid South Africa. As those ripples cross each other from a million different centers of energy, they build a current, "which can sweep down the mightiest walls of oppression and resistance," he said. That's what it felt like in the early years of the Bush administration. All across the planet, the spirit of change soared in the air.

It started in China, where the world watched in inspired amazement as a brave man, in a solitary act of civil disobedience, stopped an entire column of Chinese tanks. I wondered if I would ever have the courage to do the same in those circumstances. I was riveted by the images of young people standing, sitting, and partying on top of the legendary Berlin Wall while celebrating their freedom. And I wept as the beaming South African freedom fighter Nelson Mandela raised his fist in the sky as he confidently walked out of prison. It felt like time was finally on the side of righteousness, and I allowed myself to believe that the world was evolving. If people in other countries are tearing down the walls that divided them, then surely change will soon come to America, I thought. But in between the uprising in Tiananmen Square and the fall of the Berlin Wall, politics were carrying on as usual back in Washington. And as I began my first semester in law school, the president had found a new racist dog whistle to blow.

When George Bush sat at his desk in 1989 and delivered his first nationally televised address from the Oval Office to discuss what he called "the gravest domestic threat facing our nation today," he not only relaunched Nixon and Reagan's "War on Drugs," he also launched yet another battle in the ongoing racial resentment wars. Holding a clear, sealed plastic bag in his left hand, Bush announced: "This is crack cocaine, seized a few days ago by drug enforcement agents in a park just across the street from the White House." It was a memorable and dramatic moment, meant to illustrate the pervasiveness of narcotics in American life. But the White House story began to unravel a few weeks later, when the *Washington Post* reported that Drug Enforcement Administration (DEA) agents actually had to lure the suspect to Lafayette Park to make the undercover crack buy. So unusual was the drug sale in the park that the teenage suspect seemed not to know where to go to meet the DEA agent posing as a buyer. "Where the fuck is the White House?" he asked the undercover agent. A special agent in charge of DEA's Washington field office admitted it wasn't easy to get the teen to come to the park. "We had to manipulate him to get him down there," the agent said. And the commander of criminal investigations for the US Park Police, which patrols the park, told the *Post* that there was no record of any crack dealing in the park ever before. "We don't consider that a problem area," he said. "There's too much activity going on there for drug dealers. . . . There's always a uniformed police presence there."

The Black high school senior entrapped by the White House plot, Keith Jackson, was arrested and put on trial in federal court. The jury could not reach a verdict. A microphone that was supposed to record the drug transaction did not work, and a cameraman who was supposed to videotape it failed to do so. "This is like a Keystone Kops thing," the presiding judge said in a reference to the incompetent police featured in silent film comedies. After a mistrial in December 1989, the student was retried in January 1990. In the second trial, once again the jury could not reach a verdict on the botched sting operation in Lafayette Park, but they did convict him of unrelated charges to the actual drug bust. As a result of the federal conviction, this eighteen-year-old with no prior criminal record, lured to the White House by the Bush administration, was sentenced to ten years in prison. Even the judge in the case felt the sentence was too harsh, according to the *Washington Post*, but he told Jackson, "I've got to follow the law." That law was a 1988 measure signed by President Reagan requiring mandatory minimum sentences, and as a result of it, a young Black male who had been exploited by the Bush White House as a political prop, would be sent to jail for a decade. It was a sign of things to come, as the racial grievance strategies and mass-incarceration policies of the seventies and eighties would now place a target on the heads of Black and brown bodies.

The success of Kevin Phillips's Southern strategy and Lee Atwater's scorched earth tactics taught both major political parties unfortunate lessons that would last for decades. Republicans learned there was a very small political price to be paid, and enormous political benefit, for increasingly blatant racial division. As these tactics proved more successful, the politics of racial resentment became more blatant. Until Donald Trump, no mainstream modern politician better expressed the cause of white racial resentment than Pat Buchanan. "There is a religious war going on in this country," Buchanan announced at the 1992 Republican National Convention in Houston. "It is a cultural war, as critical to the kind of nation we shall be as was the cold war itself, for this war is for the soul of America."

Buchanan challenged Bush for the 1992 Republican presidential nomination and made enough of an impact to win a speaking role at the convention. There he argued that the country needed a leader who would be a "champion of the Judeo-Christian values and beliefs upon which America was founded." He complained that an openly gay man—whom he called "a militant leader of the homosexual rights movement"—had the audacity to speak in public at the Democratic National Convention, and he accused Hillary Clinton of promoting an agenda of "radical feminism." In Buchanan's eyes, the Clintons, if elected to office, would usher in a world of "abortion on demand," "homosexual rights," and "women in combat units." "That's change, all right. But it is not the kind of change America needs," Buchanan said. "It is not the kind of change America wants," he continued. "And," he added, "it is not the kind of change we can abide in a nation that we still call God's country."

Buchanan ended his speech that night with a stern condemnation of the 1992 uprising in Los Angeles. He did not condemn the police brutality that had led to that rebellion, which took place after the acquittal of four white police officers who had been caught on videotape beating Black motorist Rodney King for at least nine minutes on a Los Angeles street. Instead, Buchanan seemed far more troubled by the violent protests that disturbed the peace than the actual racial injustice that provoked the outburst. He was not alone. As had happened repeatedly throughout history, many in white America once again prioritized peace over justice, provoking protesters in Los Angeles to respond with the chant, "No justice, no peace!"

Buchanan's speech recentered white victimhood by characterizing Black people, who were angry at and tired of years of police brutality, as a cursing mob that had senselessly burned and looted buildings, and he told a story of how "troopers came up the street, M-16s at the ready," and "the mob retreated because it had met the one thing that could stop it: force, rooted in justice, and backed by moral courage." In Buchanan's worldview, white Americans could lay claim to the mantle of justice by standing up against Black Americans who dared to demand justice in a way that made white people uncomfortable. This would become Buchanan's metaphor for how white Christian conservative America must take back the nation and reclaim white innocence. "As those boys took back the streets of Los Angeles, block by block, my friends, we must take back our cities, and take back our culture, and take back our country," he said.

Buchanan's speech alarmed many of us who were not a part of his cramped vision of America. Political columnist Molly Ivins famously quipped that the speech probably sounded better in its original German. So toxic was his language and legacy that even Donald Trump demurred when asked about Buchanan years later during an appearance on *Meet the Press* in 1999. "He's a Hitler lover," Trump said. "I guess he's an anti-Semite. He doesn't like the Blacks. He doesn't like the gays. It's just incredible that anybody could embrace this guy," said Trump. But it was Pat Buchanan who paved the way for the Republican Party to embrace Donald Trump. When Trump ran for president in 2016, he no longer condemned Buchanan's bigotry but instead praised the man he had once called a "Hitler lover." "Way to go Pat, way ahead of your time!" Trump tweeted in January 2016.

Even in 1992, it was not difficult to see the direction in which the Grand Old Party was headed. Thousands of white Republicans in Houston's Astrodome cheered Buchanan, interrupting him with repeated applause and chants of "Go, Pat, Go!" and "U-S-A." George Bush's own vice president, Dan Quayle, while sitting in the audience, gave Buchanan a thumbs-up as he left the stage. Bush did not openly identify with the growing Buchanan wing of the party, but this was the trend that he and Reagan had helped to create. Buchanan represented the firebrand conservative future of the GOP, and once the party's base finally recognized the power of this brand, they could never again be fully satisfied with a mainstream Republican.

Looking back on George Herbert Walker Bush's accomplishments in office from the present, his record on race issues seems particularly unimpressive. The man who began his political career by opposing the Civil Rights Act of 1964 would end his career by vetoing the Civil Rights Act of 1990 and forcing Congress to adopt a much more modest bill the following year to rectify recent Supreme Court decisions that made it harder for plaintiffs to sue for racial discrimination.

Although he spoke of a kinder, gentler nation, he was all too willing to forsake those values when it came to racial issues in order to win an election in 1988 or to frame a young Black man for a drug crime in 1989. As a result of the nation's "tough on crime" policies he supported, the number of Blacks in state and federal prisons increased from 274,300 at the end of 1988 to 401,700 at the end of 1992, a shocking 46 percent increase in just four years.

He did make some significant African American appointments by selecting Louis Sullivan as secretary of the Department of Health and Human Services, General Colin Powell to chair the Joint Chiefs of Staff, and Clarence Thomas to the US Supreme Court, but Black America actually took several steps backward when Thomas replaced the legendary Thurgood Marshall on the nation's highest court.

On the world stage, Bush met with African National Congress (ANC) leader Nelson Mandela at the White House in 1990, but before that time he had long refused to condemn the racist apartheid regime in South Africa. And despite Bush's responsible decision to reverse his "no new taxes" pledge, Black Americans saw their unemployment rate climb from an already elevated 11.8 percent when Bush took office to 14.1 percent when he left.

At the end of Bush's four years in office, Black Americans were clearly no better off than they had been before. One man's kinder, gentler rhetoric and occasional strokes of inclusion were not nearly enough to compensate for his party's embrace of white identity politics or to reverse a nation's long history of racism, white supremacy, and anti-blackness.

5

BILL CLINTON'S CALCULATED TRIANGULATION

O n the day I filed my papers to run for vice president of the student government at Countryside High School in Clearwater, Florida, the faculty adviser, Linda Denny, pulled me aside for a talk. "You know we already have a Black candidate running for this seat," she told me with a look of concern. "You may want to run for something else so you two don't split the vote."

It was my first introduction to racial politics.

I had never heard of vote splitting, and it never occurred to me that two Black candidates might cancel each other out on a ballot in which all the other candidates were white. I assumed Mrs. Denny meant well, but I disregarded her advice. She was a middle-aged white woman with liberal proclivities, and she had probably determined that it would be difficult for a Black candidate to win a student government election in a school that was almost entirely white. I ran anyway and won. After spending my junior year as vice president, I ran for president and won again. As I entered my senior year, I was on a lucky streak.

That all changed the day I heard about a local candidate for Congress who piqued my interest. His name was George Sheldon, a thirty-five-year-old state representative from Tampa, who was running in the newly created Ninth Congressional District. It was a bit quixotic for a liberal Democrat to try to win a seat in this increasingly conservative part of central Florida in the Reagan era, but I believed he had a chance. With America's unemployment rate hovering above a record-breaking 10 percent and President Reagan's Gallup approval rating slumping down to 42 percent, the national momentum in 1982 clearly favored Democrats. So I walked into the George Sheldon for Congress office and volunteered. It hadn't required much thought at the time, but it turned out to be one of the most consequential decisions of my life.

As a young Black kid with a big greasy Jheri curl, I stood out from the rest of the team of mostly white volunteers, and the candidate and his campaign staff took an early interest in me. I licked envelopes and made phone calls like everyone else, but because I clearly enjoyed the retail politics of canvassing in the district, I was assigned an exciting new task in the campaign's final days. I found myself in what I considered to be the extraordinary position of actually speaking for the candidate in public. It wasn't exactly Lincolnesque oratory that was required of me, but the opportunity was thrilling for a high school senior. I screamed self-created campaign slogans through a bullhorn in a pickup truck that drove across the district. "If you make more than $100,000 a year, then don't vote for George Sheldon," I yelled. "But if you make less than that, Sheldon is your man for Congress." I was articulating what I thought was the principal difference between Democrats and Republicans—that Democrats cared more about the poor and the middle class. And, since there were far more low- and middle-income Americans than rich ones, I assumed that message would resonate with voters. What I did not fully grasp at the time was that Republican messaging around tax cuts was never completely an argument about money; it was also about race.

Reagan was in the middle of a dramatic tax-cutting initiative that reflected changes taking place in his party. In the four Republican presidencies since the Great Depression, the top rate for the superrich dropped from 92 percent under Eisenhower to 77 percent under Nixon to 70 percent under Ford and 28 percent under Reagan. I didn't buy the Reagan administration's argument that the tax cuts would "trickle down" to ordinary workers and pay for themselves by stimulating growth, and I was right. But what I did not realize was that the huge deficits created from the enormous drop in federal revenue would actually help Republicans achieve their goals. It was like an evil-genius strategy that I was too young to understand—cut taxes, raise the deficit, and use the very deficit that your own tax cuts created as a justification to further reduce government services.

The strategy did not pay off immediately. In the midst of a deep recession, Democrats performed quite well in the 1982 midterm elections. They retained control of Congress and picked up twenty-six seats in the House of Representatives. In Florida, Democratic senator Lawton Chiles and Democratic governor Bob Graham were both easily reelected. But in the first election for the member of Congress of the Ninth Congressional District, newly created by congressional reapportionment, things turned out differently. Republican Michael Bilirakis beat Democrat George Sheldon by 4,312 votes out of 185,742 votes cast. My candidate lost.

I was painfully disappointed by the defeat, but the political bug stayed with me and inspired a lifelong career with campaigns, elections, and government. Electoral politics was the one place where I—as a seventeen-year-old who was not yet eligible to vote—could still help to change the world, I thought. Even as Republicans were slowly gaining ground across Florida and the South, I knew there was hope for the future, and I knew I would one day work on yet another election for another Democrat.

I did not have to wait long. By 1984, I was a college student in New Hampshire with front-row seats to the Democratic primary process as a reporter for *The Dartmouth* newspaper, the student daily at Dartmouth College. As a young journalist, I met or interviewed nearly all the presidential candidates, from Alan Cranston of California to

Walter Mondale of Minnesota. I identified most with Jesse Jackson as a candidate, but I harbored doubts as to whether white America would vote for a Black civil rights leader to become president. I also appreciated the liberal views of George McGovern, but I wondered if he should be running again after losing in a landslide in 1972. The candidate I thought had the best chance of winning was Mondale, who had served for four years as vice president under Jimmy Carter. After considering the choices, I volunteered for his campaign months after the primary ended and I no longer had to cover him. But, in November of 1984, Walter Mondale lost.

Two years later, while spending the summer in Atlanta, I decided to volunteer for another campaign. Two civil rights legends were facing off in an epic Democratic congressional primary race. The first was Julian Bond, who had notoriously been denied a seat in the Georgia House of Representatives in 1966 because he spoke out against the Vietnam War. The other was John Lewis, who had been beaten by police at the infamous 1965 "Bloody Sunday" march across the Edmund Pettus Bridge in Selma, Alabama. Lewis lacked Bond's polish and legislative experience, and Bond was the clear favorite to win. I volunteered for Bond's campaign, thinking he would be easily elected. But in September 1986, Julian Bond lost.

The following year, I tried my luck in politics once again. In June 1987, I drove down to Boston to meet with Governor Michael Dukakis in his office at the Massachusetts State House for my interview. "Don't ever write down anything on paper you don't want to see in the *New York Times* or *Boston Globe*," he told me. It's the only thing I remember from that meeting. His campaign hired me as a press aide and paid me $250 a week to work twelve-hour days in his Boston headquarters, located near the old "Combat Zone" (the so-called adult-entertainment district in the 1960s) by Downtown Crossing. I had no idea how I would repay my college loans on a $1,000/monthly salary when the six-month grace period would end that winter, but I happily accepted the offer. I worked in Boston,

Iowa, New Hampshire, Ohio, and Georgia during the primaries, and after Dukakis won the Democratic presidential nomination, I was promoted to a new job traveling on the governor's campaign plane for the general election. Three months after the August convention, Mike Dukakis lost. My losing streak had notched another disappointment, though I was far from ready to give up politics.

The next year in St. Louis, Missouri, my grandmother recommended that I do some work for a friend of hers who was running for local office, so I volunteered on the campaign of a candidate for license collector. To this day, I am still not sure what a license collector actually does, or why this is an elected position, but I had nothing to lose by supporting her. Not surprisingly, after working on the front lines of a national campaign, the local election didn't excite me. It was also not surprising, given my past experience, that my candidate met the same fate as the other candidates for whom I had worked. She, too, lost her election.

But the politics bug wouldn't quit. A few months after graduating from law school, while I was studying for the bar exam in California, I received a phone call from a press secretary named Dee Dee Myers. We had worked together in the 1988 Dukakis campaign, but we had not spoken since that time. She called with an offer I could not refuse. Would I be interested in working for the campaign of a Democrat named Bill Clinton? I accepted immediately.

Although I had not started my new job in San Francisco, I told the hiring partner at the McCutchen, Doyle, Brown & Enersen law firm that I would be taking a leave of absence through the election, and he supported my decision. My family, on the other hand, was not as accepting. They could not understand why I would abandon a high-paying legal job for another low-wage political campaign position. After all, Harvard Law School graduates were expected to become successful lawyers, not failed political activists. They had waited three years to see me graduate from law school, and they expected I would reap the benefits afforded to those in the exclusive club I had just joined. Besides, after five consecutive losses, no one thought it was a good idea for me to join another campaign.

Outside of my family, even one of my political heroes had discouraged me. During a clerkship the previous summer at Patton, Boggs and Blow law firm in Washington, DC, I had a meeting with Ron Brown, the chair of the Democratic National Committee, who was a partner at the firm. Maybe he was just doing his job to recruit Black lawyers for the firm, but he discouraged me from pursuing politics after law school. He told me to make some money instead. I did not care for his advice, and as I watched the Democratic National Convention on television that summer, I felt left out of the excitement. Sitting in my apartment in Oakland, I wanted desperately to be in the convention hall in New York City. It reminded me of the energy I felt when I walked around the convention floor in Atlanta in 1988, and I could not resist the urge to be involved once again.

I felt a glimmer of hope as I arrived at the Clinton headquarters, housed in an old newspaper building once owned by the *Arkansas Democrat-Gazette* newspaper. Maybe Clinton knew the way Democrats could win again. I certainly did not know. I had survived eight years of Ronald Reagan and nearly four years of George Bush, and I was desperate for change. But none of the candidates I supported for public office ever won. Clearly, I was doing something wrong, I figured.

My early personal political failures mirrored those of the Democratic Party of my youth. Neither of us had been very successful. By 1992, I was twenty-seven years old, and Democrats had lost all but one of the presidential elections in my lifetime. They lost to Nixon in 1968. They lost again to Nixon in a landslide in 1972. They barely won in 1976, but only with the weight of the Watergate scandal burdening Nixon's successor, Gerald Ford. They lost to Reagan in 1980. They lost to Reagan again—this time in a landslide—in 1984. They even lost to Reagan's weaker vice president, George Bush, in 1988. After losing five of the six last presidential elections, Democrats were desperate to find their way back to the White House. The most recent Democrats to win the presidency were both Southerners—Jimmy Carter and Lyndon Johnson—so Democrats found another Southerner named Bill Clinton to be their nominee. It was worth a shot. And when Election Day finally arrived on the first Tuesday of November in 1992, no one was more surprised than I was that my candidate actually prevailed. After years of dashed hopes, finally, it seemed, there was a way forward, though victory came with compromises and problems of its own.

Bill Clinton would come to personify the cautious politics of incrementalism and triangulation that defined the Democratic Party over the course of four consecutive presidential elections. He began his first term with a bold Keynesian economic relief package, a progressive push for health care reform, and a promise to lift the ban on gays in the military. He ended his administration with a crime bill that promoted mass incarceration, a welfare reform bill that parroted Republican talking points about dependency, a financial deregulation law that repealed New Deal–era protections for consumers, and a Defense of Marriage Act that federalized state-sanctioned homophobia. Despite these disappointments and the embarrassment of a politically charged impeachment, Clinton emerged from his presidency with the highest end-of-career poll ratings of any president since World War II. His approval with African Americans was even more impressive, soaring to 90 percent in a January 2001 ABC News/*Washington Post* poll. But how did he do it? How did Clinton's calculated triangulation strategy fail so badly at advancing his party's policy agenda and succeed so dramatically in public approval at the same time? To answer this question, you have to understand the man and the times, and examining the shifting racial and political trends from the 1990s helps understand how we got to where we are now. Bill Clinton's story provides the perfect vantage point.

William Jefferson Clinton was born in the small town of Hope, Arkansas, in the segregated South of 1946. In a contrast to the pampered upbringing of the man he would ultimately defeat for president in 1992, Clinton grew up in a troubled household with an alcoholic stepfather. He worked his way up to Georgetown University, a Rhodes Scholarship at Oxford, a degree from Yale Law School, and an election to attorney general of Arkansas at only thirty years old. In 1978, Clinton won his first governor's race and was elected again in 1982, in the same year my candidate, George Sheldon, lost his race for Congress in Florida. Particularly impressive was the fact that, as Ronald Reagan won his forty-nine-state victory in 1984, Clinton had still managed to win reelection against his Republican challenger by a 25-percentage point margin, even though Reagan would easily carry his state and the rest of the South. While Democrats were repeatedly losing national presidential elections and slowly losing ground in the former Confederate states, Clinton continued winning his elections in Arkansas in 1986 and 1990.

With his youthful good looks, boyish charm, and an accomplished and outspoken wife, everything about Clinton's style and demeanor seemed to represent a change from the old conservative ways of the Reagan-Bush era. As a sixteen-year-old high school student, Clinton had been photographed shaking the hand of President John F. Kennedy at the White House in 1963, and this image came to represent a passing of the torch from one generation to the next. Just as Kennedy had been the first American president born in the twentieth century, Clinton hoped to become the first president born after World War II. He became, in the skillful hands of the marketing gurus, "the man from Hope." This Kennedyesque appeal allowed the forty-six-year-old governor to inspire various factions of the Democratic Party, but it was his record of defying the political odds that impressed those who were most desperate to win back the White House. The Clinton campaign billed the candidate as "a different kind of Democrat" with a Yankee education and a Dixie background, who could talk to Northerners and Southerners, who was fluent with Black and white audiences, and who could appeal to liberals and conservatives.

Many of the liberal Democrats who had concerns about Clinton came to embrace his candidacy and the early years of his presidency with a bit of a wink and a nod. The man could "feel your pain" and communicate his support for your interests or constituency almost telepathically, and his supporters became witting coconspirators in the plot. We knew, or thought we knew, that Clinton could not say everything we wanted him to say in support of our liberal causes, so we gave him wide latitude because we thought he was on our side and trying his best to defeat our common adversaries. As a result, when he endorsed policies with which we disagreed, some of us were often far too forgiving of his transgressions.

Black Americans also fell prey to this trap. Many of us liked Bill Clinton and wanted him to succeed. Almost from the beginning, there was something about him that distinguished him from his rivals. None of the other 1992 Democratic primary candidates appealed to Black Americans in a way that Clinton did. Former California governor Jerry Brown was seen as sort of a bohemian long shot. Former Massachusetts senator Paul Tsongas came across as an aloof intellectual. Iowa Senator Tom Harkin was a populist favorite, but he, like Nebraska Senator Bob Kerrey, appealed more to whites in middle America, and both represented states with very few Black people. Of all the candidates, Clinton had the strongest natural connection to Black voters. He was the youngest candidate in the field, the only sitting governor and the only Southerner, and he had an ability to "code switch"—he could speak the Queen's English to policy wonks and then turn around and talk like "Bubba" to the "good ol' boys" in the South—that could be comforting or troubling, depending on your perspective. His Southern heritage also gave him a proximity to Black culture that white politicians from Iowa and Nebraska tend to lack. When he played his saxophone on the popular *Arsenio Hall Show* in the summer of 1992, Black voters interpreted his gesture—which today would be dismissed as performative pandering—as a genuine effort to relate to our community. Before Clinton, we had never seen a presidential nominee for a major political party who seemed to understand or appreciate Black culture or Black music. Most previous Democratic presidential nominees obligatorily made the rounds, showing up to NAACP conventions and Black churches and visiting all the usual suspects. Clinton went beyond those traditional spaces, and he understood one truth in 1992 that future candidates from his party would fail to recognize as late as 2020—modern Democrats can't win the presidency without winning and inspiring the Black vote.

Part of Clinton's success was his familiar background. Southern culture had long been intimately connected to Black culture. The food and drinks, the accents and dialects, even the speaking styles of pastors and politicians bore similarities derived from centuries of interrelatedness. The most gifted white politicians in the South could communicate to Black audiences with a sense of cultural familiarity. Black voters in the South rewarded these colorful politicians, like Democrat Edwin Edwards, the flamboyant, scandal-plagued white Cajun, who could speak at a homecoming for Black students and alumni at Southern University, kiss the Black homecoming queen, and march off to cheers as the band played. When he ran against Republican David Duke, a former Ku Klux Klan (KKK) Grand Wizard, during Louisiana's 1991 gubernatorial race, Edwards wryly noted, "The only thing we have in common is we're both wizards under the sheets."

Bill Clinton represented a new, Northern-educated generation of that Southern Democratic tradition, fully capable of charming audiences from Hampton University in Virginia to Harvard University in Massachusetts. I witnessed his skills firsthand when I returned from a US trade mission to Zimbabwe in the summer of 1997, and Reverend Jesse Jackson walked our entire delegation across the tarmac to greet Clinton for an unplanned meeting as he boarded Air Force One. Without prompting, Clinton greeted every member of the nearly all-Black delegation by name. It did not surprise me that he knew leaders like Jackson, Coretta Scott King, Dorothy Height, and David Dinkins, who were on the trip. Nor was I surprised that he knew his own transportation secretary, Rodney Slater (although President Reagan once failed to recognize his only Black cabinet member, Housing and Urban Development Secretary Samuel Pierce, in 1981). Clinton also knew George Haley, a lawyer who worked on the 1954 *Brown v. Board of Education* case and was the brother of *Roots* author Alex Haley. And he knew Michael Brown, whose father, Commerce Secretary Ron Brown, had died in a plane crash on a similar trade mission to Croatia the year before. He knew every person on the tarmac, and he knew something about each person's background. As for me, by 1997, I had left the White House to work for a nonprofit organization and doubted I had made a huge impression on somebody as busy as the president. But Clinton didn't miss a beat. "Good to see you again, Keith."

Bill Clinton was the only politician I've ever met who could look in the eyes of almost anyone he met—Black or white, straight or gay, male or female—and make them feel that he cared about them. It reminded me of the first time I saw him work his magic the day I walked from my Cambridge apartment at 29 Garden Street to see him speak at Harvard's Kennedy School of Government in October of 1991. At the end of his prepared remarks, a student in the audience asked a question. If elected, would you lift the ban on gays and lesbians serving in the military? Clinton said he would.

The answer surprised me. I had not expected that from a white Baptist Southern Democratic politician in 1991. Clinton's position was far more progressive than the "Massachusetts liberal" I worked for in 1988. In the final three months I traveled with Dukakis on the campaign trail, watching every single speech he delivered, I cannot recall a single instance in which he even mentioned lesbian, gay, bisexual, transgender, and questioning or queer (LGBTQ) people. While Jesse Jackson had consciously included gays and lesbians in his Rainbow Coalition during his 1984 and 1988 campaigns, no

Democratic nominee for president had ever publicly endorsed federal action to protect LGBTQ people from discrimination in the military. Clinton's position marked a sea change for Democrats and a recognition that the party that had become associated with civil rights for Blacks would soon be associated with civil rights for other oppressed groups as well. By the end of the campaign, every 1992 Democratic presidential candidate endorsed the idea of lifting the ban on gays in the military. That was a stunning development for a cautious political party, but as for Clinton, it made me believe he was actually a liberal in conservative Southern clothing. Prior to that day, I preferred Paul Tsongas, primarily because he had graduated from Dartmouth, as had I. But Tsongas never inspired me as a candidate. After Clinton's speech that afternoon, I knew he would be the Democratic nominee.

My perception of Clinton had come to be shaped by an emerging aspect of my young identity that added a new dimension to my racial consciousness. I was a second-year student in law school when I first started to understand and appreciate my sexual orientation. After weeks of reflection and journaling, I walked into a bookstore in Harvard Square one day and searched for a book to help me understand and articulate what I was feeling. Nervously looking over my shoulder, I thumbed through the books in the gay and lesbian section until I found one that I wanted to buy. I discreetly carried the book to the counter, purchased it, and slipped it into my backpack to take home. That night, instead of reading for my classes, I read that entire book, and for the first time in my life, at twenty-five years old, I knew I was gay.

That discovery gave me a new sense of intersectional awareness of how racism operates and overlaps with other prejudices that I had never fully appreciated. I took a course on sexual orientation in the law and realized that many of the legal arguments used to justify discrimination against the LGBTQ community in the 1990s—religious freedom, consumer preference, unit cohesion—were identical to the legal arguments used to justify discrimination against African Americans in the 1950s and 1960s. As my early thinking evolved, I came to see sexual orientation issues as a useful but imperfect indicator of how straight white politicians would approach sensitive race issues. If they were afraid to think deeply about sexual orientation, they probably could not be trusted to do so when it came to race. And if politicians could not be relied on to defend the basic concept of non-discrimination toward gays in the military, I decided, they probably could not be relied on to defend the concept of affirmative action for African Americans, either. Both were sensitive subjects for those who were wary of a changing America, and both would require leadership and education to persuade the public.

A year and a half after Clinton's Harvard speech, I sat with him in the Oval Office as he took part in a historic first-ever meeting with leaders of the nation's largest LGBTQ organizations. It was April 1993, and I had become one of the two highest-ranking openly gay people in the White House. It would have been an unlikely place for me to be just two years earlier, when I walked into the Harvard Square bookstore to discover my own identity. But as sure as I was changing and adapting to new circumstances, the world around me was struggling to catch up. Three months before that historic meeting, a Federal Bureau of Investigation (FBI) agent called me into his office on the fifth floor of the Eisenhower Executive Office Building for a follow-up interview to my background check. We have reason to believe that you may be leading an alternative lifestyle, the agent said. "Alternative to what?" I asked, knowing exactly what he meant. The clearly uncomfortable agent told me he had uncovered evidence that I might be gay. This was hardly a secret, and I wondered why the FBI hadn't discovered this information earlier. Then I wondered why it was even a question. Apparently, undisclosed sexual orientation creates opportunities for potential blackmail or extortion, I was told. I suppose that makes sense, but my sexual orientation was not something I had hidden in my interview with the White House. Nobody ever asked. I assumed it was not an issue for a young new president who had pledged to hire gays and lesbians in the federal government and to build an administration "that looks like America."

Clinton kept his commitment in hiring and appointments, but he broke his promise in more substantive matters. In public, Clinton professed continued support for his pledge to lift the ban on gays in the military, but behind closed doors, the White House sought to make the issue go away. The groundswell of opposition to Clinton's proposal caught the new administration off guard. It had barely registered as an issue in the fall campaign, but opponents of the plan began organizing against it the moment Clinton won. Once elected, questions about "gays in the military" seemed to intrigue the media even more than Clinton's economic proposals, and those questions threatened to overwhelm the president's broader agenda on jobs and health care.

It was still not clear how Clinton planned to carry out his promise when he sat down in the White House with the eight LGBTQ leaders that afternoon in April 1993. Asked a question about his legacy, Clinton said he thought he would be remembered in history for two things: health care reform and lifting the ban on gays in the military. But, as history would unfold, he would accomplish neither of these two goals.

It did not help that conservative Southern Democrats like Georgia Senator Sam Nunn joined with Republicans in objecting to any change in military policy that might undermine "unit cohesion." Nunn even went so far as to stage an elaborate photo opportunity with thirty reporters on board a submarine at Norfolk Naval Base in Virginia to demonstrate "the very close quarters." The opinions of the sailors he spoke to that day were mixed, but the impact of the visual image was unmistakable. The next day, a four-column, above-the-fold photo of Nunn and Republican Senator John Warner of Virginia, bending down to talk to sailors in the lower section of a cramped bunk bed, appeared on the front page of the *New York*

Times. It was just a few weeks after Clinton's historic meeting, and Nunn had successfully deployed the same scare tactics that segregationist Senator Strom Thurmond had unsuccessfully used to oppose the integration of the armed forces in 1948.

The Clinton administration's inability to lift the ban on gays in the military was a colossal failure that all of us should have seen coming, and it would become emblematic of a larger problem for the new administration. As the early media focus on gays in the military seemed to eclipse other important issues that the new administration hoped to tackle, the senior White House staff became increasingly wary of the discussion. One day, when White House aide Rahm Emanuel complained in a morning meeting that reporters only wanted to talk about "fags in the foxhole," I began to question whether my colleagues shared my ideological beliefs.

For some time, I had naively assumed the president would keep the promise he made when I saw him speak at the Kennedy School. But I should have known he was retreating from that pledge the day in March of 1993 when I stood in the back of the East Room of the White House and watched him answer a question at a news conference. Asked if he would consider a proposal to segregate gay and lesbian troops in the armed forces, Clinton responded: "I wouldn't rule that out, depending on what the grounds and arguments were." I couldn't believe it. Any talk of segregating troops was sure to enrage activists and prompt memories of the military segregating African Americans before 1948, but it seemed as if the president and senior staff had no idea his response would provoke a controversy. That's when I volunteered to work on the team to communicate the president's efforts to the community.

I believed in Bill Clinton, and I assumed I could make a positive impact on the policy he chose and help to communicate it more effectively to the community. In my new unofficial capacity, I spoke almost daily with LGBTQ leaders at the White House as the Defense Department studied the military issue to determine how to implement the plan. Then, early one morning in July 1993, the phone rang in my apartment, and I woke up to a surprise. It was Air Force One telling me that I had a call from George Stephanopoulos. George was my boss in the White House, and he was on his way back from the G7 summit in Tokyo with President Clinton. He asked me to prepare a memo to the president outlining all the public statements he had made about gays in the military. I was told to deliver it as soon as possible. I got up, rushed to the office, and began researching and writing the memo, determined that my words would somehow influence the outcome of the policy debate and persuade the president to carry out his original promise.

But my memo made no difference, and the president announced his "compromise" proposal just days later. The policy was called "Don't ask, don't tell, don't pursue." The military would stop asking enlistees about their sexual orientation, and, in return, gay and lesbian troops could remain in the armed forces as long as they didn't talk about it, either. It was not the policy the LGBTQ community wanted nor the policy that Clinton had promised, and yet I somehow allowed myself to believe that it was the best he could do—that it was a noble compromise in difficult circumstances. It was not the plan I wanted, but it was a step in the right direction on the path toward a full repeal of the ban.

Looking back, I can't believe I actually thought that. Almost immediately, the policy was ridiculed and condemned by both sides. Liberals saw it as a betrayal of Clinton's promise, and conservatives saw it as a sign of hostility against traditional American values. Yet, it would take me months to recognize the dangerous precedent established by the policy. And, as the military continued to violate the spirit of the agreement by discharging gay and lesbian service members over the course of the coming years, it would eventually become painfully obvious that the compromise was wholly unworkable.

I was troubled by the outcome of the gays in the military controversy, but as time passed, I realized that the deeper problem was what the experience said about me. How did I allow myself to rationalize a broken promise as the best we could do? Yes, the odds were stacked against us from the beginning, but we never really fought for the cause in which we believed. We never tried to explain to the public why it was important to treat all service members with equal dignity and respect. Instead, we fought to avoid the controversy that Clinton's promise had brought to the administration. I found there was something about the culture of the White House that encouraged a troubling groupthink among political appointees in service of the president. The question I found myself answering, directly or indirectly, whenever I raised a controversial issue, was the same: "Does this serve the president's agenda?" But the question we all should have been asking ourselves was different: "Is this the right thing to do?" Often, the president's agenda aligned perfectly with what I considered the right thing to do. But other times, I felt as though we sacrificed our own identity and political values because we convinced ourselves that the larger cause of the administration was just. Like a platoon of soldiers fighting in the trenches in a pitched battle, we dutifully executed our objectives without the luxury of reflection to consider the wisdom of our mission. Only when I was able to step off the battlefield years later and walk away from the adrenaline-fueled rush of daily political combat was I able to fairly assess if it was worth it.

So disastrous was the gays in the military policy rollout that the White House seemed determined to avoid LGBTQ issues in the near future. A year later, when the Senate held hearings on a bill that would outlaw sexual orientation discrimination in the workplace, White House officials held an unusual meeting to determine whether to allow the assistant attorney general for civil rights, Deval Patrick, to testify in favor of the bill. We debated the issue in the White House Roosevelt Room with George Stephanopoulos of the communications office, Alexis Herman of the public liaison office,

Joel Klein of the White House counsel's office, and several other top White House officials I admired and respected. Despite the fact that President Clinton was already on record supporting the legislation, virtually no one in the room thought the assistant attorney general for civil rights should testify. Only Deval Patrick and I argued in favor of it. No one else did. It was a midterm election year, and the White House had been so shell-shocked from the gays in the military experience that no one wanted to touch another hot gay topic. And, thus, it was decided that Patrick would submit written testimony instead of appearing before the congressional committee. A cop-out.

It was a troubling pattern, repeated time and time again. When Clinton drew fire from conservatives for nominating the brilliant critical race theorist Lani Guinier to be his first assistant attorney general for civil rights, he pulled her nomination. "I would gladly fight this nomination to the last moment if nobody wanted to vote for her if it were on grounds I could defend," Clinton explained to the media. "The problem is that this battle will be waged based on her academic writings, and I cannot fight a battle that I know is divisive, that is uphill that is distracting to the country if I do not believe in the ground of the battle." This prompted a sharp rebuke from Reverend Jackson. "If President Clinton and Senate Democrats had stood by Lani as President Bush and the Republicans stood by Clarence Thomas, she would be confirmed," he told the Associated Press.

The next year, when US Surgeon General Joycelyn Elders came under fire, Clinton faltered again. While answering a question from a psychologist at a World AIDS Day conference, Dr. Elders was asked whether there should be "more explicit discussion and promotion of masturbation" to slow the spread of the epidemic. "I think that is something that is a part of human sexuality, and it's a part of something that perhaps should be taught," she said. But, she added, "we've not even taught our children the very basics." Critics pounced, arguing that the Clinton administration wanted to teach schoolkids how to masturbate, when that was clearly not the point she was making.

Yes, there would be a price to pay if the administration defended her. It would require time and energy in an already heated political environment to explain the actual context of her words. But there was also a price to pay in the failure to defend her. It would send a signal that Clinton was unwilling to fight for yet another Black woman.

With both Guinier and Elders, Clinton claimed ignorance that each woman might prove controversial. I found these excuses implausible. He had known Guinier since their Yale Law School days, and he had known Elders since he appointed her director of the Arkansas Department of Health. He must have known that political and social conservatives would balk at their nominations, and that their willingness to speak truth to power is exactly what made them heroes to progressives. But in December of 1994, Clinton fired his surgeon general. "Dr. Elders's public statements reflecting differences with administration policy and my own convictions have made it necessary for her to tender her resignation," he said in a statement. The announcement, coming just months after the collapse of Hillary Clinton's health care reform plan and only weeks after Republicans won control of the House of Representatives, signaled a tragic turning point for Clinton's presidency. The window of opportunity for progressive change in the Clinton administration was now all but closed.

These experiences left me with unanswered questions. What was the point of assembling this diverse new coalition of African Americans, Hispanics, women, and LGBTQ people if the president wasn't willing to fight for them in difficult circumstances? Had we gotten so caught up in the symbolism of diversity in allocating appointments that we had lost sight of the substantive policies that would most help the people in the various communities we represented? And what was the value in electing a president who could speak to both Southern moderates and Northern liberals if he could not use those talents to promote a Democratic agenda? The preelection promise of Bill Clinton was that the man from Hope could convince other Southerners to accept progressive change. But the postelection Clinton took over a country that was becoming increasingly divided, that would put up bitter resistance against even his modest ideas, that would actively discourage Republicans from compromise, and that would cause him to learn the wrong lesson from his failures.

The remainder of the Clinton administration would be characterized by the mercurial vicissitudes of political reality. Clinton's accomplishments would come from appointments, compromise legislation, a robust economy, and small-bore policy changes, while his failures would come from his inability or unwillingness to advance a progressive agenda. The paradox of the Clinton presidency is that his most enduring progressive legacy is not connected to any piece of legislation that passed during his administration. Ironically, it was his historic appointments of women and Blacks that may have made the most impact. He appointed Ruth Bader Ginsburg to the Supreme Court, Madeleine Albright as secretary of state, Janet Reno as attorney general, Ron Brown as commerce secretary, and Mike Espy as agriculture secretary. And he appointed Justice Department officials like Eric Holder and Deval Patrick, who would later go on to become the first Black attorney general and the first Black governor of Massachusetts, respectively.

But for every step forward, it seemed there was a step backward. Clinton would go on to sign the Defense of Marriage Act in 1996, which allowed states to refuse to recognize same-sex marriages in other states. He signed a bill the same year to "end welfare as we know it" that reduced the number of people who qualified for benefits and created limits on how long someone could receive assistance, even in a deep recession. And he signed a crime bill in 1994 that contributed to the philosophy of mass incarceration, even though it had a negligible impact on actual incarceration rates.

It would not be accurate to say that the Black community was united on the crime bill in the 1990s. In the House of Representatives, twenty-six of the thirty-eight voting members of the Congressional

Black Caucus (CBC) supported the bill, but only after Congress rejected the CBC's much more progressive proposal for a Racial Justice Act. The politics of the crime bill were also complicated by the inclusion of an assault weapons ban, funding for community policing in underserved neighborhoods, and the passage of the Violence Against Women Act. However, even among the Congressional Black Caucus members who supported the bill, I don't recall any advocating the "tough on crime" approach that conservatives endorsed to lock up criminals "and throw away the key." Almost everyone in the Democratic Party knew the crime bill was an imperfect compromise, but I think many of us mistakenly convinced ourselves that the good would somehow outweigh the bad. As time passed, however, and the legislation was reexamined in the light of new circumstances, we would all regret that calculation.

The question of marriage equality was also complicated. The issue divided the Black community, but many Black elected officials supported LGBTQ causes even as Black ministers took the opposite position. While the homophobic Defense of Marriage Act passed the House by an overwhelming 342–67 margin, leading CBC members like John Conyers, Ron Dellums, John Lewis, Charles Rangel, Maxine Waters, and others all voted against it.

Clinton's welfare bill was different. "Today, we are ending welfare as we know it," the president announced at the 1996 bill-signing ceremony for the law that ended the federal government's six-decade-long guarantee of cash assistance to the poor. It passed almost exclusively with Republican votes. Democrats voted against it, 165–30. But on the day of the bill signing, Clinton sat at a desk in the White House Rose Garden surrounded by a sea of white men and two young Black women on each side of him—Lillie Harden and Penelope Howard. Harden had participated in one of the welfare-to-work programs Clinton had initiated as governor of Arkansas, and she explained how the transition helped her. "Going to work gave me independence to take care of my children and to make sure there was always food on the table and a roof over their heads," Harden said at the ceremony. It was an attempt to use a Black woman who had benefitted from a completely different state law as a spokesperson for a federal law that would end up hurting other Black women. Liberal Democrats quickly condemned the new law. Children's Defense Fund president Marian Wright Edelman, a longtime friend and ally of the president, released a statement calling the bill "pernicious" and warning that it "makes a mockery" of Clinton's pledge not to hurt children.

Eight years after the 1994 ceremony, long after the spotlight had moved away from her, Lillie Harden suffered a stroke. It left her unable to qualify for Medicaid and unable to pay her $450 monthly prescriptions, according to a report from *The Nation*. In March 2014, she passed away at age fifty-nine. And that job that she was so proud to hold in 1994? "It didn't pay off in the end," Harden told a journalist.

At the end of eight years, Clinton's legacy was a booming economy, historic appointments, and a series of measures that made things just a little less bad than what they would have been if Republicans had held the reins of power. The results were often more symbolic than substantive. Clinton appointed legendary Black historian John Hope Franklin to chair a presidential initiative on race, for example, but the project produced unimaginative boilerplate recommendations like "anti-discrimination measures must be strongly enforced." The administration did manage to reframe some of the most divisive social issues of the day by splitting the difference. When conservatives wanted to kill affirmative action, Clinton's response was "mend it, don't end it." When they wanted to restrict women's reproductive rights, Clinton argued that abortion should be "safe, legal and rare." And, when it came to gays in the military, he tried to appease everyone with a message of "don't ask, don't tell, don't pursue." It was hardly the message of hope that had lifted him into office.

The coup de grâce for 1990s liberalism came when Clinton announced a new approach to government in his 1996 State of the Union address. He warned that "big government does not have all the answers," and that "there's not a program for every problem" and repeated lines that could have been credibly delivered by any Republican at the time. To hear them from a Democratic president was concerning, but one of the next lines was most troubling of all. "The era of big government is over," he declared.

Big government had bankrolled America's westward expansion, fought the Civil War, preserved the union, educated our children, legislated the forty-hour workweek, built the highways, subsidized suburban housing, created the safety net, enforced the minimum wage, integrated public schools, protected the right to vote, and provided financial assistance and health care to seniors and medical care for low-income Americans. Suddenly, at the very moment when America was becoming more complex and diverse, the very tools needed to manage that complexity and diversity were being abandoned. Clinton's declaration would turn out to be a premature capitulation to the loud and mostly white voices of American conservatism that were unrepresentative of his party or the future of the nation. Decades later, President Joe Biden would sign a $1.9 trillion federal stimulus bill in his first two months in office, and up to 75 percent of the American public would support it, according to opinion polls.

Many establishment Democrats of the 1990s were not as bold, and they did not believe they could win on the strength of their own ideas. Clinton offered a "third way" that did not fit neatly into left and right boxes, and he followed the calculated strategy of "triangulation" to bypass the liberal-conservative divide. As he was constantly oscillating between left and right, Black and white, he was harder to define. So, why did Black Americans stand by him so consistently?

At the height of the 1992 presidential primary, Governor Clinton signed a death warrant for a convicted felon named Ricky Ray Rector, an African American with a mental capacity so impaired that he chose not to eat the dessert in his last meal because he was saving it for later. A few months later, he denounced Black rap artist Sister Souljah at Reverend Jesse Jackson's Rainbow Push Coalition convention, after she had been quoted as saying, "If black people kill black people every day, why not have a week and kill white people?" No one took her comments seriously as a threat to white people, but Clinton compared her to America's most famous racist. "If you took the words 'white' and 'Black,' and you reversed them, you might think David Duke was giving that speech," he said. It was another calculated move designed to position Clinton as a heroic politician who could stand up to his own base, but if he was unwilling to fight for that base, how did it serve the community to start a beef with a twenty-eight-year-old rapper?

What saved Bill Clinton was not his politics, but his enemies. He became a hero to Democrats in the 1990s, in large part, because he and his wife were the targets of the slings and arrows of outrageous conservative attacks. Hillary Clinton was vilified for refusing to abide by the conservative norms of political wifedom. "I suppose I could have stayed home and baked cookies and had teas, but what I decided to do was to fulfill my profession," she responded to critics.

And as for Bill Clinton, despite his efforts to distance himself from unpopular liberal causes, Republicans continued to blame him for every controversial liberal personality, idea, or failure. As Toni Morrison explained in her 1998 essay for *The New Yorker*, Clinton's affiliation with African Americans was born of a shared and symbolic sense of persecution. It was, after all, in the middle of the White-water investigation when "one heard the first murmurs: white skin notwithstanding, this is our first Black President," Morrison wrote. Clinton was described as "Blacker than any actual Black person who could ever be elected in our children's lifetime." Yet another Black author, Ishmael Reed, described Clinton as "a white soul brother." It was a late 1990s consensus of reality among African Americans that reflected an understandable but profoundly distorted view of the country. White conservatives had convinced us that America was a fundamentally right-of-center nation that would never fully accept us and that the best we could hope for was to blunt the damage from time to time with small, incremental steps forward. Republicans convinced Democrats of this messaging, even as the slowly changing demographics of the country foreshadowed an inevitable political and cultural shift on the horizon. It is much easier to recognize this today in a way that was not apparent in the 1990s, but our greatest failure of that era may have been our inability to believe in and articulate our own vision for America.

Only when Republicans overplayed their hands and impeached President Clinton over an admittedly inappropriate consensual adult affair did our power become apparent. Clinton was not the bold reformer that many wanted him to be, but he was the public face of the Democratic Party. An attack on Clinton, led by a group of white Southern Republicans, felt like an attack on women and minorities.

At the end of Clinton's two terms in office, his presidency did not lend itself to an easy verdict for Black America. From a purely economic perspective, many Blacks were better off after Clinton. The booming economy helped to cut the Black unemployment rate from 14.1 percent to a record low of 7.0 percent in 2000. Meanwhile, the federal minimum wage rose by 21.0 percent during his two terms. And despite his spectacular perfidy in abandoning Guinier and Elders, Clinton deserved credit for the numerous other political appointees and judicial nominees he did hire. But for the people who were left behind because of the politics of mass incarceration and welfare reform, it's hard to balance their deprivation of basic liberty or resources against the economic advancements for middle-class and upper-income African Americans. For the vast majority of Black people at the time, Clinton was neither transitional nor transformative, but he was the best we thought we could do under the circumstances. It was an argument that seemed to make perfect sense in the 1990s. Reexamining the Clinton administration some decades later, it seems we were wrong.

6

GEORGE W. BUSH'S
"SOFT BIGOTRY"

The Fire Island Ferry moved quietly past the boats docked along the marina, until we reached the end of the Browns River. There, the first roar of the engine abruptly alerted me that the journey had begun for what would be the last major celebration of my thirties. As we raced into the Great South Bay between New York's Long Island and Fire Island that Friday afternoon, the seemingly endless expanse of water crashing against the crisp blue skies reminded me just how tiny was my place in the universe.

There had always been something about the water—that beautiful but powerful presence that covers more than 70 percent of the earth's surface—that both fascinated and frightened me. As a child in my hometown of St. Louis, I was drawn to the towering arch that rose from the banks of the Mississippi River. In college, I led a canoe trip for new students along the Connecticut River. Even after I had almost drowned on a stolen paddle boat in the Mediterranean Sea during a foreign study program in Spain, I still loved the water. But nothing I had ever experienced felt as special as the ride from Sayville to Fire Island. At the very moment the ferry enters the bay, the body relaxes, the worries disappear, and, for twenty minutes the troubles of the outside world vanish into the air, vaporizing into the gusts of wind that blow the American flag on the bow of the speeding vessel.

I had a few days left to enjoy my thirties when I stepped onto the wooden planks of a quaint little community called "the Pines." No cars or bikes are allowed on this part of the island, and so I dutifully carried my bags to the gates of a handsome waterside home with a swimming pool and jacuzzi facing the bay. The home belonged to a friend, who generously provided it for the event, and, for that weekend, it would be the location for an early celebration of my fortieth birthday. As dozens of my friends joined for food and drinks and camaraderie, I was successfully distracted from the recognition that I was getting older. In addition, the birthday party in "the Pines" represented the first time I had seen so many Black people in one space, and I felt a slight sense of accomplishment that we had collectively helped to make this beautiful, but notoriously white, island just a little bit more welcoming for a diverse crowd.

Nearly 1,400 miles away, a close friend was preparing for his own life transition. Dr. Anthony Pinder had been the associate dean for global studies at Dillard University in New Orleans, and he was just a few weeks from relocating to Atlanta to start a new job at Morehouse College. Where Fire Island had a reputation as a haven of whiteness, New Orleans and Atlanta were both Black cities with proud histories and rich cultural traditions. Dr. Pinder had lived in the Crescent City for six years, had seen storms pass New Orleans many times before, and was not particularly concerned when a tropical depression formed far away in the Bahamas on Tuesday afternoon. It was five days before my birthday, and Pinder's focus was on selling his house in the Black middle-class neighborhood of the Seventh Ward called Gentilly. By Friday, the tropical storm from the Bahamas had been upgraded to a Category 2 hurricane headed to New Orleans, and the governor of Louisiana, Kathleen Blanco, declared a state of emergency. The following day, Saturday, August 27, New Orleans mayor, Ray Nagin, received a phone call from Max Mayfield, the director of the National Hurricane Center. "Mr. Mayor, the storm is headed right for you," Mayfield said. "I've never seen a hurricane like this in my 33-year career. And you need to order mandatory evacuation."

While Dr. Pinder was busy prepping his house for the storm, I turned on the television to see a breaking news story on CNN. Mayor Ray Nagin stood at a podium in a white polo shirt emblazoned with a small blue fleur-de-lis that symbolized his city. With his shiny shaved head and surrounded by ten sober-faced government officials, Nagin slowly read a mandatory evacuation order he had just issued for New Orleans. "The storm surge most likely will topple our levee system," the mayor warned. He told residents to get out of the city but announced that the Superdome was opening as a "refuge of last resort" for those who could not evacuate. Even the famous football stadium would not be a comfortable place, he cautioned, because the hurricane would likely knock out all electricity in the city. It was Sunday, August 28, 2005, my fortieth birthday, and the mayor's alarming announcement told me that all my thoughts of celebration would soon be swept away with the rising waters of tragedy in New Orleans.

Dr. Pinder was by now well aware that the situation was dire, but not all of his neighbors shared his level of concern. Just a day earlier, the skies had been clear when one of his neighbors told him that he did not want to evacuate his elderly mother because she only had one leg and would be difficult to move. It had been forty years since a major hurricane had struck New Orleans, and many residents wondered whether Katrina would be yet another in a long line of hurricanes that had threatened the city but failed to materialize. But after the mayor and the governor spoke at the press conference Sunday morning, there was nothing left to wonder.

Pinder grabbed everything in the house that he could fit into his Saturn sport utility vehicle and secured his dog—a chow chow named Moka—into the front passenger seat for a drive to Atlanta. With a number of gas stations closed for the storm and traffic piled up on the highway, what was normally a six- or seven-hour trip on Interstate 10 instead lasted twenty-five hours. By the time he arrived at his destination in Georgia, a levee had broken at the London Avenue Canal back in Louisiana, sending billions of gallons of water into the Gentilly neighborhood. Long before he had time to find a home in Atlanta, his old home in New Orleans had already been destroyed; 80 percent of the city was under water. And when it was all over, his neighbor's mother was dead.

Unfortunately, Dr. Pinder's story is not unusual. Nearly half a million residents of pre-Katrina New Orleans were devastated by the storm. Hundreds of thousands were forced to leave their homes. Huge swaths of the city were flooded. More than a thousand people died. Entire neighborhoods were virtually wiped off the map. And despite the failure of local officials to evacuate all of their residents, the persistent impression left by the crisis was that the federal government allowed a major American city to drown. And not just any city. It was New Orleans, a crown jewel of the South, known for its music, its food, and its culture, and known to be a Black city with a thriving middle class. The damage was incalculable, and the city never fully recovered. Nearly fifteen years after that catastrophic hurricane, much of the physical structure of the city had been rebuilt, but nearly one hundred thousand Black residents never came back. One out of every three Black people who lived in New Orleans before Hurricane Katrina had gone.

Of course, this is not just a story about the powerful waters of a hurricane. It is a story about the federal government's relationship to its most powerless citizens. There is no better example that reflects the sense of neglect that many African Americans felt during the presidency of George W. Bush than the mismanagement of the Hurricane Katrina crisis. While images of Black people wading in waist-deep water, rowing boats through city streets, camping on rooftops, and stuck in the squalor of an un-air-conditioned Superdome filled the news for days, the president of the United States remained on holiday, quietly secluded at his 1,600-acre ranch in Crawford, Texas. He waited until August 31, two days after the hurricane hit New Orleans, before finally halting his twenty-nine-day summer vacation. On his way home to Washington, a White House photographer snapped a photo of President Bush peering out the window of Air Force One, examining the ruins of the devastated Gulf Coast like an emperor surveying his destitute peasants beneath him. The image stuck. When Bush finally showed up on the scene on September 2, he walked into an airport hangar in Mobile, Alabama, and held a press conference. Surrounded by white men who did not reflect the vast majority of the victims in the disaster, the president indulged in a moment of gratuitous praise for his own team leader. "And Brownie, you're doing a heck of a job," Bush told Federal Emergency Management Agency Director Michael Brown. It was as if Bush had learned nothing from his famously failed "Mission Accomplished" photo op on board the *USS Abraham Lincoln* aircraft carrier in May 2003, when he prematurely declared, "In the battle of Iraq, the United States and our allies have prevailed." As Michael Brown stood in khaki pants and white Oxford shirt listening to Bush's praise, it felt as though the president had been completely oblivious to the national mood. Ten days later, Michael Brown resigned in disgrace.

Bush was not the only elected official guilty of heaping praise on undeserving colleagues. When CNN anchor Anderson Cooper, while on location in Waveland, Mississippi, interviewed Democratic Louisiana senator Mary Landrieu via satellite in Baton Rouge, he asked her if the federal government bore responsibility for the Katrina crisis. Landrieu unsuccessfully tried to deflect the question. "Anderson, there will be plenty time to discuss all those issues about why and how and what and if," she said. Standing in a dry parking lot, she glibly rattled off a list of politicians from both political parties she wanted to thank "for their extraordinary efforts" and was about to praise Congress for taking action. Anderson Cooper couldn't take it any longer. "Excuse me, senator, I'm sorry for interrupting. I haven't heard that because for the last four days I've been seeing dead bodies in the streets here in Mississippi, and to listen to politicians thanking each other and complimenting each other, you know, I got to tell you, there are a lot of people here who are very upset."

Cooper was right, and many of those people were African American. I was one of them, and I cheered at the television as the CNN
anchor spoke truth to power. "Finally!" I screamed at the TV. It felt
like a pivotal moment, the first time I could remember a television
journalist dressing down a politician on live television for reciting
anodyne talking points in the face of crisis. Landrieu's assertion that
"there will be plenty time to discuss all those issues" was a classic
and cowardly political deflection. Whenever there was a mass shooting, a white domestic terrorist, or a national tragedy that did not
lend itself to a convenient political explanation, cautious politicians
would demand time before commenting on the assignation of blame
or appeals for justice. But they did not exercise the same restraint
when faced with other crises that allowed them to engage in quick,
demagogic solutions.

Black Americans did not need time to determine whom or what
to blame. After centuries of watching the nation's leaders neglect,
disrupt, and destroy our communities, the pattern was all too familiar. Two weeks after the storm hit, a CNN/USA Today/Gallup poll
found six in ten Black people blamed race for the federal government's slow response in New Orleans. In stark contrast, only about
one in eight white respondents believed the government responded
slowly because the victims were Black. For African Americans, both
in and outside the region, the pain felt personal and familiar. When
the same consortium conducted another poll four weeks later, it
found 63 percent of Black respondents feared for their lives during
the hurricane, compared to only 39 percent of whites. More than
half of Blacks in the area also reported that they had gone without
food for at least a day during the storm, while less than a quarter of
whites had the same experience. Black residents were also far more
likely than white residents to report that they had been worried about
an elderly relative during the crisis. Once again, a major tragedy in
America had disproportionately impacted Black people, and once
again, the nation found itself divided about the impact of race.

Four days after Katrina struck New Orleans, NBC aired a hurricane relief telethon, featuring musical performances and celebrity appearances to help raise money for victims. During one segment, film star Mike Myers looked earnestly into the camera and read a script to viewers explaining how the breach of the levees in New Orleans had changed the landscape of the city "dramatically, tragically, and perhaps, irreversibly." When he finished his lines, his partner on stage began to speak. "I hate the way they portray us in the media," Kanye West said. Myers turned abruptly to West, clearly noticing that the rapper had gone off script. "If you see a Black family, it says they're looting. If you see a white family, it says they're looking for food," West continued. His words tumbled out after that, as he began to ramble about a number of issues, including his own sense of guilt for shopping instead of donating. At the end of West's unscheduled, one-minute speech, Myers attempted to return to the script, hurrying through his remaining lines without addressing West's remarks. "The destruction of the spirit of the people of southern Louisiana and Mississippi may end up being the most tragic loss of all," Myers said. But when it came time for West to speak again, he blurted out the now famous words that would come to haunt the White House: "George Bush doesn't care about Black people."

The producers quickly cut the segment. They switched the camera to comedian Chris Tucker, who was clearly not prepared for the early handoff. But it was too late. Kanye West had already spoken and articulated what Black Americans had been saying all across the country. We had been complaining about the dueling media narratives of Black and white hurricane victims and the demonization and criminalization of Black poverty. The persistent and inescapable televised images of Black suffering caused by the storm had opened an unhealed wound for our people, just as the Flint, Michigan, water crisis would do a decade later, once again reminding us that our lives are disposable in the eyes of the larger white society. Kanye West's extemporaneous candor, no matter how untimely or inelegantly presented, had its desired effect. It prompted yet another national conversation on race and stamped a brand on the president that would remain for the duration of his tenure in office. As Bush would later acknowledge in his 2010 memoir, *Decision Points*, the accusation of racism directed at him during the Katrina crisis "was the worst moment of my presidency."

It hadn't always been that way for George W. Bush. When the Texas governor secured the Republican nomination for president in 2000, he portrayed himself as a "different kind of Republican" who had worked successfully with Black leaders in his own state. He was following the playbook of Bill Clinton's handlers, who had depicted him in 1992 as a "different kind of Democrat" who had worked successfully with Republicans in Arkansas. Both Bush and Clinton were all too familiar with the baggage that their party identifications carried, and they made efforts to distinguish themselves from some of the more polarizing leaders of their respective parties. During the Clinton presidency, Republican House Speaker Newt Gingrich shut down the government in 1995 and 1996 and impeached the president in 1998. But George W. Bush tried to send a different and less divisive signal.

You could feel the difference when Bush walked on stage in a Baltimore convention hall in July 2000 to speak to the NAACP. He entered the room with NAACP President Kweisi Mfume, NAACP Chair Julian Bond, and NAACP Chair Emeritus Myrlie Evers-Williams. Bush politely shook the hands of the officials on the dais, received a standing ovation as he was introduced, and had the political savvy to begin his remarks with self-deprecating jokes to soften the crowd. Although he faced a mostly Democratic audience, he did not hesitate to describe the tension in the room. "I recognize the history of the Republican Party and the NAACP has not been one of regular partnership," he said. This was not entirely true. The NAACP was founded, in part, by Republicans in 1909. But that was a different Republican Party that could still claim close ties to the leaders who fought to save the union from the Confederacy. Bush acknowledged this reality in his speech when he admitted that "the party of Lincoln has not always carried the mantle of Lincoln."

For a moment, it seemed as if Bush got it. "Discrimination is still a reality, even when it takes different forms," he said. Black Americans had never stopped saying this, of course, while much of white America, including Bush's own party, pretended that racism had ended with the passage of civil rights laws and the accomplishments of a few high-profile Black Americans. But Bush sounded different from other Republicans that day. "Instead of Jim Crow, there's racial redlining and profiling," he said. "Instead of separate but equal, there is separate and forgotten," he added. The Texas governor promised the NAACP that "strong civil rights enforcement" would be a "cornerstone" of his administration.

The most obvious problem with Bush's promises, and those of other Republicans who sought the White House, was that the Grand Old Party remained stubbornly opposed to all new civil rights laws to protect African Americans. Virtually any civil rights legislation designed to end racial discrimination was deemed unnecessary, at best, or "reverse discrimination," at worst. Even as Republican Party leaders paid lip service to historic civil rights legislation, as they did with the Voting Rights Act of 1965, Republican-appointed judges were laying the groundwork to vitiate the law.

This contradiction would become apparent in the midst of the Katrina crisis, on Saturday, September 3, 2005, the day after Bush visited Alabama, with the death of Chief Justice William Rehnquist. Having recently nominated John Roberts to fill the seat for retiring Justice Sandra Day O'Connor, Bush renominated Roberts for the new opening to replace Rehnquist as chief justice and later nominated conservative Samuel Alito to replace O'Connor. These two justices would soon join more senior Reagan-Bush appointees—Antonin Scalia, Anthony Kennedy, and Clarence Thomas—in striking down

Section 4 of the Voting Rights Act in the 2013 case, *Shelby County v. Holder.*

It would not matter that the reauthorization of the Voting Rights Act was signed into law under President Bush after an overwhelming and bipartisan vote in the US House of Representatives and a rare unanimous vote in the Senate. Bush's own judges would strike down a critical enforcement mechanism of the very same civil rights law that he would sign. What had once been a central juxtaposition for Republican presidents in the nineteenth century had returned again for Bush in the twenty-first century: a Republican president who publicly claimed to support civil rights laws had appointed judges who ruled against those very same civil rights laws.

On that summer day in Baltimore when Bush spoke to the NAACP, there was one line in the governor's speech that stood out above all others. After scoring points for acknowledging the existence of redlining and racial profiling, Bush promised to confront yet another form of bias. He called it "the soft bigotry of low expectations." As he vowed to "close the achievement gap" in America's schools, he declared that "no child in America should be segregated by low expectations, imprisoned by illiteracy, abandoned to frustration and the darkness of self-doubt." Bush's stated goal was admirable, and almost every Black person in the audience could surely support his vision for an American society in which children of all races achieved relatively equal outcomes in public education. In fact, the very point of this book is that our racial justice policies must focus on equal outcomes instead of just slightly better outcomes. But Bush's solution was shamefully, inexcusably, and perhaps, purposely, unimaginative. He argued that America could "raise the bar of standards" simply by adopting the platitudes of "education reform"—"expect every child can learn"; give schools flexibility; "measure progress"; insist upon results; "blow the whistle on failure"; and, of course, give parents charter schools and school choice.

At no point did Bush address the inequity of resources in Black and white schools. In fact, his only mention of public school funding came in a statement that "resources must go to the parents so that parents can make a different choice." Nor did he bother to interrogate the underlying causes that contributed to the nation's centuries-long disparities in educational outcomes—the absence of jobs, the lack of quality health care, the legacy of housing discrimination, the environmental racism that targeted Black and brown communities with polluted air and drinking water, a justice system that criminalized Black and brown youth, and state property tax funding mechanisms that directed public education dollars to the communities that were already most well-off. In fact, Bush outright dismissed these root causes. "Whatever the causes," he told the NAACP, "the effect is discrimination."

What Bush proposed to the NAACP was not a fix for public education; it was an outright abandonment. It was as if the federal government committed to develop a cure for cancer merely by telling patients to expect that they can get better and that they should "blow the whistle on failure," while the government redirected its dollars away from cancer research and instead encouraged cancer patients to figure out the cure in the free marketplace. If a public official gave a speech to cancer patients and told them, "Whatever the causes of cancer, let's just focus on solutions," no one would take the official seriously. After all, how could you develop a solution to the problem if you don't know what caused the problem in the first place? Yet here was the Republican nominee for president telling his Black audience that whatever the causes of racial disparities in education, we should turn our attention to solutions instead.

There was a certain form of condescension inherent in Bush's Baltimore remarks. One might even call it a "soft bigotry" that was not overtly hostile to the interests of African Americans, and, in fact, actually purported to serve those interests, but in reality, was designed to ignore the stated concerns of the vast majority of Black people and redirect the conversation to other concerns that were more palatable to Republican audiences. Instead of centering racial discrimination as a subject of concern by focusing our attention, for example, on the school-to-prison pipeline that disproportionately punishes young Black students, Bush moved the discussion to school choice, which allowed Republicans to elide broader and more uncomfortable conversations about race by shifting the burden to struggling Black families who were somehow supposed to remedy centuries of state-sponsored racist socioeconomic policies with a voucher or a tax credit.

Bush's facile approach to race was no surprise from someone who had spent his entire life blithely ensconced in the comfort of white privilege. I've never met the man, but almost everyone I know who has met George W. Bush describes him as a "down-to-earth" guy with an amiable personality that allows him to interact comfortably with people of all races. That's why I would not be surprised or troubled years later by his unlikely postpresidency friendship with Michelle Obama. Bush was, after all, the guy voters wanted to "have a beer with" compared to his stuffy Harvard-educated 2000 opponent, Al Gore, and his stodgy Yale-educated 2004 opponent, John Kerry. Never mind the fact that Bush, himself, graduated from Yale and Harvard. The problem is we shouldn't be electing presidents to be our drinking companions in the first place. We elect them to run the country, and that job requires competence and leadership skills, not just a pedigree and a pleasing personality.

George W. Bush's unusual life story of personal advantages and second chances would also make a mockery of the conservative argument that affirmative action stigmatizes its beneficiaries. His entire career was a product of affirmative action for rich white men from famous families. He was the son of a president and the grandson of a senator and was educated in the pampered prep schools of Texas, went to boarding school at the prestigious Phillips Academy at Andover, and then attended college at Yale University. In May 1968, nearly two weeks before his college graduation—and the end of his student draft deferment from Vietnam—Bush applied to join the

Texas Air National Guard, a post that would keep him out of the deadly, raging war. The commander, noting that Bush's father was then a US congressman, overlooked a long waiting list and Bush's low 25 percent score on the pilot aptitude test, and swore him in as an airman the very same day.

An admittedly mediocre student in college, Bush tried to return to academic life by applying to attend the University of Texas Law School. He was rejected in 1970. Then, in August 1972, Bush was suspended from flying with the Texas Air National Guard and never flew again with the unit. But as his father's influence grew as US ambassador to the United Nations and later chairman of the Republican National Committee, the young Bush's fortunes rose as well. A year later, he was discharged from the National Guard to attend Harvard Business School. While thousands of young men who did not have famous fathers were still fighting the war in Southeast Asia, Bush acknowledged later that he "chased a lot of pussy and drank a lot of whiskey" during those years. He would continue on in that vein, drinking and partying, drifting from one failed business venture to another, until his fortieth birthday celebration in July 1986, when he woke up one day with a hangover at the historic Broadmoor Hotel in Colorado Springs, Colorado. Bush decided that day to give up alcohol for good.

When I think about the special privileges and opportunities afforded George W. Bush and the reckless and repeated mistakes that he made in his first forty years, I can only imagine how differently I, or any other Black person, would be viewed under those circumstances. On the day of my own fortieth birthday party, as I gazed at the perfect sunset on the still waters of the bay, I realized I had led a relatively quiet life. I had no thoughts of running for public office that day, but if I had, surely, I would have known that I would never be president of the United States. For a Black person to be taken seriously for that office, she or he would have to be flawless. Bush, on the other hand, had been an unimpressive person for most of his life, known for his difficulty with the English language and not even considered to be the smartest among his siblings. Yet he parlayed his family privilege and white male entitlement into the governorship of Texas and the presidency of the United States. His failures made him "relatable," particularly to white Americans who described him as the type of person they'd like to "have a beer with." It would be hard to imagine an inarticulate, intellectually incurious African American politician with a past drinking problem who would be taken seriously as a gubernatorial candidate, much less a presidential one. Every failed business venture, every suspicious military deferment, every National Guard suspension, every allegation of nepotism, and every episode of raucous adult drunkenness would create serious consequences for a Black candidate. But here was George W. Bush, just fourteen years after that last hangover in Colorado, standing before the NAACP, only five months before he would become president, in an election that would itself become a sore subject within the Black community.

Despite Bush's charm offensive with the NAACP, Vice President Al Gore won 90 percent of the Black vote and won the national popular vote by a 544,000 vote margin. Yet Bush narrowly won the electoral college, as the presidency was decided by a mere 537 votes in the state of Florida. For the first time in more than one hundred years, the candidate who lost the popular vote had won the election. That bitter pill was made even harder to swallow by the thirty-seven-day ordeal that allowed it to happen. Once again, Bush's family came to the rescue. His brother, Florida governor Jeb Bush, worked to influence the outcome of the election in the state, while his father, former president George H. W. Bush, had appointed the one justice, Clarence Thomas, who would cast the deciding vote in the Supreme Court case that effectively stopped a recount of ballots.

By the time Congress was prepared to certify the electoral college vote for Bush in January 2001, a dozen members of the Congressional Black Caucus stood up in Congress to object. They argued that the certification of the results should be blocked because of the disputed election results in Florida. In a final humiliating exercise of the democratic process, Gore presided over the Senate for the certification process. One by one, members of the Congressional Black Caucus stood at the podium in the House chamber and denounced the antidemocratic election process. But each time someone rose to object, Gore asked the speaker if the objection was in writing and signed by a member of the House and the Senate, as required by law. One by one, each Black caucus member who spoke was forced to acknowledge that not a single member of the US Senate was willing to stand with them. "The objection is in writing, and I don't care that it is not signed by a member of the Senate," Representative Maxine Waters thundered.

The spectacle of certifying the popular-vote loser as the actual winner in a presidential election in what is supposed to be the world's greatest democracy exposed structural obstacles embedded deep in the framework of the republic that would bedevil the Democratic Party in the years to come. The fundamental problem is that our eighteenth-century Constitution cannot power a twenty-first century democracy. Decades after the 2000 election debacle, this problem was still not fixed. The composition of the Senate would remain unreflective of the diversity of the nation. A state like California, for example, with nearly forty million people and a population larger than the twenty-one smallest states combined, received the same number of senators in 2020 as tiny Wyoming, with barely six hundred thousand residents. The two Dakotas, with a combined population of 1.6 million people, receive four US senators, while the island of Manhattan, with about the same number of people, has to share its two senators with the nineteen million residents of New York state. And the District of Columbia, with a population larger than Vermont or Wyoming, has no senators at all. The beneficiaries of this arrangement are states with small populations of overwhelmingly white residents, and the victims are the residents of larger states with urban city centers and the most diverse populations. The electoral college only exacerbates the problem, diluting the impact of millions of Black and brown voters in the nation's largest states by giving a disproportionate voice to white voters in the nation's smallest states. Yet George W. Bush showed no intention of addressing any of these issues in his time in office.

The nation's forty-third president inherited a deeply divided country that was riven by the culture wars of the 1990s, by the Republican-led impeachment of Bill Clinton in 1998, and by the Supreme Court's controversial 5–4 decision in the *Bush v. Gore* case. But nothing would shape the Bush presidency more than a Tuesday morning in late summer that changed the nation. Halfway through his first year in office, on August 6, 2001, the intelligence community presented a warning in the president's daily briefing. The title was clear: "Bin Ladin Determined To Strike in US." Despite the warning, and what officials later claimed was a lack of "actionable intelligence," the Bush administration took no significant new steps to protect the homeland. Just over a month later, on Tuesday, September 11, a well-coordinated group of nineteen terrorists hijacked four airplanes along the East Coast, slamming two of them into the twin towers in Manhattan, one into the Pentagon outside Washington, and a fourth into the ground in Pennsylvania.

The most impressive moment of the Bush administration, for me, came a few days after this tragedy. Just a week after the September 11 attacks, Bush visited the Islamic Center in Washington, DC, and quoted from the Quran: "Evil in the extreme will be the end of those who do evil." As he made his brief but eloquent remarks, surrounded by Muslim leaders, he made a point to recognize that "Muslims make an incredibly valuable contribution to our country," and he added that "they need to be treated with respect." I held back tears as he spoke. It was, in my opinion, Bush's finest moment as president and represented the kind of inclusive America that made me proud.

But soon afterward, I found myself predictably disappointed as he launched two wars against Muslim countries.

The September 11 attacks gave Bush an opportunity to prove he was a different kind of Republican; his approval rating soared in the wake of the tragedy. But despite his campaign promise to be a "compassionate conservative," Bush largely governed like a traditional Republican, dramatically increasing the defense budget, initiating the construction of a new seven-hundred-mile border fence, and pushing through two massive tax cut laws that depleted the Clinton surplus he inherited, expanded the national debt, and exhausted the country's available resources to invest at home while fighting wars abroad.

All that really changed was the rhetoric. It was a time when the conservative brand, under the direction of Southern Republicans like Lee Atwater, Newt Gingrich, and Trent Lott, had become so coarsened that "public opinion gurus" were hired to sell the party to a wary public. Just as the first President Bush had broken his promise of a "kinder, gentler nation," the second President Bush would do the same with "compassionate conservatism." The very use of the term, itself, suggested an awareness of the party's increasingly toxic reputation in some quarters. But as cable news and social media created new information bubbles for conservative consumers, talk radio hosts like Rush Limbaugh, conservative television commentators like Bill O'Reilly, and entire conservative television networks like Fox News developed a right-wing media infrastructure to amplify the Republican Party's message.

Like his father, Bush's record on racial and social justice issues was built on a legacy of symbolism that was often contradicted by policy. Bush appointed two prominent Black Republicans—Colin Powell and then Condoleezza Rice—for one of the highest positions in his cabinet, secretary of state, but he deployed them to help justify the war with Iraq. He claimed to "strongly support diversity of all kinds" but then ordered his Justice Department to file a brief against the University of Michigan for using affirmative action policies that were needed to achieve diversity. He said he supported civil unions for gay and lesbian couples but then called for an unprecedented constitutional amendment to ban all gay marriages.

As Bush attempted to present a compassionate face and voice to mask the cruelty of the Republican Party's aggressive new twenty-first-century conservatism, some of his GOP colleagues didn't even bother to try. When South Carolina Republican Senator Strom Thurmond turned one hundred years old in December 2002, Republican Senator Trent Lott of Mississippi praised Thurmond for his racist 1948 campaign for president:

> I want to say this about my state: When Strom Thurmond ran for president, we voted for him. We're proud of it. And if the rest of the country had followed our lead, we wouldn't have had all these problems over all these years, either.

Here was the Senate Republican leader, of what was once the party of Lincoln, openly praising a racist political campaign in the twenty-first century, bragging that his state voted for a segregationist in the presidential election, and arguing that America would be better off if a bigoted Southern Democrat had won the presidency in 1948. Lott was forced to apologize for what he called "a poor choice of words," but the impression was indelible. It would be impossible to ignore how the Republican Party had changed over the course of the previous four decades. Bush did little to remedy this.

During the Bush administration, a country that had previously enjoyed peace and prosperity under a Democrat would be plunged into two wars and economic collapse under a Republican. It would be a time of unbelievable headlines, from the very first year when terrorists hijacked four civilian passenger jets and crashed them into the World Trade Center and the Pentagon, leading the country to war, to the third year, when the administration launched a second war that killed hundreds of thousands of Muslim civilians in a country that had never attacked the United States, on the false premise that Iraq was hiding weapons of mass destruction. At the end of his first term, Bush faced a similarly divided nation. The man who came to the presidency by 537 votes in the state of Florida was narrowly re-elected because of 118,000 votes in the state of Ohio.

By his fifth year in office, when Hurricane Katrina claimed nearly two thousand lives and washed away New Orleans, the wars in Iraq and Afghanistan had dragged on long enough to weigh down the president. Bush found himself on thin ice. His Gallup public approval rating, which had risen to 89 percent after the September 11 attacks, dropped to 31 percent in 2006. By November, Democrats recaptured control of Congress, and in January 2007, Nancy Pelosi was elected as the first woman to serve as Speaker of the House of Representatives. Momentum was shifting quickly. When Bush finally limped to the last year of his presidency, a once-in-a-lifetime financial crisis submerged the economy into the worst recession since the Great Depression. Then, in one last memorable insult, during Bush's "valedictory trip" to Iraq a month before he left office, the president had become so loathed in the international community that he was forced to duck and hide as a local journalist hurled a shoe at his head.

In some areas, Bush did move in a slightly more compassionate direction during his presidency, but his party—and, perhaps, his own instincts—would only allow him to go so far. He called for an end to racial profiling in his first address to Congress in 2001, but a bill to do so garnered little support after the 9/11 attacks. Instead, in 2003, Bush issued vague "policy guidance" on racial profiling in federal law enforcement that was so filled with exceptions that the American Civil Liberties Union condemned it as "little more than rhetorical smoke and mirrors." He also signed a controversial prescription drug bill for Medicare, but he created no funding mechanism to pay for it, thus blowing a hole in the deficit that would encourage Republicans to call for other vital government programs to shrink. And his crowning achievement, the No Child Left Behind Act, which tried to reform American education by raising standards and imposing rigorous testing requirements, had to be replaced a dozen years later due to teacher and parent complaints of too much testing. By 2015, a report from the Council of the Great City Schools found that students took an average of 113 standardized tests between prekindergarten and twelfth grade. And despite all that testing, the racial achievement gaps barely budged. The math and reading gaps for African American and Latino students actually "shrank far more dramatically before No Child Left Behind—when policies focused on equalizing funding and school integration, rather than on test scores," former *Mother Jones* education correspondent Kristina Rizga wrote at the time.

Given the circumstances in which the Bush presidency ended, it would be hard to argue that Black Americans were better off when he left office than when he was inaugurated. During Bush's two terms, Black unemployment climbed from 8.2 percent in January 2001 to 12.7 percent in January 2009. Black homeownership rates declined. Black wealth disappeared. Thousands of Black soldiers were killed or wounded in Iraq and Afghanistan. And President Bush's signature law, the No Child Left Behind Act, did little to eliminate the achievement gap between Black and white students. The "soft bigotry of low expectations" that Bush decried in 2000 turned out to be more of an apt description for his own administration than for the problems facing Black Americans.

Of course, the Bush years were defined by a series of unanticipated tragedies—the September 11 attacks, the war in Afghanistan, the war in Iraq, the failure to find weapons of mass destruction, the response to Hurricane Katrina—but as his presidency came to a close, one more final tragedy loomed on the horizon. In September 2008, an economic crisis, caused by risky investments in America's housing market, forced some of the nation's leading financial institutions to collapse. Investors were shocked. Stocks plummeted. Trillions of dollars in market value vanished overnight. Housing prices tanked. Automobile manufacturers slashed their workforces and threatened to close down for good. And US companies laid off millions of workers in a matter of months.

Only under these dramatic conditions, after the worst terrorist attack in American history; after two long, deadly, and costly wars; after the failure to find weapons of mass destruction in Iraq; after thousands were killed in Hurricane Katrina; after the beginning of the worst recession since the Great Depression, did America finally elect a Black president.

7

BARACK OBAMA'S UNRECIPROCATED OPTIMISM

I was a first-year student at Harvard Law School when I walked into a campus building one afternoon ready to shake things up. I had come to participate in a student-organized vigil for campus diversity that was taking place outside a faculty meeting in Pound Hall. At the end of the meeting, while we stood at attention silently holding our signs outside the door, our law school professors walked out of their room and awkwardly filed past us. A few quietly signaled their support with smiles and warm gestures. Others simply ignored us. Then came the dean of the law school, his face directed toward the ground as though urgently watching his feet move each step along the way. He walked right by me, escorted by a school security official.

I had never met Dean Clark before, and I had only seen him once or twice on campus. My only real memory of him was that he had given a disappointing welcome speech to my class of first-year students a few weeks earlier, in which he seemed to suggest that our principal role as lawyers would be to grease the wheels of commerce and that we should not be ashamed to seek high-paying corporate law firm jobs. This advice seemed to contradict the values of Dean Pound, the namesake of the building in which we stood, who wrote in the *Notre Dame Law Review* in 1944 that the legal profession should be "guided by something better than the desire for money rewards."

I subscribed more to Dean Pound's view of the legal profession than to Dean Clark's. Inspired by a line I read years earlier in my college brochure that emphasized students who will make a "significant, positive impact on society," I resented the message of unrepentant careerism that Dean Clark seemed to push. And, thus, at that moment when I stood with my classmates at the faculty vigil, I felt as though the dean had purposely slighted our group by failing to acknowledge our presence, and I launched into an unscripted outburst.

"Hey Dean Clark, why don't you come back and talk to us?" I shouted.

There was no reply. The dean did not even acknowledge the question. I asked again, more loudly than before.

"Hey, why don't you come back and talk to us?" I yelled.

Still, the dean ignored me and kept walking toward the door.

At this point, something inside me was so offended by what I perceived to be a brush-off, that I decided in that moment to take action, stepping out of the carefully prepared script for the event.

I picked up my backpack, swung it over my shoulder, placed my protest sign under my arm, and marched toward the dean as he approached the door. Unbeknownst to me, other students in the protest had also begun to follow me toward the door. I suppose that is what startled the dean and his security escort, because something unexpected happened next. When he saw us coming toward him, the dean of the Harvard Law School bolted out the door and began sprinting across the campus to get away from us.

I was shocked. I had never expected him to flee, and I had no idea where he was going or what would happen next. But I knew this was a moment not to be missed. I had run on the varsity track teams in my high school and college, and I was not afraid of a good race. With my backpack still swinging on my shoulder, I caught the door leading out of Pound Hall and chased the dean across the campus. As he approached the International Law Center, he lifted his hands to hide his face from the photographers who were covering the event. I continued yelling right behind him as he moved past the west wing of Langdell Hall and retreated into the lower level of the school's administration building at Griswold Hall. The campus security officer then blocked us from entering. We were unable to corner the dean, and I had no idea what I would have said to him if I had caught up with him, anyway. But as a tuition-paying student in the law school, I believed the dean had a duty to acknowledge and address our concerns. And simply by forcing the law school's top administrator to flee from us, we had put the institution on notice that we would not be ignored.

The media played its part in amplifying that message, too. On this particular occasion, one of the media outlets we had invited to cover our protest was the *Boston Globe*, and the next day a story appeared in the metro section of the newspaper. Along with it was a photo. There I was, in black and white, chasing the dean of the Harvard Law School across the campus as he covered his face in embarrassment.

It was a time of intense controversy on campus, when faculty members, divided by politics, openly fought with one another in the pages of the *New York Times* and *Boston Globe*. One of Harvard's first Black professors, Derrick Bell, had just taken a leave of absence to protest the school's failure to hire a woman of color. That was the point of our vigil that day—to advocate for greater diversity in the faculty that taught us. While the student population had become increasingly representative of the larger population of the country, the faculty lagged behind in diversity.

It was in that environment that I had joined an organization called the Harvard Coalition for Civil Rights, whose goal was to push the law school to hire more women, people of color, and other highly qualified candidates from underrepresented groups. The coalition consisted of seven different student affinity organizations—representing Black, Latinx, Asian American, Native American, women, LGBTQ students, and students with disabilities—united for a common purpose. We conducted teach-ins, distributed literature, and held a one-day classroom strike to protest the lack of diversity. But after the faculty meeting incident, we escalated our tactics. We took over the dean's office twice, sitting on the floor and demanding that the dean meet with us and take action to hire women and people of color. We even tried to take over the university president's office, but we were blocked at the door when someone tipped off the staff that we were coming. The law school never budged. Finally, we tried the one action we thought Harvard Law School would understand—we took them to court.

In my second year of law school, I joined with ten other students to file a lawsuit against Harvard University for discrimination in the selection of the law school faculty. We argued the case ourselves as students, all the way up to the Massachusetts Supreme Judicial Court. The court ruled against us because we did not have the legal standing to bring the suit as students. Although our tuition dollars helped pay the salaries for the professors who taught us, Harvard's lawyers described us as mere incidental third-party beneficiaries of the relationship between the school and the faculty. The justices agreed, and although we lost our case in the court of law, we won in the court of public opinion by forcing the institution to defend its abysmal hiring record to the nation.

At some point during the campus diversity movement, I kept hearing about a student with a slightly unusual name. He was in the graduating class ahead of me, and I'm sure I must have bumped into him several times on campus, but it was not until he was elected the first Black president of the *Harvard Law Review* that I seriously took notice of who he was. His name was Barack Obama.

Although we shared only a few mutual friends, did not take any classes together, and were not active members of any of the same organizations, our paths—although distinctly different—were destined to cross. I had become a student activist fighting for faculty diversity, and he was the embodiment of what Harvard said it was looking for in recruiting faculty members of color.

The law school had often explained its dismal track record at recruiting women and people of color by citing the absence of candidates who met their demanding qualifications. Harvard only wanted to hire top graduates of elite schools who served on top law review journals and clerked for top judges on the federal bench. And here was Obama, who had graduated from Ivy League Columbia University, was a student at one of the nation's top law schools, had served on the *Harvard Law Review*, and had become the first Black president of the hundred-year-old institution.

With that background, Obama could have gotten a clerkship with any of the top judges or justices in the federal court system. Whether or not he wanted it, he was on a career track that would have made him perfectly suited to teach at Harvard. It was a godsend to our campaign for faculty diversity. He did not take part in our sit-ins at the dean's office. He did not get disciplined, as some did. And he was not involved in our controversial lawsuit. But he did not need to be. His mere existence came to symbolize everything we had been arguing in our case against the law school.

In a speech after he was elected to his post at the law review, Obama stood outside the student center with Professor Derrick Bell at one of our campus rallies and articulated his support for greater diversity on the faculty. His presence alongside Bell communicated our message that there were qualified candidates available to be hired. And all he had to do was stand up and introduce the professor to a multiracial crowd of classmates, faculty, and media. Wearing a simple button-down blue Oxford and khaki pants, Obama recalled an encounter when Bell spoke at a welcome session organized by the Black Law Students Association for first-year students. In what would become the now familiar cadence of Obama's speaking style, he praised the professor for the "excellence of his scholarship," which he said had "opened up new vistas and new horizons and changed the standards for what legal writing is about." It was classic Barack Obama, always able to thread the needle between various communities and adept at addressing even the most controversial public issues with a measured tone of reason and civility.

The next time I remember seeing Obama was four years later, after we had both graduated from law school, when he had just published his first book, and I had just finished writing mine. Harvard Law Professor Charles Ogletree invited the two of us to campus to talk about writing and politics. Obama was running his first campaign for public office as a candidate for the Illinois State Senate, and I had been working at the White House in the Clinton administration. After that event, Obama would go on to win a state senate race, but he did not succeed that first time he ran for Congress in 2000. The loss was not a great surprise—Alexandria Ocasio-Cortez and Cori Bush notwithstanding, it is very difficult to defeat an incumbent member of Congress. Perhaps that's why Obama would later describe his decision to challenge the incumbent as "stupid" in his memoir *A Promised Land*. But that loss to Representative Bobby Rush, in a district that was overwhelmingly Black, prepared him for questions about his identity that would follow him into the 2008 presidential campaign and beyond.

The former president recalled some of the whispers in his memoir: "Obama's an outsider. He's backed by white folks. He's a Harvard elitist. And that name. Is he even Black?" As Chicago political expert Paul Green told National Public Radio (NPR) in 2007, Bobby Rush "basically had a campaign in which the argument was, 'Obama's not one of us.'" He was a transplanted Chicagoan who had been educated at Columbia and Harvard with a base of support near the prestigious University of Chicago in Hyde Park, while Rush was a longtime civil rights activist who had founded the Illinois chapter of the Black Panthers in the 1960s.

But what may have appeared to be an embarrassing defeat in 2000 would actually turn out to be an unexpected gift. Losing to Rush may have been the best thing that ever happened to Obama's career. The loss of the campaign helped to prevent him from being typecast by a white America that would have reduced him to the label of a

Black congressman. In white identity politics, whiteness is portrayed as normative and universal, while Blackness is considered suspect. White people are assumed to be neutral and unbiased and fully capable of representing the whole, while Black and brown people are presumed only to hold loyalty to their own. White members of Congress from overwhelmingly white states—even people who've never had any meaningful interaction with a Black person—are seen as viable national figures. Black members of Congress, who often rely on white donors and supporters to help sustain their campaigns, are characterized as biased and rarely afforded the same credibility that white members are given when speaking on issues beyond the interests of their Black constituents. This remains the case even though people of color are required to interact with white people in order to function in our white-dominated society, while white people themselves are often able to distance themselves from people of color and remain oblivious to the struggle and experience of Black and brown Americans.

While serving as a US senator representing the overwhelmingly white state of Illinois, Barack Obama would still face these predictable, and sometimes contradictory, questions about his loyalties. As the son of a Black father from Kenya who spent his childhood in Hawaii and Indonesia, he was foreign. As a Chicago politician who attended a controversial Black church, he was just another radical militant. Even the man Obama would choose as his 2008 running mate had once described him as "the first mainstream African-American who is articulate and bright and clean and a nice-looking guy," a comment that casually dismissed the historic significance of Shirley Chisholm in 1972, Jesse Jackson in 1984 and 1988, and Reverend Al Sharpton and Carol Moseley Braun in 2004. Obama's presidential campaign would challenge politicians and journalists to come to terms with their cramped notions of Blackness.

For many white observers, Obama was an anomaly, a unicorn, a mystery, not just because of his blended background, but because he did not reaffirm the existing tropes of Black identity. For Black people, however, Obama was impressive, but not spectacular. As Ta-Nehisi Coates explained in *TIME* magazine in 2007, what white observers "fail to understand is that African-Americans meet other intelligent, articulate African-Americans all the time." When white politicians or journalists swoon over a Black person for speaking English properly, their reaction suggests what limited experience they have had with educated Black people.

Keenly aware of America's racial history, African Americans approached Obama's presidential campaign with cautious optimism. Most Black Americans had very little knowledge of Barack Obama when he announced his campaign on a cold day in Springfield, Illinois, in February 2007. Contrary to assumptions, they did not reflexively support him because he was Black. In a country where we make up only 13 percent of the population, we have a long history of supporting viable white candidates. It was the reason I had worked for Michael Dukakis after college instead of joining Jesse Jackson's campaign. Most Black people have learned to be political realists in a society where our options are often limited.

One day in late 2007, I took a train from New York to Washington, DC, and caught a cab from Union Station to my destination. The cab driver, an older Black man, struck up a conversation with me. I rarely see Black American cab drivers where I live in New York City, so I was particularly interested to hear what he had to say. He told me that most of the cab drivers in the nation's capital were not Black Americans. As a longtime DC resident, he described himself as part of a dying breed. We talked about our respective cities and chatted about trivial things. And then the subject of politics came up. He told me he supported Hillary Clinton for president. I did not disclose my own choice. I was a TV commentator and had not publicly stated my preference at the time, although I knew which candidate I supported. I had met Clinton and Obama, and I liked them both. As a forty-two-year-old Black man, however, I felt more connected to the forty-six-year-old Black senator. I planned to vote for him, but I would have been satisfied if either candidate had won.

I also knew who I did not want to win. After forty-three consecutive white men as president, I did not want to elect another white man. White men were just 29 percent of the nation's population but 100 percent of all our presidents. I had even contributed to that trend by supporting Dukakis over Jackson in 1988. But in the two decades that had passed since that campaign, America had changed, and it was hard for me to see how we could continue electing white guys over and over again in a country that was becoming increasingly diverse.

"And what do you think about Barack Obama?" I asked the cab driver. "I wish he would take his marbles and go home," he responded. His comment stunned me even though I knew that Hillary Clinton enjoyed strong support among Black voters. As late as October 2007, Hillary Clinton held a twenty-four-point lead over Barack Obama among Black Democrats in a CNN poll. But I did not expect the driver to be so dismissive of the candidacy of a Black man who was running a viable campaign and raising a significant amount of money.

Many Black voters admired Obama for his accomplishments but felt the young senator should "wait his turn." Some wanted to support him but thought white America would never vote for a Black man for president. Others imagined he would be better suited as Clinton's vice president. And almost every Black person I knew feared for Obama's safety, worried that an assassin might end his candidacy or his presidency if he advanced too far. Considering America's troubled racial history, even the most optimistic of Obama's Black supporters surely must have harbored some doubts as to whether this impossible dream might become a reality.

Having watched his rise from Harvard to the United States Senate, I had confidence in Obama's abilities to win the support of liberal white voters. But Clinton impressed me too with her grit and tenacity. I saw her as a fighter, and after years of Democrats who seemed afraid to fight for what they believed in, I liked the idea of electing someone who was not afraid of conflict, and at that time, no one had more battle scars than Hillary Clinton. Even when it became clear that Clinton would not win her party's nomination in the late spring of 2008, she continued to fight on in a way that both impressed and infuriated me. It infuriated me because I felt she might divide the party on the eve of Obama's nominating convention, but it impressed me because it was exactly the kind of determination that I had wanted to see from Al Gore and Democrats during the lost battle over the disputed 2000 election. The persistence with which Hillary Clinton fought to the end in 2008 is the way I imagine she would have fought against George W. Bush, his brother Jeb Bush, and the five-member majority of the Supreme Court in 2000. Even though I strongly disagreed with her Senate vote to authorize the war with Iraq, I would have gladly supported her if she had won the nomination in 2008.

Obama was different. His recent arrival on the national political stage served as an asset that left him unburdened by decades of baggage that Clinton brought to the campaign. My concern about him was that a candidate with his professorial instincts might be steamrolled in the rough and dirty world of national politics. Then one day during the primary season, I made a comment on television criticizing something he said. Not long afterward, I received an ominous phone call from a law school friend and Obama associate who warned me to be "on the right side of history." I doubt that Obama knew anything about the call, and I was not intimidated by the message, but in a strange way I felt reassured that there were at least some people in Obama's corner who understood the gravity of the challenge he faced. Just four years earlier, Republicans had deployed a massive disinformation campaign to portray Senator John Kerry, a decorated Vietnam War veteran and 2004 Democratic presidential nominee, as a traitor to his country. Even though Kerry's opponent had avoided the draft with educational deferments, this did not stop Republicans from deploying a group of "swift boat veterans" from Vietnam to attack Kerry's character. If Republicans could "swift boat" a rich, established white guy like Kerry, I could only imagine how they would try to destroy a Black newcomer like Obama.

It was only after Obama won Iowa in early January 2008 that many African Americans first believed he could win. After the Iowa caucuses, Clinton's twenty-four-point lead among Black voters evaporated, and by mid-January, Black voters in the CNN poll supported Obama by twenty-eight points. Despite the argument that I and others had been making for years to replace the Iowa caucuses with a more representative state, a Black presidential candidate had just won a crucial victory in one of the whitest states in the country.

Although Obama argues in his memoir that he never avoided race in his 2008 campaign, he clearly never tried to engage on that topic until he was forced to do so. The common consensus, he acknowledges in *A Promised Land*, was that "too much focus on civil rights, police misconduct, or other issues considered specific to Black people risked triggering suspicion, if not a backlash, from the broader electorate." In order to make a difference on those issues, he explains, he first had to win the election. "I needed to use language that spoke to all Americans and propose policies that touched everyone," he writes.

One consequence of that approach was that it contributed to the very postracial narrative that Obama despised. When he won the South Carolina primary in late January 2008, Obama walked onto the stage in an auditorium in Columbia and heard the crowd chanting, "Race doesn't matter! Race doesn't matter! Race doesn't matter!" It was a moment of pure elation, Obama remembers in his memoir. "They deserved a victory lap," he writes, "which is why, even as I quieted the crowd and dove into my speech, I didn't have the heart to correct those well-meaning chanters—to remind them that, in the year 2008, with the Confederate flag, and all it stood for, still hanging in a state capitol just a few blocks away, race still mattered plenty, as much as they might want to believe otherwise."

A few months later, we would all be reminded just how much race really mattered. I was live on television, sitting in a flash-cam studio on the MSNBC set in New York's Rockefeller Center one day when I was told of a video that had just been released. The video showed a clip of the Reverend Jeremiah Wright delivering a sermon denouncing American racism and imperialism. That, by itself, was not news. What made it significant was that Wright was the pastor at Barack Obama's Chicago church, and now his words had finally forced the conversation that many people had been avoiding. I did not know Reverend Wright personally, but I had previously attended services at his Trinity United Church of Christ in Chicago. For some reason, it did not occur to me when we were on the air that this was the same church and pastor. The network anchor played two video clips. In one clip, Wright said "God Damn America." In the other, he said: "We bombed Hiroshima, we bombed Nagasaki, and we nuked far more than the thousands in New York and the Pentagon, and we never batted an eye."

After the video played, the camera turned to me, and I was asked for my reaction. I knew the video would not be helpful to Obama's campaign, but I completely misjudged the gravity of the controversy. Except for the "God damn America" line, I didn't find anything Wright said to be particularly controversial or unusual. He's right, I said. The United States did bomb Hiroshima. We did bomb Nagasaki. We are the only country in the history of the world to use nuclear weapons on civilians. I had only seen a short, edited clip of the sermon at the time when I was asked to give an opinion, but even after I saw the rest of the sermon, I failed to grasp the significance. Wright had identified a series of America's sins and commented about them honestly: "When it came to treating her citizens of Indian descent fairly, she failed. She put them on reservations. When it came to treating her citizens of Japanese descent fairly, she failed.

She put them in internment prison camps. When it came to treating her citizens of African descent fairly, America failed. She put them in chains."

I heard nothing in Jeremiah Wright's sermon that I had not heard in dozens of other sermons at Black churches over the years. It was the same litany I had heard in hundreds of conversations of Black people throughout my life. My Black aunts and uncles, cousins, and grandparents in St. Louis, Missouri, would often chastise the country for the racism deeply embedded in it or complain about the racist white people they encountered in their lives. I had an uncle, who worked for a major defense contractor, who told stories of how white people had committed genocide against African Americans. I had an aunt, who worked for the public school system, who frequently called in to a local Black radio show to complain about racist white people. I had a grandmother who spent her entire career working for the federal government but never trusted white people. And I had a great grandfather who was a lifelong St. Louis Cardinals baseball fan, who would sit back in his La-Z-Boy recliner with his chewing tobacco and tell stories of the white people he had encountered as a child in racist Mississippi in the early 1900s or as an adult in segregated St. Louis. Even my own mother, who spent her entire career working for the Department of Defense, had story after story to share of how her white coworkers had often been treated better than the Black employees.

What were we supposed to say? Were we supposed to deny the horrific history and ugly reality of racism to make white people feel more comfortable with their privilege? Our criticism of our country made us no less patriotic. In fact, it made me proud to know that my ancestors, in the face of white supremacist opposition, had been fighting for generations to make America live up to its promise. They had fought against tyranny in our nation's wars abroad only to return home to a country that treated them as second-class citizens. They had pledged allegiance to a flag that represented a republic that purposefully excluded them from the vast resources built from their own toil. They sang a national anthem that celebrated a battle for a country that enslaved them. And after all the indignities and injustice that they had witnessed and experienced, America should have been grateful that they only wanted equality and not revenge.

Black people knew all too well from personal experience that the sacred founders and heroes of the nation were deeply flawed men, tainted with the stain of slavery, segregation, and racism that they allowed to persist at our expense. And yet the fragile shell of white supremacy depended on our collective historical amnesia, asking us to ignore the genocide of Indigenous people, the enslavement of Black people, the incarceration of Japanese Americans, and the bombing of hundreds of thousands of innocent civilians in Japanese cities. I suppose it is easy to ignore or downplay that history when your people are the perpetrators and beneficiaries of such crimes, but it is much more difficult to do so for people of color who have been the victims of white supremacy and anti-blackness. For white America to ask us to move on and stop talking about the past is like a serial killer asking his victims' surviving families to stop talking about the people he murdered.

For African Americans, our rage was also complicated by our reality. Because we live in a white-dominated society, many Black people have learned not to communicate our true thoughts on racism in the company of most white Americans. For the purposes of survival, we have trained ourselves not to express our fury in public to our white bosses and managers, to our white coworkers and colleagues, to white police officers and judges, and to others who may have power over us. We talk about these things in safe spaces in private, at family reunions and cookouts, at dominoes and spades games, at barber shops and beauty salons, at Black colleges and universities, in Black fraternities and sororities, in heartfelt conversations with our loved ones, and in our Black churches.

Obama himself acknowledged the existence of these conversations when, in the midst of his presidential campaign, he was finally compelled to deliver a speech on race to address his pastor's remarks. Speaking to an audience at the National Constitution Center in Philadelphia, Obama delicately and compassionately explained both sides of the race discussion in a way that only he could. "The fact that so many people are surprised to hear that anger in some of Reverend Wright's sermons simply reminds us of the old truism that the most segregated hour of American life occurs on Sunday morning," Obama told the audience. He acknowledged that the anger expressed in Black communities is "real" and "powerful," but in his words, it was "not always productive." In a flourish that would prove to be characteristic of Obama's racial equipoise during his presidency, he balanced his condemnation of racism with a recognition that "a similar anger exists within segments of the white community," where he said "most working- and middle-class white Americans don't feel that they have been particularly privileged by their race."

I applauded the seriousness and sensitivity with which Obama approached his speech that day, but I disagreed with what appeared to be an assignation of moral equivalency to the ordeals experienced by the two communities. His careful analysis seemed to discount the reality that, although Black Americans experience the same angst that struggling white Americans do, Black suffering is compounded by the unique and additional burden of racism.

I have to admit that I also had a uniquely personal experience that informed my perspective on his speech that day. Obama stood on the same stage where I had stood just four years earlier as a participant in the Showtime reality television series *American Candidate*. I was one of ten candidates who traveled the country, giving speeches, holding rallies, answering questions at press conferences, and participating in debates as part of a simulated presidential campaign contest. When my campaign recorded a TV commercial in Washington, DC, I chose the Lincoln Memorial as the location for my spot. It was a special location for me because it was where Dr. King had delivered his famous "I Have a Dream" speech, and I was born on the same day, exactly two years later. But when I mentioned this fact in my commercial, some members of the focus group that reviewed my ad attacked me for "exploiting" my race. Just by mentioning Dr. King's dream, I was somehow being racially divisive. "If America is truly to be color blind, then we shouldn't even be considering his race," a white man complained. "America won't be color blind for the next 100 years," a Black man shot back. He was right, and I was pissed. I wanted to argue with the white people who challenged me, but I could not. I was doing very well on the show and had won several of the campaign contests in previous episodes, but that focus group felt like a turning point. Just days after the incident, I stood on the stage at the National Constitution Center for one of the final debates of the show, and by the end of the episode, I was voted off.

What Obama did not acknowledge in his 2008 Philadelphia speech, although he did discuss it in his 2020 memoir, is that white Americans are more often permitted to express their disapproval or outright condemnation of the country without being questioned or policed about their patriotism. When a white person criticizes the country, mainstream white society rarely interprets that critique as a threat to the structure of its existence. I thought Obama might make that point in his race speech when he acknowledged that he already knew that Reverend Wright had been a "fierce critic of American domestic and foreign policy." From there, however, Obama compared his church experience to that of other religious Americans who often disagree with their faith leaders. "I'm sure many of you have heard remarks from your pastors, priests, or rabbis with which you strongly disagreed," he said. But then Obama tried to separate Wright's latest statements from his past controversial sermons. The latest remarks, according to Obama, "weren't simply a religious leader's effort to speak out against perceived injustice." Instead, Reverend Wright "expressed a profoundly distorted view of this country—a view that sees white racism as endemic, and that elevates what is wrong with America above all that we know is right with America," he said. Needless to say, I disagreed.

Obama's sense of optimism about America's potential to overcome its problems had become standard political rhetoric for twentieth-century presidents. From Franklin Roosevelt to John F. Kennedy, Ronald Reagan to Bill Clinton, politicians were always pushing the fantasy that there was nothing wrong with America that could not be fixed by what is right with America. It was also, conveniently, the language deployed by Dr. King in his "I Have a Dream" speech, when he called the nation to "rise up and live out the true meaning of its creed." Democrats had once embodied this sense of political optimism, but by the 1980s, they had become increasingly sensitive to charges that they were unpatriotic and took great offense when former United Nations ambassador Jeane Kirkpatrick delivered a speech at the 1984 Republican National Convention alleging that Democrats always "blame America first."

Conventional wisdom dictated that successful presidential candidates must not disparage America, and, surely, this sense of political reality is part of what motivated Obama to disavow his own pastor. But this rule would not apply to a white man in 2016, when Donald Trump would run an entire presidential campaign denouncing America. While Barack and Michelle Obama were repeatedly required to prove their loyalty and patriotism to their country, Trump and his immigrant wife, Melania, were not. Obama was forced to denounce a pastor not associated with his campaign for saying "God damn America," while Trump was able to be elected president while using language attacking America that Obama never could. In February 2017, when Fox News host Bill O'Reilly interviewed Trump and complained that Russian President Vladimir Putin is "a killer," Trump continued to defend the Russian autocrat. "There are a lot of killers," Trump responded. "You think our country's so innocent?"

Is it possible to imagine a scenario in which President Obama, or any Black president, could justify his support for a shift in American foreign policy by citing America's history of crimes? This is exactly what Trump was allowed to do in his first month of office, and yet white America never questioned his patriotism for saying so. On the other hand, is it possible that a Black president could even be elected to the presidency if the public knew that the candidate was supported by the aid of a foreign government? Or that he or she openly encouraged that government to interfere in the election by hacking emails from an opponent's campaign? Is it in any way conceivable that a Black candidate with that baggage could be elected president of the United States?

The implicit loyalty oath that the Obamas were forced to affirm suggested that many white Americans did not believe that a Black president could represent the interests of the entire country without seeking revenge against the white majority. This remained true even as white candidates were free to run political campaigns that represented the interests primarily of white Americans while largely ignoring the concerns of minorities.

Barack Obama was required to prove himself in a way that his predecessors and his immediate successor did not. Any one of the many major controversies that plagued the Trump campaign would have ended Obama's campaign. Obama had to be squeaky clean to bear the burden of representation for all Black people. If he had entered his presidential campaign, as Trump did, with no prior political experience, no one would have taken him seriously. If he had a history of six bankruptcies, five draft deferments, and a $25 million fraud settlement on his record, he would never have won a single primary. If Obama had five children from three different women, he would have been denounced by evangelicals. And imagine what white America would have said if he had married an immigrant who had appeared nude on the cover of a magazine.

Barack Obama could not have spent five and a half years lying about a white president's birth certificate. He could not have paid hush money to a Playboy Playmate or an adult-film star to keep them from speaking about his adulterous affairs. He could not have had a lawyer, campaign chairman, and a national security adviser who were convicted of federal crimes, and he would have lost support from his own party if he tried to pardon them. The truth about Obama and Trump is that Trump turned out to be all the things that white Americans feared that the Black president would be—lazy, vulgar, loud, gaudy, unprofessional, incompetent, immoral, and corrupt. These were the traits that racist white people consistently derided in Black Americans but boldly defended in Donald Trump.

For many white Americans, it did not matter that Obama was president of the United States. He was still a Black man in a white-dominated society, and they expected him to know his place. In fact, his very presence in the White House threatened centuries-old rules of white supremacy and would inspire some racists to go to great lengths to turn back the clock in their race against time. The reaction to Obama made this clear to those who chose to pay attention. Racism was not just an old problem of the past. It was a looming new crisis for the foreseeable future.

From the very beginning of his presidency, Obama would face fierce resistance and unprecedented disrespect, and any attempt he made to initiate civil discourse about race was met with stiff opposition from conservatives who accused him of being hostile to the interests of white people. When a white police officer in Cambridge, Massachusetts, arrested Black Harvard professor Henry Louis "Skip" Gates Jr. for breaking into his own home in July 2009, Republicans questioned Obama's commitment to law enforcement just because he said the police "acted stupidly." The criticism was so severe that the president was reduced to hosting a "beer summit" with Sergeant James Crowley and Professor Gates on the South Lawn of the White House to make peace. Yet in 2020, when President Trump tweeted an angry complaint about "29 gun toting FBI Agents" raiding the home of his convicted associate Roger Stone, Republicans didn't say a word.

Two months after the beer summit, President Obama faced another unprecedented insult. It happened in the middle of Obama's health care speech to a joint session of Congress, when South Carolina

Republican Representative Joe Wilson yelled, "You lie!" It was a shocking breach of decorum. Yet, when President Trump actually did lie to Congress in his 2020 State of the Union speech that he had protected patients with preexisting conditions, no one in the Republican caucus bothered to correct him.

Although it is difficult to discern how much of the opposition Obama faced was based on race instead of politics, he did encounter a new level of disrespect in office. In an October 2010 interview in *National Journal,* Senate Republican Leader Mitch McConnell declared that "the single most important thing we want to achieve is for President Obama to be a one-term president." On the surface, this was not a terribly controversial remark. At some level, every legislative opposition leader wants to defeat the incumbent president in office. What's different is that this type of political hostility is rarely communicated publicly as a party's top priority. Typically, leaders couch their language in policy terms that disguise their political motivations. We want to stimulate the economy with tax cuts and deregulation, Republicans might say, and the only way to accomplish that is to elect a Republican president. McConnell, on the other hand, dispensed with the pleasantries and launched directly into the politics.

With a Black president in office, Republicans found themselves increasingly strident and more overtly political. Former House Speaker Newt Gingrich even labeled Obama "the food stamp president." It was a reminder of just how naïve President Clinton had been in 1996, when he negotiated a compromise with Republicans for a welfare reform bill. "After I sign my name to this bill, welfare will no longer be a political issue," Clinton claimed that day. He couldn't have been more wrong. The Republicans' antiwelfare rhetoric would continue into the 2020s, and the confrontational politics of demonization that Gingrich brought to Congress in the early 1990s became the rule instead of the exception for the party. President Obama watched the GOP's divisive politics play out through his last days in the White House, with Senator McConnell's unprecedented refusal even to consider the president's nomination of Judge Merrick Garland to the US Supreme Court. McConnell had argued that Antonin Scalia's seat should not be filled because the vacancy occurred just nine months before election day. Four years later, however, when Justice Ruth Bader Ginsburg died, McConnell allowed Trump to nominate a replacement. The Republican-controlled Senate confirmed Amy Coney Barrett to the Supreme Court just over one week before Election Day. Every argument that McConnell and his party had used to block a vote, or even a hearing, on Obama's nominee had been a lie.

Of course, double standards are routine in politics, and politicians have been known to hold their adversaries to a higher level of accountability than they do their own allies. The sanctimonious Republicans who rushed to impeach Bill Clinton for hiding a consensual adult affair would spend four years without even investigating Donald Trump for adultery, infidelity, illegal hush money payments, or multiple allegations of rape. And, of course, the Republicans who spent sixteen years complaining about deficits under Presidents Clinton and Obama would conveniently ignore the astounding rise in federal deficits under Presidents George W. Bush and Donald Trump.

Yes, double standards have been common in politics, but the double standards in the Obama era seemed not just to enforce political norms but also to reflect racial biases. In fact, it appeared that many of the Obama-era double standards were specifically designed to police the behavior of the new Black family in America's White House. As Obama had learned from his experiences with Jeremiah Wright and Skip Gates, he would be questioned and criticized whenever he spoke about race in any way that did not alleviate white guilt.

It happened again in March 2012, when the president was asked a question about Trayvon Martin. "If I had a son, he'd look like Trayvon," the president said. "When I think about this boy, I think about my own kids," he told the reporters in the Rose Garden press conference, and he called on the nation to do some "soul searching" about our laws and the circumstances that led to the case. Despite what was a transparently innocuous remark, conservatives pounced on the president. Right-wing radio talk show host Rush Limbaugh argued that Obama should never have mentioned anything about Trayvon Martin's race. "It is the least important thing, what the kid looks like," Limbaugh said. Republican strategist Karl Rove accused Obama of politicizing the tragedy "by injecting himself into it," even though Obama had merely answered a question at a news conference. "We need a president to bring us together, not rip us apart," Rove pleaded, in an argument that would be conveniently forgotten when Obama's successor took office. Republican congressman Steve King of Iowa complained that Obama "turned it into a political issue that should have been handled exclusively with law and order." And conservative political cartoonist Gary McCoy drew an image of Obama sobbing over Trayvon Martin's tombstone in a staged photo op for the press.

The idea that a Black father expressing normal human remorse and empathy at the tragic and unnecessary death of a Black teenager would be portrayed as a publicity stunt reflects the depraved cynicism of modern American conservatism. But it also indicated the lengths to which white political leaders would go to police the conduct of the nation's first Black president, to shrink his megaphone and to generate fake controversies to question his legitimacy, undermine his authority, and hamper his ability to govern.

There was the feigned outrage at the photo of President Obama working in the Oval Office, leaning back in his chair with his shoes on his desk, which critics slammed as "disrespecting" the White House, a complaint that was unheard when Presidents George W. Bush or Gerald Ford or other white men had been photographed casually relaxing their shoes on the same desk in the past. Those critics also ignored the rules of decorum when Trump's counselor Kellyanne

Conway would be photographed sitting cross-legged with her feet on the Oval Office sofa while she scrolled through her cell phone and ignored a group of visiting Black college presidents.

There were the complaints about Michelle Obama's sleeveless dresses, which were considered unbecoming of her office, despite the fact that other first ladies, including Jacqueline Kennedy, had also worn sleeveless dresses. Those of us in the Black community knew it was more than just a dress that upset them. As one Virginia woman told NPR's Ari Shapiro, "She's far from the first lady. It's about time we get a first lady in there that acts like a first lady and looks like a first lady." American-born Michelle Obama, who worked her way up from her modest upbringing in Chicago to Princeton University and Harvard Law School and became a devoted wife and mother, was treated more disrespectfully by white conservatives than the Slovenian-born first lady who would follow her in the White House.

There was the time when President Obama appeared in a Buzz-Feed video mocking himself by holding a selfie stick. Critics called it "undignified" and "not presidential." Fox News anchor Lou Dobbs described Obama as a "self-absorbed ass clown," and at least one Fox News critic contrasted Obama and Reagan by falsely claiming that Reagan refused even to remove his jacket in the Oval Office.

There was the infamous Obama "bro hug" scandal, in which the president was attacked for friendly physical contact with his outgoing chief of staff Rahm Emanuel, when Emanuel left his job to return to Chicago. I remember being on the set of CNBC with anchor Larry Kudlow that night to discuss the impact of Emanuel's departure, but as soon as our segment began, Kudlow started complaining about the message being sent by seeing the president of the United States hugging another man in the White House instead of doing a formal handshake.

There was the infamous tan-suit scandal, which took place in the course of one afternoon when Obama simply wore a light-colored suit into the White House briefing room on a summer day in 2014.

Admittedly, I, too, did not care for the suit or the way it fit the president, but I hardly felt it was scandalous. Dobbs, on the other hand, called it "shocking" and blamed it on a "desperate" White House hoping to turn around Obama's poll numbers. Another Fox News commentator called it "unpresidential."

But no other fake controversy was more pernicious than the one spearheaded by Obama's soon-to-be successor, Donald Trump. From March 2011 to September 2016, Trump led a nationwide public relations campaign, complete with dramatic live press conference events, to undermine the legitimacy of America's first Black president. During this multiyear time span, he questioned the existence of President Obama's birth certificate; claimed to have sent investigators to Hawaii who "cannot believe what they're finding"; demanded Obama produce his birth certificate; refused to accept the veracity of the birth certificate once produced; and then, finally, two months before the 2016 presidential election, reluctantly admitted that Obama had been born in the United States, after all. Trump never once apologized for his five-and-a-half-year crusade of lies.

For anyone who might have believed in those early days of November 2008 that the election of Barack Obama had ushered in a new postracial era in America, the America of November 2016 should have shattered that myth. Eight years in office had deeply circumscribed Obama by race. The man who had reluctantly but eloquently discussed racism during his presidential campaign found no more freedom to do so even after he occupied the highest office in the land. One of the final ironies of the Obama era was that the Black man whom Republicans feared would center Black concerns above others had actually spoken less directly about racism than the white Democratic nominees who followed him. It was Hillary Clinton, after all, in 2016 who became the first major party nominee to use the term "systemic racism" in her official convention acceptance speech. And it was Joe Biden in 2020 who chose the first African American woman to be a running mate on a Democratic presidential ticket and pushed through a stimulus bill in 2021 that included targeted financial aid for Black farmers.

Obama, himself, had reacted defensively to the implication that he had not prioritized Black concerns during his time in office. "I'm not the president of Black America. I'm the president of the United States of America," he told *Black Enterprise* in the summer of 2012. While he championed all-inclusive policies that redounded to the benefit of African Americans, he rarely spoke of those policies in language that gave the impression that he was focused primarily on Black progress. Yet under Obama, the Black unemployment rate was cut from a high of 16.8 percent in March 2010 to 7.4 percent when he left office. More African Americans gained health insurance because of his Affordable Care Act. He appointed sixty-two Black judges and added more Black women to the federal bench than any president in history. The number of Blacks in prison declined and the Black incarceration rate dropped. And he granted 1,927 presidential pardons and commutations, more than the previous five presidents combined.

Other actions were more symbolic, including his administration's proposal to put Black abolitionist Harriet Tubman on the twenty-dollar bill. But even that symbolism represented a profound threat to the existing order, as evinced by the Trump administration's decision to rescind the changes to the nation's currency. Obama also defied conservative criticism when he invited rapper Kendrick Lamar to perform at the White House after Fox News personality Geraldo Rivera attacked Lamar by claiming "that hip-hop has done more damage to young African Americans than racism in recent years." Years later, when Donald Trump allowed Trump-supporting rapper Kanye West to call himself a "crazy motherfucker" in a ten-minute, profanity-laced monologue in the Oval Office, many conservatives remained curiously silent. Just as they did when Trump posed for an Oval Office photo op with rock star Ted Nugent, who had previously stood on a public stage with a "machine gun" and called

President Obama a "piece of shit" and Hillary Clinton a "worthless bitch." The invisible rules of presidential decorum that had been used to restrict Obama's freedom in office did not apply to his white Republican successor.

In the face of so much blatant racial hypocrisy and inconsistency, it was difficult for me to understand how President Obama could remain so positive and optimistic. For many Black Americans, we could clearly see that he was being treated differently from other presidents. In our eyes, nearly every olive branch he extended to his critics and opponents was a wasted effort. His adversaries would never allow him to govern, and they would not only block his policies but also silence his voice. Surely, he appeared friendly and nonthreatening to the vast majority of white Republican leaders in Congress, but to the impassioned and indignant base of voters that elected those Republicans, he represented an existential threat. Even as Obama's own supporters complained that he was too reasonable and too eager to seek bipartisanship with Republicans, his fiercest critics condemned him for being unreasonable and divisive. And for his most vocal opponents, Barack Obama's very presence in the White House personified the fear that white America was losing its four-hundred-year grip on national power.

Obama's reluctance to engage in divisive racial debates allowed him to be elected and reelected and to maintain his popularity with a significant percentage of white voters, but it also left a gaping hole at the highest levels of national public discourse at precisely the moment when activists developed the Black Lives Matter movement. African American martyrs like Trayvon Martin, Michael Brown, Tamir Rice, Sandra Bland, Eric Garner, and John Crawford would become household names during the Obama administration, and the existence of a Black president and two consecutive Black attorneys general did not save their lives. Of course, it was unfair to expect that any individual Black political figure or law enforcement officer could unilaterally end systemic racism or police brutality.

These patterns had existed for centuries, but Obama had the mixed fortune of coming to office at exactly the time when new technology allowed us to record these incidents on our phones and rapidly disseminate the images on social media. In earlier years, high-profile cases like the beating of Rodney King, the sexual assault of Abner Louima, or the shooting of Amadou Diallo took more time to rise to the public consciousness and had to be filtered through mainstream media. By the end of the Obama era, these cases seemed to be documented almost weekly.

At the same time when private citizens, vigilantes, and law enforcement officers were caught on video policing Black bodies on the street, the political class in Washington policed the two most famous Black bodies in the White House. That part was easy to recognize. But in the intoxicating energy of the fight against Obama's racist critics, I was slow to recognize that President Obama himself slipped into the act of policing Black bodies from time to time, particularly when he addressed Black audiences.

When Obama became the first sitting president to give the commencement address at historically Black Morehouse College, for example, he warned the graduates that "too many young men in our community continue to make bad choices." In explaining the obstacles that the young men would face after graduation, Obama told them: "Nobody cares how tough your upbringing was. Nobody cares if you suffered some discrimination." That scolding tone raised questions for a number of Black critics. "It is hard to avoid the conclusion that this White House has one way of addressing the social ills that afflict Black people—and particularly Black youth—and another way of addressing everyone else," writer Ta-Nehisi Coates observed in *The Atlantic* at the time. "I would have a hard time imagining the president telling the women of Barnard that 'there's no longer room for any excuses'—as though they were in the business of making them." As Coates concluded, "Barack Obama is, indeed, the president of 'all America,' but he also is singularly the scold of 'black America.'"

Obama's rhetoric of personal responsibility was not new or unique to him. Black parents, religious leaders, and community activists had been expressing similar sentiments in public forums for as long as I could remember. Young African Americans were repeatedly lectured to stay in school, stay off the streets, support their families, and support Black-owned businesses. We were taught at an early age that racism was ineradicably embedded in the DNA of American society and that we had to be "twice as good" in order to be half as successful as our white counterparts. President Obama's words to Black audiences barely deviated from that long-established guidance, but much of that advice had been premised on the assumption that African Americans would never access control of the levers of power that could free them.

What made Obama's remarks different is that Obama controlled the very instruments of government that legions of Black parents and pastors had long critiqued. Yes, racism was inevitable for Black people in America, but for eight years, a Black man actually ran the government that had the power to do something about it. Was it the young people's responsibility to acquiesce to the inevitable oppression of racism or was it the president's responsibility to try to stop it? And if Black college students had an obligation to accept personal responsibility, then shouldn't the Black president of the United States have had an obligation to use every tool at his disposal to fight racism?

Personal responsibility had been a consistent theme with Obama long before he was elected president. Years earlier, in his first major speech to a national television audience, Obama initiated a public conversation on personal responsibility. As the keynote speaker at the 2004 Democratic National Convention, the new rising star in the party called on "inner city" parents and children to do their part instead of relying solely on government. "Go into any inner-city neighborhood, and folks will tell you that government alone can't teach kids to learn," Obama said. "They know that parents have to parent, that children can't achieve unless we raise their expectations and turn off the television sets and eradicate the slander that says a Black youth with a book is acting white."

Perhaps we should have seen it then. Those of us who expected Obama to transform into a vehicle for revolutionary racial progress once in office had either misread the moment or the man. Perhaps we had inserted our own assumptions into the blank slates of "hope" and "change" that his campaign symbolized. But Obama the candidate made it clear who he was all along. He did not support reparations for African Americans. He did not support marriage equality for gay and lesbian couples. He did not support legalizing marijuana. Nor did he support the abolition of the death penalty. He preferred an employer-based health care system over a single-payer government health insurance model. And on immigration, he was far from radical. "We simply cannot allow people to pour into the United States, undetected, undocumented, unchecked, and circumventing the line of people who are waiting patiently, diligently, and lawfully to become immigrants in this country," Obama declared in 2005, in a speech where he also called for border security agencies to "deport illegal immigrants."

Despite the obvious signals of moderation long before he became president, many in progressive communities assumed that Obama was a closet radical. He had reportedly supported gay marriage years before he ran for president, and few of our mutual law school classmates really thought he was opposed to it in 2008. He had also spoken positively about government-run health insurance long before he ran for president. And by his own admission, he had smoked marijuana and taken drugs as a young person. As he wrote in his first memoir, *Dreams from My Father*, "If the high didn't solve whatever it was that was getting you down, it could at least help you laugh at the world's ongoing folly and see through all the hypocrisy and bullshit and cheap moralism."

As a Black man married to a Black woman, both of whom attended a Black church run by a controversial pro-Black preacher, many Black people also assumed that Obama secretly held radical views of Black liberation. Despite his benign public demeanor, maybe there was a secret revolutionary side we missed. I remember during the Democratic National Convention, walking through downtown Denver in August 2008, when my former professor Charles Ogletree cornered me and pulled me aside for a quick conversation. He was worried that the media had gotten access to a video of Obama in law school with law professor Derrick Bell. He remembered that I had been involved in the diversity movement and asked what I knew. I reassured him that the parts of the video I had seen were innocuous and unlikely to affect Obama's campaign.

Still, there was a sense of trepidation that Republicans had some secret weapon ready to release on Obama at any moment after he secured the nomination. Republican operative Roger Stone even claimed that there was a tape of Michelle Obama referring to white people as "whitey"—a term I had never heard any Black person use in my life—that was about to emerge at any moment. To add to the heightened suspicion, a July 2008 cover of *The New Yorker* magazine featured an illustration of a gun-toting, Afro-wearing Michelle Obama fist-bumping her husband who wore Muslim headdress and clothing; they stood in the Oval Office next to an American flag burning in a fireplace below a portrait of Osama bin Laden. That was far from subtle. But even Obama's name raised questions for some. The very idea that America might elect a Black man named Barack Hussein Obama—after fighting a war against an Iraqi dictator named Hussein and an al-Qaeda terrorist named Osama—aroused suspicion in some quarters.

With his Kenyan-born father and "exotic" background, perhaps Obama was a closet radical, conservatives feared. And even in Black America, and in other Democratic circles, many of us approached Obama's moderate views with a wink and a nod. Those were words he had to say or things he had to do to get elected, we reasoned; while deep down in our bones we knew that he actually shared our values and our beliefs. We understood the game we thought he was playing. We knew that America would not allow a Black man who openly described himself as pro-Black to become president, so we allowed Obama to play the role of being pro-everyone. Surely, we told ourselves, that was the point of his 2004 convention speech, when he resisted the efforts to divide America into red states and blue states. "There's not a Black America and white America and Latino America and Asian America; there's the United States of America," he said. No one I knew actually believed that. It was aspirational, at best. As much as politicians talk about unity, we all know the country had been divided since the beginning.

But, perhaps, Barack Obama was different. Maybe this child of a white woman from Kansas and a Black man from Kenya actually did believe in this message of racial unity. We had no way to know for sure. Obama ran for president "on two contradictory platforms," Emory University professor Drew Westen wrote in an August 2011 *New York Times* op-ed, "as a reformer who would clean up the system, and as a unity candidate who would transcend the lines of red and blue." He could not be both, but because he presented as a blank slate just being introduced to millions of Americans, voters were free to choose which platform they would embrace.

Barack Obama was, in effect, a Rorschach test. In him, people could see whatever they wanted, depending on who they were as much as who he was. He reflected the person looking at him. Hidden behind the inspirational "Yes, we can" celebrity music videos and iconic one-word poster images, there was an Obama for everyone. You could vote for Obama the reformer in the "Change" poster or Obama the unifier in the "Hope" poster, depending on which made you more comfortable. For his own part, Obama pursued the platform that was "most comfortable" with his character, according to Westen, "consistently choosing the message of bipartisanship over the message of confrontation."

At the end of eight years in office, it had become abundantly clear that Barack Obama was never the radical revolutionary racial fighter that progressives dreamed of or that conservatives feared. He helped to pull the country out of the twin crises of war and recession that he inherited and set a positive example of Black leadership and "Black excellence," but he did not radically change America. Nor was this ever his goal. From his very first day in office to his last, Obama governed with the message that prioritized "hope" over "change." Even after the devastating results of the November 2016 presidential election, while stunned Democrats shrieked in horror, Obama exuded his characteristic optimism in throwing his support behind his archrival Donald Trump. "We are now all rooting for his success in uniting and leading the country," Obama said. "We have to remember that we're actually all on one team."

The presidency had been a humbling experience for Barack Obama, and his two terms in office had been an eye-opening experience for America as well. If anyone had ever held the mistaken belief that one Black president could dismantle hundreds of years of racism and white supremacy, that idea should have been destroyed by the lived experience of the Obama era. If anyone felt that a Black president, for whom most white Americans did not vote, could serve as adequate compensation for centuries of racial injustice, that notion should have been dismissed long ago. And if anyone believed that America had magically evolved into a postracial society because of the election of one biracial Black official, that myth was shattered well before his eight years had lapsed.

As a realist, Obama knew from the beginning that he could only accomplish a few big things in his presidency. But as an optimist, he understood at the end of his presidency that the work would go on. "I think of this job as being a relay runner," Obama said after the disappointing 2016 election. "You take the baton, you run your best race and hopefully by the time you hand it off, you're a little further ahead, you've made a little progress." Yes, it was just "a little progress" in the eyes of some, but it was deeply threatening to others. He clearly did not advance racial justice as far as many of us would have liked. And yet, he just as clearly threatened millions of nervous white Americans that the race against time had reached a critical juncture that threatened to dislodge them from power. As America continued to become Blacker and browner, fearful white people worried that they would soon lose control of their country unless they took dramatic steps to limit the growth of or to disenfranchise the new emerging majority. For them, a crisis loomed, and the time had come to make one last-ditch effort to preserve white patriarchal privilege in society.

In walked Donald J. Trump.

8

DONALD TRUMP'S WHITE NATIONALISM

The glow of jubilation from the night before had barely begun to dim when the phone rang in Denver. I had spent Thursday evening—my birthday night—on the field of a football stadium with eighty thousand people around me to watch my former schoolmate accept his party's nomination for president of the United States. I covered the national convention for Black Entertainment TV that night. I had expected to wake up on Friday to celebratory newspaper headlines and positive television coverage of Obama's soaring acceptance speech. The convention had achieved its goal. It had successfully consolidated warring factions of Democrats for a common purpose. The party was finally united. The wind was at their backs. Then came the news that would ruin the day.

Late Friday morning, I learned that Obama's opponent had selected a running mate. The announcement was purposefully timed to steal the thunder from the Democrats at the end of their convention. Republican presidential nominee John McCain was expected to reveal his choice at a rally in Dayton, Ohio, that afternoon. And the person who would take the stage that day? A little-known forty-four-year-old mother of five who had struggled to graduate from college and never traveled outside the United States until a year before she was nominated. At the time she was picked, she had been governor

of Alaska for less than two years. Her only completed term in government had been as mayor of small-town Wasilla, Alaska, with a
population of about ten thousand people.

"For God's sake, this woman is totally unqualified," I complained
on *CNN Headline News* that day. "And for the Republicans, who
have been arguing all along that experience is the most important
issue, this is an outrage," I said. Republican strategist Chris Wilson
shot back: "Keith, I really hope all the Democrats are as dismissive
and condescending toward this pick as you are because I think what
it's going to do is show the attitude, the true attitude, that Democrats
and many of the Barack Obama supporters have had towards women
throughout this campaign." Wilson's attempt to conflate criticism
of the woefully unqualified Sarah Palin with criticism of all women
struck me as a transparent deflection. It had been Democrats who
selected Geraldine Ferraro in 1984 as the first woman to be a major
party nominee for vice president, twenty-four years before Republicans nominated Sarah Palin. And it had been Democrats who gave
Hillary Clinton eighteen million votes for president in 2008, long
before any Republican woman would come close to winning the
GOP's presidential nomination. What the Palin selection actually
revealed was the Republican Party's own dismissive and condescending attitude toward women. Instead of picking a qualified, talented
Republican woman with experience in government, McCain chose a
noisy lightweight to compensate for his own failure to excite his base.
His approach toward diversity reflected the same condescending and
dishonest attitude George H. W. Bush had displayed in picking the
inexperienced Black Republican Clarence Thomas to replace the legendary civil rights icon Thurgood Marshall on the Supreme Court.
Bush chose Thomas because he was Black like Thurgood Marshall,
and McCain chose Palin because she was a woman like Hillary Clinton. Bush and McCain both denied the real reason behind their se-
lections. We were supposed to believe it was just a coincidence that
Bush chose a Black man to replace a Black man and that McCain

chose a white woman after a white woman had just run a historic campaign for president. This disingenuous Republican approach to "identity politics" fundamentally misunderstood that Democrats had selected highly qualified Blacks and women, while Republicans were simply playing politics.

Before he was appointed to the Supreme Court, Thurgood Marshall had served as executive director of the NAACP Legal Defense and Education Fund and had argued successful cases before the court, including the famous *Brown v. Board of Education* case. He had also served as US solicitor general and a federal judge on the US Court of Appeals for the Second Circuit. His Republican-appointed replacement, Clarence Thomas, had never argued a case before the Supreme Court and had only served a year as a judge when Bush nominated him to a lifetime seat on the highest court in the country. Putting Clarence Thomas in Thurgood Marshall's seat was like substituting an amateur boxer to fill in for Muhammad Ali.

The same held true for Sarah Palin. She had been chosen, in large part, in direct response to the energy and excitement generated by Hillary Clinton's historic 2008 campaign. But Clinton, unlike Palin, came to her campaign with decades of experience, including her service as a staff member on the House Judiciary Committee during the 1970s Watergate scandal. Before her husband was even elected president in 1992, Clinton had twice been named as one of the one hundred most influential lawyers in America by the *National Law Journal*. She served eight years in the White House as the most politically engaged First Lady in history and served nearly eight years in the US Senate. Even putting Sarah Palin in the same sentence with Hillary Clinton was like comparing a failed first-round *American Idol* contestant to Barbra Streisand.

Palin, a self-proclaimed "hockey mom," would go on to embarrass herself repeatedly on the campaign trail. She claimed she had foreign policy experience because "you can actually see Russia from land here in Alaska." She could not name a single newspaper or magazine that she read when asked by journalist Katie Couric. And she wrote crib notes on the palm of her left hand to answer questions when she spoke at one of her events. But on that Friday afternoon, as I watched John McCain introduce her to the adoring crowd of white people, as I watched them cheer for her and wave their American flags at a campaign rally outside of Dayton, Ohio, I had a hunch that she represented something much bigger than herself. It did not matter if she won the election or not. The energy in that room told me that her brand of snarky, demagogic politics would be the future of the Republican Party. She was the opposite of Obama and Clinton, with their Ivy League degrees, intellectual curiosity, and federal government experience. She could speak to that elusive group of working-class white people that Democrats and Republicans ceaselessly courted. And she was the culmination of decades of Republican politicians who had sought to dumb down their party for the masses.

In Sarah Palin, I could see the future of the Republican Party. The John McCains and the Mitt Romneys who practiced the old-school politics of collegiality and bipartisanship would soon become extinct. They would be replaced by political neophytes, opportunists, and conspiracy theorists who openly embraced the extremists in their party. As renowned political scientists Thomas E. Mann and Norman J. Ornstein observed as far back as 2012, the Republican Party has become "an insurgent outlier" in American politics. "It is ideologically extreme; scornful of compromise; unmoved by conventional understanding of facts, evidence and science; and dismissive of the legitimacy of its political opposition," they wrote in the *Washington Post*. It was during this time, in the midst of the Obama era, that the Republican Party had become so divorced from reality and so obsessed with racial grievance that the road to Donald Trump seemed inevitable.

As America was becoming more inclusive of women and people of color, John McCain's selection of Sarah Palin to be his running mate represented a generational shift for Republicans. The country club establishment wing of the party had tried for decades to disguise its plutocratic agenda with white resentment populism and specious arguments of anti-elitism, but it needed fresh new voices to represent its interests for the changing times. It was a transition that had been decades in the making, as when Bush chose forty-one-year-old Indiana Senator Dan Quayle to be his running mate in 1988. Bush strategists openly admitted to the press that the blond-haired politician, who was said to resemble the actor Robert Redford, had been chosen, in part, for his looks. They argued to the *Los Angeles Times* that Quayle "would bring glamour to the ticket." Even John McCain openly predicted that Quayle's alleged good looks might appeal to women. "I can't believe a guy that handsome wouldn't be attractive in some respect," he said. But Quayle was clearly a lightweight—he would later become famous for miscorrecting a student on the spelling of the word "potato"—who needed to reassure the public of his competence. In his vice presidential debate with Texas senator Lloyd Bentsen, Quayle foolishly invited a comparison of himself to young John F. Kennedy when he ran for president. Bentsen was not impressed. The sixty-seven-year-old Texan turned to face Quayle, who refused to look Bentsen in the eye, and addressed him like a schoolboy. "Senator, I served with Jack Kennedy. I knew Jack Kennedy. Jack Kennedy was a friend of mine. Senator, you're no Jack Kennedy."

The audience roared. I sat in a press room near the auditorium in Omaha that night thinking that Bentsen's zinger might resurrect Dukakis's flagging campaign and expose the Republican senator for the empty suit that he was. The sound bite made great television, but I soon realized that it did not affect the campaign. Republicans were never seriously worried about Quayle's lack of experience or intelligence. This had become the brand of modern conservatism. It was part of the same anti-intellectual tradition that chose the former B-list actor Ronald Reagan as governor of California and then president of the United States. It was the tradition that had once led Richard Nixon to denounce Democratic presidential nominee Adlai Stevenson as an "egghead." And it was part of the tradition that motivated conservative intellectual William F. Buckley to denounce Ivy League academics: "I would rather be governed by the first 2,000 people in the Boston telephone directory than by the 2,000 people on the faculty at Harvard University," said the famous Yale graduate.

While Democratic presidents like Kennedy sought "the best and the brightest" for their teams, Republicans found an opportunity to characterize them as elitists who were out of touch with everyday people. It did not matter that the vast majority of presidents of both parties had attended elite institutions, or that every Republican presidential nominee from 2000 to 2020 had been born into privilege with a famous father. The Republican argument was about tone, not reality. It fit with the party's Southern strategy by appealing to the racial resentment of white Americans who felt they had been left behind and betrayed by liberal elitists in their own racial ranks. In language both coded and uncoded, Republicans learned to speak to non-college-educated white people without offering any serious solutions beyond blaming nonwhite people for their problems.

The conservative strategy was to "starve the beast," as they referred to the government. They would cut taxes that support the government, simultaneously comforting the country club Republicans, who could keep more of their income, and the white working-class Republicans, who were misled to believe that government services were primarily enabling Black and brown people. Any Republican president could implement this strategy—a second-rate actor, a failed oilman, or a bankrupt real estate developer. As antitax activist Grover Norquist admitted in a 2012 speech to the Conservative Political Action Conference, "We just need a president to sign this stuff. We don't need someone to think it up or design it." Norquist's only rule was to "pick a Republican with enough working digits to handle a pen to become president of the United States."

With the bar set so low, it is not hard to understand how a national party that once nominated experienced statesmen like Barry Goldwater and Richard Nixon would eventually come to nominate actors and performers like Ronald Reagan and Donald Trump. You could trace the origins from Reagan's rehearsed lines to the studied seriousness of the lightweight Dan Quayle, from the malapropisms of the oilman George W. Bush to the willful ignorance of the hockey mom Sarah Palin. After nominating such a progressively worse string of candidates, you could see the Republican Party's devolution to the incompetent narcissism of the game show host Donald Trump. He was not an aberration from Republican history, but a direct extension and natural evolution of decades of conservative bigotry and anti-intellectualism.

From the day Donald Trump descended the escalator into the lobby of his New York skyscraper to launch his unlikely presidential campaign, the Trump operation became a spectacle of buffoonery and bigotry. "I will be the greatest jobs president that God ever created," he not so humbly predicted. "I will build a great, great wall on our southern border. And I will have Mexico pay for that wall," he promised. "When Mexico sends its people, they're not sending their best," Trump complained. "They're bringing drugs. They're bringing crime. They're rapists. And some, I assume, are good people," he said.

Trump's rambling announcement speech reflected a stunning departure from political norms, but it would become characteristic of his chaotic leadership style in office. He would zigzag from topic to topic, reeling off sound bites that reflected his transparent ignorance of the topic discussed, but before anyone could process the nonsense of his remarks, he was onto another topic and another sound bite, another scandal and another controversy. He spoke not from evidence, but from intuition, and, more specifically, from the intuition of a privileged septuagenarian white man accustomed to enthralling adoring audiences and unaccustomed to being challenged. Chaos was his survival skill in life, in business and in politics. It successfully diverted attention from one scandal after another. For those who had never paid serious attention to Trump, his antics were, perhaps, shocking to watch in real time. But for those who knew of his long history of ill-informed, inappropriate, and inflammatory language, it was, sadly, nothing new.

As Trump became more popular among Republicans, his defenders tried to conceal his history of racism and xenophobia. Look, he has Black friends, they explained, pointing to photographs of Trump with Don King, Rosa Parks, Jesse Jackson, and Al Sharpton. For millions of African Americans, who had grown tired of such "Black friends" arguments, the collage of photos that suddenly appeared on social media did nothing to alleviate their concerns. And for millions of New Yorkers, who knew the brash real estate developer from years of outrageous newspaper headlines, his self-serving photo ops did nothing to erase the decades of racism in his public history.

When a thirty-three-year-old Black nurse from Harlem tried to rent a one-bedroom apartment in Queens, the building's rental agent talked to his boss, Fred Trump, to ask him what to do. "Take the application and put it in a drawer and leave it there," he responded. It was 1963, and the elder Trump was grooming his son, Donald, to take over the family business. The young Donald Trump, according to the *New York Times*, was "spending much of his free time touring construction sites in his father's Cadillac, driven by a Black chauffeur." Ten years later, Trump had become president of his father's business when a front-page story in the *Times* exposed him: "Major Landlord Accused of Antiblack Bias in City," the headline blared. The Nixon administration, not known for aggressive civil rights enforcement, had accused Trump of racial discrimination, in violation of the Fair Housing Act of 1968. Trump's scheme reportedly involved a coding system, in which applications from people of color were marked with a large "C," while applications from whites were not. A lawyer in the Justice Department told *The Atlantic* that

Trump even admitted to her, "You know, you don't want to live with them either." When Trump finally settled the case, he told the *Times* that he was satisfied with the agreement because it did not compel his company "to accept persons on welfare as tenants unless as qualified as any other tenant." Even in defeat, Trump perpetuated racist stereotypes that conflated race—the subject of the lawsuit— with poverty, an argument he would repeat decades later in the final weeks of his 2020 reelection campaign.

Trump's racist behavior would continue for four decades in public life, often obscured by the glitzy spectacle of his tabloid lifestyle. By the 1980s, as Trump expanded his business to Atlantic City casinos, he took his racism along with him. As former Trump casino worker Kip Brown told *The New Yorker* in 2015, "When Donald and Ivana came to the casino, the bosses would order all the Black people off the floor." It was a pattern of discrimination that would continue in his casino business until at least the next decade.

In 1989, Trump launched his most famous racist diatribe when a twenty-eight-year-old white woman was raped while jogging in New York's Central Park. Rather than allowing the criminal justice process to provide the accused defendants a fair trial and administer justice, Trump stoked white fears with a bitter public relations campaign. "You better believe that I hate the people that took this girl and raped her brutally," he told a press conference. "You better believe it. And it's more than anger. It's hatred. And I want society to hate them," he said. While positioning himself as the defender of white women's virtue, Trump manipulated the public by using his wealth, race, and social status to lead the charge against the five unknown, low-income Black and brown defendants, ultimately taking out full-page advertisements in New York City newspapers, calling on the government to "bring back the death penalty."

The four African American teenagers and one Latino teen who had been falsely accused never stood a chance. Despite the conflicting and coerced confessions from the boys about the alleged events, the absence of any physical evidence connecting them to the crime scene, and the lack of even a single witness—including the victim—who could identify any of them as a perpetrator of the heinous crime, they were all convicted and sent to prison. Yet even after Antron Mc-Cray, Kevin Richardson, Yusef Salaam, Korey Wise, and Raymond Santana were exonerated by DNA evidence; even after the real rapist, Matias Reyes, later confessed to the crime; and even after New York paid a $41 million settlement for wrongful imprisonment, Trump continued to claim the five Black and brown victims of his lynch mob were guilty of a crime they did not commit. He never apologized for leading his ugly crusade against them.

A former Trump employee shared yet another disturbing story in a 1991 book called *Trumped!* Author John O'Donnell recalled a lunch conversation in which Trump complained about one of his Black workers. "I think that the guy is lazy," Trump said. "And it's probably not his fault, because laziness is a trait in blacks. It really is, I believe that. It's not anything they can control." In the same conversation, Trump reportedly complained about his Black accountants. "Black guys counting my money! I hate it. The only kind of people I want counting my money are short guys that wear yarmulkes every day." Trump acknowledged the remarks in a 1997 *Playboy* interview. "The stuff O'Donnell wrote about me is probably true," he said. But two years later, Trump denied the story during a TV interview on *Meet the Press* after he had announced his unsuccessful Reform Party campaign for president.

Trump's casinos would remain a continuing source of racial tension throughout his career. When a high-rolling gambler arrived at his Atlantic City casino, management removed a Black dealer from his station to accommodate the gambler's racist preferences. The New Jersey Casino Control Commission forced Trump to pay a $200,000 fine in that case. In another case, Trump testified to Congress in 1993 that some Native American casinos should be blocked because he doubted the authenticity of their ancestry. "If you look at some of the reservations that you've approved," Trump told a congressional committee, "I will tell you right now, they don't look like Indians to me." When another Native American casino worried Trump, advertisements appeared in local newspapers with an inflammatory headline: "How Much Do You Really Know About the St. Regis Mohawk Indians?" The words ran below a grainy image of hypodermic needles, lines of cocaine, and drug paraphernalia. "The St. Regis Mohawk Indian record of criminal activity is well documented," the ad said. "Are these the new neighbors we want?" The ad claimed to be paid for by a group called the New York Institute for Law and Society, but, as the *New York Times* later reported, it was actually bankrolled by a competing casino operator. His name was Donald Trump.

After four real estate bankruptcies in the 1990s, Trump turned to television, but controversy followed him there as well. Predicting that racial conflict would be good for ratings, Trump came up with an idea to create a battle of the races—Black people versus white people—on his TV show, *The Apprentice*. "Whether people like that idea or not, it is somewhat reflective of our very vicious world," he said. Race issues also proved problematic when a Black contestant on the show was kicked off for being too smart. Kevin Allen, a Wharton graduate, would later explain that Trump "doesn't like educated African Americans very much." It was not surprising. Years earlier, Trump told NBC's Bryant Gumbel that "a well-educated Black has a tremendous advantage over a well-educated white in terms of the job market." Although "a Black may think that they don't have an advantage," Trump knew better. "If I were starting off today, I would love to be a well-educated Black, because I believe they do have an actual advantage," Trump said. Contrary to the revisionist history of the Trump presidency that African Americans never complained about Trump's racial politics before he ran for president, African American film director Spike Lee appeared on the same 1989 NBC program moments after Trump and condemned the real estate developer's ignorance. "I certainly don't agree with that garbage that Donald Trump said," Spike Lee told NBC's Bryant Gumbel. Lee could not believe Trump actually said that on national television, and as he shook his head in disgust, Gumbel and the audience laughed.

The laughter was the problem. Until he was elected president, no one took Donald Trump seriously as a political figure. As a garish, self-promoting playboy, he had earned a regular spot in the scandal-seeking New York tabloids and had become a punch line in comedians' jokes. His alleged wealth also afforded him the privilege of eccentricity, and that, in turn, insulated him from questioning that would have been directed at more serious political figures. Yet the public acquiescence of that eccentricity came with an expectation that the real estate developer would stay in his lane. He was allowed to share his ridiculously sexist, racist, and xenophobic opinions in public forums because he was perceived to be harmless as long as he was merely entertaining with his stupidity and not governing with it. But here he was in 1989, a privileged white man, who had been born into wealth, who had dodged the draft in Vietnam with his family's help, who had inherited his father's successful real estate company and racist business practices, who had already failed in several business ventures, and who was on the verge of his first of six bankruptcies—none of which prompted the slightest moment of public introspection or humility—appearing on national television to lecture Black people that they were, in fact, the privileged ones.

After Trump's well-documented, four-decade-long history of racial hostility and insensitivity, it was no surprise when he launched a racist campaign against the nation's first Black president. Trump told NBC's Meredith Vieira in 2011 that he had dispatched investigators to Hawaii to research Obama's origins, "and they cannot believe what they're finding." He promised ABC's George Stephanopoulos that he would release his income tax returns if Obama released his birth certificate. And when Obama did release his birth certificate, Trump still refused to release his tax returns, telling CNN's Candy

Crowley, "it's not a birth certificate." He only backed down after he won the Republican nomination, more than five years later, in 2016. "President Barack Obama was born in the United States," he told a press conference. He never apologized.

Trump had learned a valuable lesson. There was great political and personal benefit for him in stirring up public outrage. By angering Black and brown people, he could win the support of disaffected white people. Attacking the nation's first Black president without suffering any personal consequences taught Trump that he could continue these attacks on others. If he could go on live national television and lie about the president of the United States with impunity, what could stop him from attacking anyone else? In fact, he discovered he could actually grow in popularity among a certain segment of white Americans by continuing to attack people of color and the causes they supported. And this he did.

In 2014, he called for a ban on all flights coming from West Africa after an Ebola outbreak in three countries there. "KEEP THEM OUT OF HERE!" Trump tweeted in all caps in July 2014. "THE UNITED STATES HAS ENOUGH PROBLEMS!" he tweeted a month later. It was, in Trump's words, "Obama's fault," as he tweeted in October 2014. "Obama should apologize to the American people & resign," he tweeted. There were only eleven cases of Ebola and two deaths in the entire United States when Trump called for Obama to resign, but in January 2021, when Trump left office as president with nearly twenty-five million coronavirus cases and more than 400,000 Americans dead, he had not only refused to resign, he had applauded his own shameful record of failure.

In 2015, he turned his attention to another group to demonize. "Donald J. Trump is calling for a total and complete shutdown of Muslims entering the United States until our country's representatives can figure out what the hell is going on," he announced. Trump wanted to ban nearly two billion people on the planet from coming to America. It was all part of a predictable pattern of offering simplistic solutions to complex problems, but in the eyes of Trump supporters, the problems were never that complex. The central problem was the loss of privilege. How do you deal with the absence of a white man in the Oval Office? Delegitimize the Black president. How do you handle Ebola? Ban flights from Black countries. How do you stop unwanted immigration? Build a wall with Mexico. How do you stop terrorism? Ban Muslims. How do you reduce the trade deficit or fight a pandemic? Blame China. It was no accident that the targets of these attacks were almost always people of color. In Trump's worldview, people of color were nearly always the villains, and white Americans were nearly always the victims.

It was a convenient interpretation of history that allowed Trump's mostly white audiences to ignore their ancestors'—and their own—contributions to the problems they purportedly sought to fix. By attacking President Obama, they could avoid explaining why every American president before him had been white and male in a country where white men made up only about 29 percent of the population. By demonizing the failure of Black countries in West Africa, they could ignore the long history of white European plunder that robbed the continent of its resources and left the people of Africa under the boot of faraway imperial rule. By vilifying undocumented immigrants, they could disregard the American imperialism that destabilized Latin American countries and overthrew democratically elected leaders to install puppet regimes to benefit US corporate interests and Cold War politics. And by focusing on Islamic terrorism, they could absolve themselves of culpability for their own government's decades-long role in propping up ruthless dictators in the Middle East, like the Shah of Iran, whose brutal rule enabled the Islamic revolution that followed.

Trump's "Make America Great Again" (MAGA) campaign theme reminded his supporters of a mythical, unspecified time in the past when America was thought to be strong and respected and seemingly unconcerned about the negative impact of its actions in the world.

He was not visibly troubled by the blatant hypocrisy of the MAGA message, having spent his own career outsourcing American jobs. Trump deployed the theme like a cudgel to attack his opponents. MAGA represented a time when white men could build empires on the backs of Black and brown bodies and when white male dominance seemed impervious to critique or challenge. Trump never explained exactly when he thought America had been great in the past. If there was a particular year or time period he had in mind, he never said. This was part of the marketing genius of the MAGA slogan. The ambiguity of the phrase gave the candidate plausible deniability of what the words actually meant. In much the same way the Southern strategy allowed post–civil rights era Republicans to connect with disaffected white voters, the MAGA slogan enabled Trump to signal his synergy with white voters who were worried or resentful about what they perceived to be their diminishing social dominance over the country.

Trump's audacious lack of specificity regarding his campaign slogan left the country free to speculate about what he really meant. For those who shared Trump's beliefs, they were free to envision some imaginary time out of intolerant 1970s television hero Archie Bunker's theme song, when "girls were girls and men were men" and mediocre white guys "had it made." But for those who did not picture themselves in Trump's vision, returning to the past was a scary prospect. Did he want to return to the time when the land was stolen from Indigenous people? Or the time when African Americans were enslaved and deprived of basic freedom? Could it have been the years when women were not allowed to vote? Or when Japanese Americans were locked up in internment camps? Did he want to return to Jim Crow when public schools segregated water fountains and classrooms by race? Or to the time when LGBTQ Americans could be arrested for the "crime" of sodomy? For those who were not cisgender, heterosexual white men, the thought of making America "great again" by going back to virtually any time in the past almost certainly meant returning to a time when they were treated as second-class citizens in their own country.

What exactly did "MAGA" mean to Trump? "This will be the last election that the Republicans have a chance of winning," he told the Christian Broadcasting Network in September 2016. "You're going to have people flowing across the border, you're going to have illegal immigrants coming in and they're going to be legalized and they're going to be able to vote, and once that all happens you can forget it." It was a call to arms for white nationalism.

After all the evidence, there were still people who required more proof of Trump's bigotry. A few weeks before the 2016 election, speculation turned to the possibility that Trump's former TV producer, Mark Burnett, was sitting on incriminating video evidence that would finally prove Trump's racism. The speculation was fueled by the release of the *Access Hollywood* audio, in which Trump bragged that "when you're a star . . . you can do anything," including grabbing women by their private parts. The *Access Hollywood* scandal resurrected questions about other tapes that might have existed, including the possibility that *The Apprentice* creator Burnett could have video of Trump using the N-word. Some activists and writers called for Burnett to release the tapes, and Burnett responded that he could not do so, but this discussion wasted time and obscured a critical point: it did not matter. Even if Trump had been caught on tape using the N-word, his supporters would have found a way to deny, excuse, or explain his behavior, just as they had done time and time again when Trump had been caught in embarrassing scandals. As Trump famously told his supporters in 2016, "I could stand in the middle of Fifth Avenue and shoot somebody, and I wouldn't lose any voters." By October 2016, his racist history had been well documented. The N-word was not the issue. His actions already spoke as loudly as any of his words ever could. With everything we already knew about Trump, why was it necessary for anyone to produce a tape to prove his racism? And why would we turn our attention to the existence or nonexistence of such a tape when there was already so much damning and compelling evidence in front of us?

What was most infuriating during this time was watching knowledgeable white political commentators assure the public that white voters had actually been attracted to Trump because of something called "economic anxiety." It was not really racism that led them to support Trump; they were concerned about their own economic well-being.

Almost every Black person I encountered knew better. We remembered the ways in which white supremacy had shrouded itself in the robes of economic apprehension since the days of slavery and segregation, and we knew such facile explanations conveniently excused and ignored a long history in which white Americans repeatedly made decisions against their own economic interests in order to perpetuate anti-Black racism. After all, we were suffering too. In fact, we were suffering worse. Our unemployment rate remained persistently higher than white unemployment rates throughout the Great Recession of 2007–2009, and we were more likely to lose our homes and our savings during that crisis. We knew what Trump meant when he said, "Make America Great Again," we knew we weren't included in this vision of America, and we knew exactly why this appealed to white voters. It was not a disconnect between the modern Democratic Party and working-class voters. The vast majority of African American voters were working-class Americans, and they consistently supported Democrats. The disconnect was not about class; it was about race. It was about white voters who worried that they were losing their status in a rapidly changing world.

Much of the available data and research confirmed what Black Americans had been saying. A 2016 survey from Public Policy Polling found that 70 percent of Trump supporters in the South Carolina primary wanted to fly the Confederate flag. A June 2017 survey by the *Washington Post* and the Kaiser Family Foundation found that

Trump's margin of support was about twice as high with voters with "excellent or good" job opportunities in their communities as in communities where the job opportunities were not good. Another study that year from researchers Sean McElwee and Jason McDaniel found "little evidence to suggest individual economic distress benefited Trump" but did find that "Trump accelerated a realignment in the electorate around racism." A similar 2017 study by Public Religion Research Institute and *The Atlantic* found that, aside from questions of political partisanship, "fears about immigrants and cultural displacement were more powerful factors than economic concerns in predicting support for Trump among white working-class voters." And an April 2018 study in the *Proceedings of the National Academy of Sciences* found that Trump voters were driven more by fear of loss of their own status in society than by economic anxiety. "It would be a mistake for people to understand the 2016 election as resulting from the frustration of those left behind economically," University of Pennsylvania professor Diana C. Mutz wrote in the study.

As for the estimated 6.7 million to 9.2 million Obama voters who reportedly switched to Trump in 2016, according to election analyst Geoffrey Skelley, it's not clear that they were motivated by economic factors either. "Vote switching was more associated with racial and immigration attitudes than economic factors," according to a study by Tyler T. Reny of University of California, Los Angeles (UCLA); Loren Collingwood of University of California, Riverside; and Ali Valenzuela of Princeton. The researchers also found that vote switching "occurred among both working-class and non-working-class whites."

I don't know any Black person who is not in academia or politics who read any of those studies. But almost every Black person I know intuitively understood the reality. Donald Trump was tapping into deep-seated fears in America and resurrecting demons that had been hidden for half a century. "He calls for a civil war," I warned on CNN in 2019. "He didn't call for a civil war," *National Review* editor Rich Lowry quickly responded from across the table. What Trump actually did was to retweet a post from one of his supporters that removing him from office "will cause a Civil War like fracture in this Nation." I called it a reckless, irresponsible threat. But Lowry laughed at me on television, claiming it was just "a bad tweet." It was one of the many times over the course of four years when Black people who warned about the corrosive effects of Trump's rhetoric would be ridiculed by dismissive white commentators who tried to minimize the president's audacious misconduct in office.

Every Black person I know understood the threat. We saw it when a white Ohio fireman boasted that he would rescue a dog from a burning building before saving a Black person because "one dog is more important than a million niggers." We saw it when a white former city commissioner in Georgia complained that he "lived next to nigger town" while speaking at a public city meeting to push for Confederate History Month. We saw it when a white man in Reno, Nevada, attacked a bilingual Latino man as a "fucking spic" and told him to "learn how to fucking speak English" because "you live in America." We saw it when a white man called a Black man "a fucking nigger" at a protest in the still Black city of New Orleans. We saw it when a chest-thumping white man in Texas yelled "Donald Trump will stop you" to an Arab family on a public beach. We saw it when the Proud Boys marched through the streets of American cities flashing white-power signs. We saw it when white supremacists marched through Charlottesville, Virginia. We saw it in Detroit and Kenosha and Portland. We saw it in Minneapolis, Louisville, and New York. We saw it with our own eyes in dozens of American cities in every region of the country. And we saw it because nearly all of these incidents were recorded on video, demonstrating the audacity of Trump-era bigotry. Donald Trump did not invent racism in America, but he clearly emboldened racists and bigots to express themselves publicly in a way that America had not witnessed in decades.

When Cesar Sayoc reportedly sent deadly pipe bombs to CNN in 2018, video emerged of Sayoc at a Trump rally in Florida in which participants chanted "CNN sucks!" When Travis Reinking was arrested for killing four people at a Waffle House in Nashville in 2018, authorities revealed that he had previously been arrested for trying to enter the White House because he wanted to meet Trump. When Coast Guard Lieutenant Christopher Paul Hasson was arrested on federal weapons charges in 2019 after developing a hit list of prominent Democrats to kill, prosecutors announced that they found searches on his computer for "civil war if Trump impeached." When Kyle Rittenhouse was arrested and charged with killing two Black Lives Matter protesters in Kenosha, Wisconsin, in 2020, video emerged of him in the front row of a Trump rally. When Adam Fox was arrested in 2020 and charged with conspiring to kidnap Michigan's Democratic governor Gretchen Whitmer, a *Washington Post* analysis found that Fox and at least five others involved in his plot had previously taken part in an April 2020 antilockdown occupation of the Michigan State Capitol to protest COVID restrictions after Trump had tweeted "LIBERATE MICHIGAN!" Even as far away as New Zealand, when Brenton Tarrant allegedly killed more than fifty people at a mosque in 2019, a manifesto believed to belong to him was discovered, calling Donald Trump "a symbol of renewed white identity." Violent political extremists had always existed on the left and the right, but Trump was the first American president in modern history to encourage and incite them.

Of course, Trump never admitted he was a racist. He didn't have to. When he spoke about Frederick Douglass during a Black History Month event at the White House, he demonstrated a willful ignorance of the very history the month was designed to recognize. When he visited Andrew Jackson's slave plantation to pay tribute to the nation's first *Democratic* president, he abandoned the legacy of the party of Lincoln. When he blamed "both sides" for the racial division in Charlottesville, he promoted a false equivalence between racists and antiracists. When he condemned professional football players who kneeled in protest against police brutality, he prioritized empty gestures of compulsory patriotism over the lost lives of African Americans. When he targeted women of color in Congress and told them to "go back" to where he thought they came from, he trafficked in one of the oldest racist tropes in white supremacy. When he attacked the predominantly Black city of Baltimore as a "disgusting, rat and rodent infested mess," he reinforced racist stereotypes of Black communities that he, himself, had promoted as a candidate. And when he released his "1776 Report" on Martin Luther King Day in 2021, in response to the groundbreaking *New York Times* 1619 Project, he communicated his contempt for Black history by telling us not to criticize slave owners for their hypocrisy because that will "damage our civic unity and social fabric." Time and time again, even as he boasted about a falling Black unemployment rate that he had, in fact, inherited from his Black predecessor, the president of the United States expressed his disdain for the concerns of African Americans.

What appeared to motivate Trump more than all else was a repudiation and attempted erasure of the nation's first Black president. This may explain his eagerness to sign the First Step Act, a criminal justice reform bill similar to a Democratic proposal during the Obama administration that Republicans had blocked. "President Obama and Vice President Biden never even tried to fix this," Trump falsely claimed when he signed an executive action on police misconduct, ignoring the Obama Justice Department's fifteen consent decrees with law enforcement agencies. But whenever Trump was challenged on his obsession with Obama or his racist actions, he responded with the most predictable racist rejoinder of all: "I don't have a Racist bone in my body," he tweeted in July 2019, reflecting a disturbing lack of self-awareness. It is inconceivable that any white man in America—especially one who had been born into privilege in a segregated country and made no effort to change it—could live for more than seventy years in this nation without absorbing at least a fragment of the racist pollution inherent in society. Any mentality that fails to acknowledge this basic reality is, itself, a form of racism, for it promotes an easy denial and diminution of the impact of racism instead of the careful analysis required to understand its lingering effects.

At the same time, it's important to acknowledge that Trump did enjoy the support of a tiny but vocal coterie of small-time pastors, reality TV villains, and washed-up actors and sports figures who happened to be Black. For the most part, they were people with little or no credibility in Black intellectual thought in the African American community, but he paraded them around as shields as though they were the direct descendants of Dr. King's legacy. After publishing a photograph of Trump with real Black heroes Rosa Parks and Muhammad Ali, conservative commentator Kyle Olson argued that "if Trump was a racist, there's no way he would have posed for a photo with those two." Such a low bar of acceptance fundamentally misunderstands the nature of racism.

First, superficial association with famous Black people provides a convenient shield to protect white people from critique and allows them to gain access to social and economic opportunities that could enrich their lives. What successful white man would not want a photograph with Muhammad Ali or Jackie Robinson or a well-known Black sports hero or celebrity? This performative tolerance has been the linchpin of the Southern strategy, facilitating generations of modern white politicians to enact racist policies as long as they speak in race-neutral terms and make efforts to be seen in the company of "respectable" Negroes.

Second, racism is not the unwillingness to associate with Black people. It is, instead, a belief system in a social order that ranks Black people as inferior to white people. Nineteenth-century slave owners interacted with Black people and raped Black women while perpetuating racist lies about Black beauty. Twentieth-century segregationists, like Senator Strom Thurmond, slept with Black women and had their own Black children. Their association with Black people did not negate their racism.

Donald Trump may have epitomized the hypocrisy of performative tolerance better than any modern politician. He made little effort to speak sensitively about race or to pursue substantive policies of racial reconciliation, but he did seem to relish the performance. "Look at my African American over here," he called out during an airport rally in California in the midst of the 2016 presidential campaign. A few months later, he stood for a photo opportunity with game show host Steve Harvey in Trump Tower during the transition before he took office. Months after that, he sat with former football player Jim Brown and rapper Kanye West for a public relations meeting in the Oval Office. He invited almost every Black person he had ever met to vouch for him on camera at his 2020 Republican Convention. And, of course, he hired reality TV star Omarosa Manigault Newman to work for him in the White House as his top Black aide.

When Trump took actions that did help Black people, his motivations were often suspect. Thankfully, he commuted the life sentence of a sixty-three-year-old great grandmother named Alice Johnson. But he did so, not to reexamine discriminatory federal drug policy—as Obama had done when he granted clemency to nearly two thousand people during his administration—but because his celebrity friend Kim Kardashian West asked him to help Johnson. When three UCLA basketball players were released from a Chinese jail after being arrested on suspicion of shoplifting during a 2017 team trip, Trump all but demanded a public expression of gratitude from the young Black men for whatever role he claimed he played in securing their release. And when Kanye West informed Trump that rapper A$AP Rocky had been arrested in Sweden in 2019, Trump boasted on Twitter that he would call the prime minister of Sweden to try to secure the rapper's release.

Helping Americans in need is the president's job. No president had ever been so boastful or demanding of acknowledgment in the execution of this basic function of office as Donald Trump. When A$AP Rocky returned to the United States and declined to thank Trump, one of the president's most prominent Black surrogates, Pastor Darrell Scott, publicly complained about the lack of credit given to the White House. "All I'm asking for you guys to do is say thank you," he said.

The demand for adulation was not surprising given Trump's transactional approach to politics. With the exception of his nativist policies toward trade and immigration, he had changed his position on nearly every major issue in his lifetime and seemed to be motivated by no other goal as much as self-aggrandizement. By all accounts, he had never bothered to think deeply about the issues that face Black people in America or to study African American literature or even to consult with the people who had devoted their lives to understanding issues of race. Trump's thinking seemed to be frozen in time at the year when he was sued by the Nixon administration for discrimination. His rhetoric reflected a 1970s mentality about race in America.

After alienating African Americans throughout his entire 2016 campaign, Trump made a belated, perfunctory, and disingenuous appeal to Black voters in August of 2016. "You're living in poverty, your schools are no good, you have no jobs, 58 percent of your youth is unemployed—what the hell do you have to lose?" Trump asked. The fact that he posed the question to a nearly all-white audience in a nearly all-white community in Michigan suggests that he was never particularly serious about reaching Black voters. Instead, his appeals were largely targeted to assuage the concerns of white swing voters in the suburbs who did not want to believe they were supporting a racist candidate. Trump promised his white audience that day, in a fatuous, self-delusional boast, that "at the end of four years, I guarantee you that I will get over 95 percent of the African American vote." He never came close.

What made Donald Trump so dangerous is not that he missed the target on his unrealistic 2016 campaign promises to Black people. It was far worse than that. He didn't just passively fail to help us; he actively tried to hurt us. Generations of presidents of both parties had paid lip service to Black voters while prioritizing white voters. We were already painfully familiar with that song-and-dance routine. But before Trump, no president in more than a century had governed with such callous disregard to the expressed concerns of African Americans.

Trump's repeated attacks on Black communities in Baltimore, Atlanta, Chicago, and Detroit perpetuated racist stereotypes of Black inferiority by failing to interrogate the root causes of persistent racial inequities in America. "Crime and killings in Chicago have reached such epidemic proportions that I am sending in Federal help," Trump tweeted in the summer of 2017. He unfairly characterized Representative Elijah Cummings's Baltimore congressional district as "rat-infested" and Representative John Lewis's Atlanta congressional district as "crime infested" and never asked why the government had orchestrated a decades-long transfer of wealth from mostly Black and brown cities to mostly white suburbs. Nor did he examine why so many "red states" that consistently vote Republican in presidential elections repeatedly rank at the bottom of the nation in socioeconomic conditions. If the poor conditions of cities represented the failure of urban Democratic leadership, then surely the poor conditions in states like Alabama, Mississippi, and South Carolina must also represent the more dramatic failure of Republican governors and legislatures. And unlike those Republican states, the Democratic cities were left relatively powerless to enact structural change to improve their condition. Many cities lacked the legal authority to raise new revenue without authorization from their state governments, leaving them at the mercy of conservative state legislators who often did not share their interests.

The big picture for Trump was to fulfill a campaign promise to his base. They were not particularly concerned about the minutiae of government policy. They were, instead, invested in Trump's appeal to their fears. What Trump offered was a plan to slow down the forces of time that threatened their privilege in society, and his entire campaign and presidency were animated by this desperate race against time. The MAGA slogan, the Muslim ban, the repeal of Deferred Action for Childhood Arrivals (DACA), the separation of immigrant families, the reversal of President Obama's policies and initiatives, the voter suppression efforts, the Census rigging, and the rushed judicial appointments had all been designed to do one thing—to protect a fragile, dwindling white majority from extinction. It was all a scheme to turn back the clock to some glorified time in the past, or, at the very least, to stop the clock from moving forward toward a more diverse and inclusive future.

For five decades, the GOP had championed a particular set of American values that united the various elements of the party. The modern Republican Party had often been likened to a three-legged stool, consisting of moral conservatives, economic conservatives, and national security conservatives. The moral conservatives wanted to bring God back into public life and to uphold Christian values. The economic conservatives demanded fiscal discipline to reduce government spending, balance the budget, and bring down the debt. And the national security conservatives wanted to use the military to extend American hegemony throughout the globe. Trump swung a hatchet at all three legs of the GOP stool, and, in so doing, he brought down the entire facade of the party.

It began with the moral conservatives, when Trump sat down for a televised discussion with Republican pollster Frank Luntz in 2015 and told an Iowa audience that he had never asked God for forgiveness and mocked the Christian sacrament of communion as simply a time where "I drink my little wine" and "have my little cracker." Later in the campaign, when asked to name a favorite Bible verse, Trump said, "I wouldn't want to get into it because to me that's very personal." In the same interview, when asked if he preferred the Old Testament or the New Testament, he hedged: "Probably equal." And although he had claimed the Bible was too personal for him to disclose his favorite passage, he had no problem bringing and waving a Bible at campaign events and bragging about how much he loved it. In one infamous incident, he even mispronounced the New Testament book of "Second Corinthians" during a speech at Liberty University. "Two Corinthians, three seventeen," Trump announced to the audience. "That's the whole ballgame."

If Trump truly believed in Christianity, his conduct suggested otherwise. He told supporters at his rallies to "knock the crap out of" protesters. He threatened to "bomb the shit out of" other countries. And he told businesses at a New Hampshire campaign event "to go fuck themselves." This was a man who had been caught on tape saying that he had grabbed women "by the pussy," kissed them without their consent, and pursued married women "like a bitch." He had repeatedly cheated on his wives and been divorced two times before marrying his third wife. He had paid hundreds of thousands of dollars in hush money to conceal his affairs and had been credibly accused of rape by dozens of women. And unlike Obama, Trump had no public record of church attendance as an adult, little evidence of any acts of Christian charity, and seemed bereft of even a basic understanding of Christian worship. He was the living embodiment of nearly all of the seven deadly sins—pride, greed, lust, envy, gluttony, wrath, and sloth. Any single one of these transgressions of personal conduct would have brought condemnation against President Obama from white evangelicals, but not Trump.

At the October 2016 Al Smith dinner in New York, Trump was photographed staring aimlessly at the crowd while Cardinal Timothy Dolan, Hillary Clinton, and other dignitaries bowed their heads in prayer. At the February 2017 National Prayer Breakfast in Washington, President Trump asked the audience to pray for the TV ratings of his former show, *The Apprentice*. "They hired a big, big movie star, Arnold Schwarzenegger, to take my place," Trump said. "And we know how that turned out. The ratings went right down the tubes. It's been a total disaster." This wasn't a celebrity-roast gala. It was a speech from the president of the United States at an annual national prayer event. But the trend continued at the December 2018 state funeral for former president George H. W. Bush, where Trump sat in silence, rocking back and forth in apparent boredom, while Presidents Obama, Clinton, and Carter and the rest of the congregation all read the words of the Apostles' Creed. And when Trump finally staged his infamous Bible photo op after gassing peaceful protesters outside St. John's Church in 2020, he didn't even have the self-awareness to be ashamed of his sacrilege.

In example after example of Trump's misbehavior and misconduct, it became increasingly clear that Trump either did not understand Christianity or did not practice it. Yet, this glaring truth had virtually no impact on his approval rating among white evangelicals. Prominent white evangelical leaders like Franklin Graham and Jerry Falwell Jr. turned a blind eye to Trump's depravity. Televangelist Paula White told Fox News that "Christianity is such a large part— his faith is such a large part of his life." Trump's energy secretary Rick Perry called his boss "the chosen one." And conservative radio host Wayne Allyn Root compared the president to "the second coming of God." Rather than ask Trump to conform to their "Christian" values, they appeared to adapt Trump's values to their own belief system. Yet no hypocrisy was as audacious as that of Vice President Mike Pence, who had once proclaimed, "I'm a Christian, a conservative, and a Republican—in that order." He stood by Trump's side after the release of the *Access Hollywood* tape. He remained by the president's side after evidence emerged showing that Trump paid $130,000 to Stormy Daniels and $150,000 to Karen McDougal to conceal his affairs. He provided Christian cover to an administration that locked migrant children in cages and separated them from their families. He never chastised the president for praising racists in Charlottesville, extorting a foreign government for his personal benefit, or telling nearly thirty thousand documented lies in office. And for all the decades of right-wing complaints about the immorality promoted in the secular liberal media, almost no one said a word as the supposedly Christian president of the United States attacked his critics with decidedly un-Christian words like "human scum," "son of a bitch," "horseface," "lowlife," and "enemy of the people."

Trump succeeded by converting self-described "values voters" into "nostalgia voters," according to Robert P. Jones in *The End of White Christian America*. Personally, I'm not sure if they needed to be converted. When Barack Obama was president in 2011, only 30 percent of white evangelicals said that an elected official could fulfill his public duties if he had committed an immoral act in his personal life, according to a poll from the Public Religion Research Institute and the Brookings Institution. But by October 2016, after Trump became the Republican presidential nominee, the figure had jumped to 72 percent of white evangelicals, who were suddenly willing to overlook a public official's immoral activities.

Given the differences in behavior and values between Trump and his predecessor, it became abundantly clear, for those who did not already know, that morality was not the guidepost of the modern Republican Party. In Trump's case, Republicans overlooked his blasphemy, his vulgarity, his infidelity, his avarice, and his lack of basic human empathy because it suited their political needs. With Obama, they started questioning his faith as soon as they heard his name. Trump's quick hatchet job had completely destroyed the first leg of the GOP stool. Those who remained loyal to Trump and pretended to be motivated by Christian morality were exposed as frauds. After all of Donald Trump's moral transgressions and his refusal to grow, learn, or apologize for them, if your faith allowed you to believe that he was a God-fearing Christian and Barack Obama was not, your faith was white supremacy.

Next came the economic conservatives. During the 2016 campaign, Trump promised to balance the budget "relatively quickly." Without offering any detailed plans or specifics, he assured Fox News host Sean Hannity you just need to "have the right people, like, in the agencies and the various people that do the balancing." But instead of reducing the deficit, Trump nearly doubled it, even before the coronavirus pandemic struck. In President Obama's last full fiscal year of 2016, the national deficit was $585 billion. By 2017, the number had jumped to $666 billion. In 2018, it reached $779 billion, And by 2019, the federal deficit soared to nearly $1 trillion. The steep rise in the deficit during the Trump administration started long before the pandemic forced the nation to shut down.

Trump also promised he would magically eliminate the entire $19 trillion national debt in two terms by renegotiating trade deals and stimulating economic growth. But at the end of his only term in office, the national debt had grown from $19 trillion to nearly $28 trillion. Even before the coronavirus epidemic hit in 2020, the debt had already grown by $4 trillion during a period that Trump falsely described as having "the greatest economy in the history of our country."

Trump was never particularly concerned about "out of control spending," which had been the alleged sin of the Obama administration when the Tea Party was formed in 2009. Trump boosted defense spending, demanded billions of dollars for a new wall that Mexico was supposed to pay for, launched a new "Space Force" program, pledged not to cut Social Security or Medicare for seniors, and promised an elusive but significant $1 trillion investment in the nation's infrastructure. This pattern, along with his $1.9 trillion tax cut that primarily benefited corporations and the wealthy, contributed to the staggering rise in federal deficits in his administration. The only two ways to balance a budget are by increasing revenue or decreasing spending. Trump refused to do either. His tax cuts reduced government revenue, and his funding priorities allowed government spending to continue unabated. But where was the Tea Party when all of this was happening? Where were the angry protests in the streets of Washington? Where were the CNBC commentators ranting about rising deficits from the floor of the nation's trading exchanges? They were gone, waiting for the next Democrat to enter the White House before they would rise again.

Just as Trump's personal depravity exposed the hypocrisy of the moral conservatives, the rise in government spending, debt, and deficits in the Trump administration revealed the economic conservatives to be frauds as well. They were never truly concerned about fiscal discipline, and the only government spending that seemed to bother them was spending on low-income people or people of color or on any other Democratic Party priority.

Trump's final attack on the three-legged stool came with the national security conservatives. For decades, Republican presidents from Richard Nixon to Ronald Reagan to George W. Bush had argued that Republicans were resolutely devoted to national security, while Democrats were portrayed as weak on defense. In the 1970s, they blamed Jimmy Carter for surrendering the Panama Canal and failing to retaliate against Iran during the hostage crisis. In 1988, they questioned Army veteran Mike Dukakis's patriotism. In 1992, they attacked Bill Clinton for a Vietnam War–era letter he wrote explaining "how so many fine people have come to find themselves still loving their country but loathing the military." By 2000, they continued the argument even as Democratic Vietnam War veteran Al Gore faced George W. Bush, who had avoided service in the war. In 2004, they attacked Vietnam War hero John Kerry. And in 2008, when Republicans nominated Vietnam War hero John McCain, they boastfully compared his military service to Barack Obama's failure to serve, even though Obama had been only four years old when the war began.

But eight years later, the same party that heralded John McCain's military service chose a nominee who derided that same service. "He's not a war hero," Donald Trump said of McCain. When pressed, Trump begrudgingly acknowledged McCain's service. "He's a war hero because he was captured. I like people that weren't captured," he said.

Trump had not only dodged the draft, he received five deferments from service, including a suspicious health-related deferment for alleged bone spurs in his feet. Yet during his campaign, in the midst of America's years-long military battle against terrorists from the Islamic State of Iraq and Syria (ISIS), Trump declared, "I know more about ISIS than the generals do," and he promised voters, "I will be so good at the military, your head will spin." His record in office suggested otherwise.

Trump refused to receive regular intelligence briefings during his transition and his presidency and compared US intelligence agencies to "Nazi Germany." Once in office, he repeatedly questioned and undermined the military and the intelligence community. Instead of taking responsibility for a failed 2017 raid in Yemen in which a US Navy SEAL was killed, he blamed the generals. And when four American soldiers were killed in Niger in 2017, it took Trump twelve days to mention it. When a flag-draped coffin of one of the soldiers returned to the United States, Trump was too busy golfing to even acknowledge the young man's sacrifice. And when Trump finally did call the African American widow of Sergeant La David Johnson, who was killed in the mission, he told her: "He knew what he signed up for."

This was the same president who contradicted his own intelligence community and flatly denied Russian interference in the 2016 US election. The same president who stood in front of the Central Intelligence Agency's (CIA) Memorial Wall of Agency Heroes and whined about the news coverage of his inauguration, bragged about how many times he had been on the cover of *TIME* magazine, and told the audience: "Trust me, I'm like a smart person." The same president who announced a change in US military policy toward transgender service members on Twitter without telling the Pentagon. The same president who met with Russian President Vladimir Putin in Helsinki, Finland, and announced that he believed Putin over his own government's military and intelligence analysts. The same president who said that North Korea's communist dictator Kim Jong-un "wrote me beautiful letters," and "then we fell in love." The same president who withheld military aid to Ukraine, a key US ally, after it had been invaded by Russia, in order to extort the Ukrainian government to dig up dirt on his potential 2020 opponent, Joe Biden. The same president who abruptly ordered the withdrawal of troops from northern Syria to pave the way for Turkish troops to invade that country. And the same president who then bragged about a US raid that killed Islamic State leader Abu Bakr al-Baghdadi, a mission that had been made more difficult because of his own decision to withdraw from Syria. US credibility was so severely damaged by the president's sudden decision to withdraw from Syria that American military officers told the *New York Times* that their country had broken its trust with the Kurds and that that they were "ashamed" of what had happened.

When Navy Secretary Richard Spencer resigned from his post in protest of Trump's decision to intervene in a war crimes case in the fall of 2019, he issued a blistering critique of Trump's conduct as commander in chief of the armed forces. "I cannot in good conscience obey an order that I believe violates the sacred oath I took in the presence of my family, my flag and my faith to support and defend the Constitution of the United States," Spencer wrote in his resignation letter.

When Trump used the chairman of the Joint Chiefs of Staff, General Mark Milley, in his infamous June 2020 church photo op after tear-gassing protesters, General Milley had to issue a public apology. "I should not have been there. . . . It was a mistake," he said. Five months later, when Trump hinted that the military might remain loyal to him as he plotted to stay in power after losing the election, General Milley was forced to issue another public statement separating himself from Trump's authoritarian power play. "We do not take an oath to a king or a queen, a tyrant or a dictator," Milley said. "We do not take an oath to an individual. . . . We take an oath to the Constitution."

Two weeks before the last day of his presidency, when Trump sat in the White House watching an unprecedented attack on democracy unfold on live national television, it become obvious that the nation's military commanders demonstrated more respect for our democracy than our civilian commander in chief. On the day of the deadly Capitol insurrection, it took the Trump administration three hours and nineteen minutes to approve an urgent request to send in National Guard troops, District of Columbia National Guard Commander William J. Walker told Congress after the incident. Yet many of the same Republicans who relentlessly attacked President Obama and Secretary of State Hillary Clinton for not sending US troops in time to save four Americans five thousand miles away in Benghazi, Libya, in 2012 were perfectly willing to absolve Donald Trump for not sending troops just two miles away to save five Americans during a deadly coup attempt at the US Capitol. With Benghazi, they conducted eight congressional investigations, held thirty-two hearings, published eleven reports, and forced Hillary Clinton to testify for eleven hours. But with a violent insurrection in their own workplace, in America's celebrated temple of democracy, Republicans simply wanted to move on.

If President Obama had acted as dishonorably toward the military as Trump did in office, Republicans would have appropriately impeached him. But with Trump, they enabled him, consistently creating new excuses to justify and rationalize their support for a man who stood for nothing that they had previously claimed to represent.

And with the third leg of the GOP stool finally slashed by Trump's self-absorbed, irrational decision-making, the modern Republican Party had nothing on which to stand. The moral conservatives, economic conservatives, and national security conservatives who continued to support Trump had sold their souls for the luxury of power. The Republican Party apparatus had become little more than a cult devoted to the worship of one man.

Trump's final year in office would also invalidate two of the Republican Party's most popular slogans—"Pro-Life" and "Law and

Order." After fearmongering senior citizens during the Obama administration with false claims that the Affordable Care Act would institute "death panels" to decide who could live or die, Republicans embraced their own form of "death panels" in 2020. As casualties mounted from the coronavirus pandemic, Texas Lieutenant Governor Dan Patrick claimed, "There are lots of grandparents out there in this country" who "don't want the whole country to be sacrificed" to keep them alive. "Let's be smart about it and those of us who are 70-plus, we'll take care of ourselves," said Patrick. This would become the attitude of numerous state and federal leaders in the "pro-life" Republican Party. They openly and repeatedly chose the economy over the lives of the American people.

Then, after spending most of the summer of 2020 chastising racial justice protesters with the slogan "Blue Lives Matter," leading Republicans incited a mob that attacked Capitol police officers during the January 6 insurrection. The "law and order" Trump supporters broke windows and knocked down doors, smashed officers' helmets, attacked them with bear spray, trashed them with flagpoles, and clubbed them with fire extinguishers. Yet even after this dramatic outburst of violence, a dozen Republicans in the House of Representatives voted against a resolution to award Congressional Gold Medals to police who protected the US Capitol. Meanwhile, Republican Senator Ron Johnson of Wisconsin, in a seemingly intentional display of cognitive dissonance, claimed he "wasn't concerned" for his safety during the insurrection because the rioters "truly respect law enforcement" and "would never do anything to break the law." But if the protesters had been with Black Lives Matter and Antifa, he admitted, "I might have been a little concerned." It was the same racist double standard that Trump expressed when he condemned Black Lives Matter demonstrators as "vandals," "hoodlums," "anarchists and agitators." "They're bad people. They don't love our country. And they're not taking down our monuments," Trump said in June of 2020. But when the violent white mob tried to take down the US government and its most conspicuous monument to democracy in

January of 2021, Trump praised the attackers. "We love you. You're very special," Trump said. "I know how you feel." For half a century, every Republican presidential nominee since Nixon had run on a promise of "law and order," and when the day finally came to protect the nation from attack, the party tacitly admitted that the promise was just a charade.

The sad truth is that nearly every leader in the Republican Party knew that Donald Trump was toxic, but they embraced him anyway because he, alone, could speak to the party's base of angry white voters. The very Republicans who had once condemned Donald Trump in his 2016 campaign were later forced to grovel for his approval. Senator Lindsey Graham of South Carolina had once described Trump as a "race-baiting, xenophobic bigot" who was "unfit for office," but he became one of Trump's most loyal supporters, even after the disastrous plot to overturn the 2020 election. Senator Mitt Romney of Utah had described Trump as "a phony" and "a fraud" and became the only Republican member of the Senate to vote to convict Trump in both of his impeachment trials, but he teetered between support and opposition during much of the president's term. Senator Ted Cruz of Texas had called Trump "a pathological liar" during the presidential campaign, but he hailed Trump's leadership once in office and offered to defend Trump before the Supreme Court in his unconstitutional scheme to overturn the 2020 election. Senator Marco Rubio of Florida had called Trump "a con artist," but he too praised the president until the end. And House Republican Leader Kevin McCarthy had once told his colleagues that Trump was on the payroll of Russian President Vladimir Putin, but McCarthy, like nearly every other Republican, simply backed down when Trump entered the White House.

Trump's own staff knew very well what kind of person he was, but they worked for him anyway. Former secretary of state Rex Tillerson reportedly called Trump a "fucking moron." White House Chief of Staff John Kelly described the president as "unhinged." Energy

Secretary Rick Perry had once called Trump "a cancer on conservatism." And United Nations Ambassador Nikki Haley had previously condemned Trump for his refusal to disavow the KKK. "That's not who we want as president," Haley said. "We will not allow that." Nearly every serious Republican in federal government must have known that Donald Trump was unstable, intemperate, and incompetent. He entered the White House woefully unprepared for the solemnity of the moment, blissfully ignorant of the responsibilities of office, and negligently unwilling to learn the essential tasks needed to perform his duties. Yet Republicans continued to elevate the man they knew, from their own words, was unfit for office.

Republicans had spent half a century mining white racial resentment that flourished abundantly just below the surface of America's political discourse. From there, they built a gold-plated monster of racism, bigotry, and xenophobia that one day they could no longer control. It was a creature larger than Donald Trump or any demagogue who might conveniently choose to harness its power for his own interest. Months after Trump was defeated, when he had left office and begun his virtual political exile in Florida, a February 2021 poll conducted by the conservative American Enterprise Institute revealed just how determined the GOP had become to resist a changing America. A majority (56 percent) of Republicans agreed with the statement that "the traditional American way of life is disappearing so fast that we may have to use force to save it," and 39 percent of the party explicitly supported Americans "taking violent actions" to achieve their goals. This would be the dangerous future of the Republican Party.

For his temperament and misconduct in office, Trump was unprecedented in American history. But in his racism, Trump was neither outlier nor aberration from past presidents. Nor was he the culmination of decades of racist Republican policies, for this language suggests that his departure from office would end the nightmare. Rather, he was the logical extension of centuries of American racism that had moved effortlessly from generation to generation, and from party to party, transforming itself along the way to fit the needs of the times in which it existed.

It had once been the Democratic Party that boldly embraced racism to defend its interests. Half a century after Republicans adopted their own cynical political strategy, they continued to feign a connection to the legacy of their party's famous Civil War president. But it was Donald Trump who hammered the final nail in the coffin of the Party of Lincoln that Barry Goldwater had begun to seal decades earlier. If Trump accomplished nothing else, he successfully and unwittingly exposed the hypocrisy of the party he led. By the time he left office, it was no longer a party of "conservative values." It had become, more clearly than ever, a party of racism.

PART THREE

LET US MARCH ON

"Facing the rising sun of our new day begun
Let us march on till victory is won."

—James Weldon Johnson,
"Lift Every Voice and Sing"

9

TILL VICTORY IS WON

It may be hard to hear this right now, but our history need not be our destiny. No matter what you've been told, we are not doomed to repeat the mistakes of the past. Just as surely as the colonists changed the course of America in the eighteenth century, the abolitionists in the nineteenth century and the civil rights activists in the twentieth century, we, too, can chart our own path, and we can finally break the cycle of progress and retreat.

But to create this change, we must first be "brave enough to see it," as Amanda Gorman, the youngest inaugural poet in US history, reminds us. Lin-Manuel Miranda, creator of Broadway musical *Hamilton*, explains it this way: "I know that we can win. I know that greatness lies in you. But remember from here on in, History has its eyes on you."

So, let's make history and imagine a vision of a possible new future.

It's now Tuesday, February 10, 2060. A Black woman with beautiful, flowing locs walks into a crowded auditorium filled with hundreds of dignitaries. She stops a few steps after she enters the chamber and waits. A white woman and a Latina notice her entrance and rise from their chairs in the front of the room. The Latina picks up a heavy wooden gavel and slowly strikes it three times against the desk. The audience quiets. All eyes turn to the back of the room to face the woman with the locs. She opens her mouth and speaks: "Madam Speaker, the President of the United States."

The audience cheers.

A beaming Indigenous woman in a wheelchair enters the floor of the United States House of Representatives, shaking hands with and fist-bumping smiling members of Congress from the fifty-two states, who stand or sit to her left and right. As she proceeds down the hall, she greets each of the eleven Black US senators, equivalent to the total number who served during the first 245 years of the nation's history. Even her opponents from the three other political parties scramble to greet her. Pausing repeatedly for photos, she takes a few minutes to arrive at the well of the House. For continuity-of-government reasons, her space secretary cannot attend tonight, but the president shakes hands with the remaining cabinet members, a dazzling and talented cross section of America. Next, the president is ushered toward the six women, four men, and one nonbinary member of the US Supreme Court. They greet her warmly. Then the Joint Chiefs of Staff salute her. All the while, applause continues uninterrupted as the president wheels herself up the accessible ramp and the automatic podium adjusts to her height.

It is a historic night. She is the third woman president, the second woman of color to hold the office, and the first Indigenous president, and this is her final address to a joint session of Congress. The Latina woman in the front of the room gavels the crowd to order and speaks for the first time: "Tonight, I have the high privilege and distinct honor of presenting to you the president of the United States." The audience roars again in applause. The president finally has reason to celebrate. Thanks to the national health care law passed decades earlier, the nation was able to mobilize quickly and vaccinate 95 percent of the population against a deadly contagious virus. The Black and Hispanic unemployment rates for the past three years remained slightly below the white unemployment rate for the first time in history. The Reparations Act of 2036 has finally started to eliminate some of the nation's racial disparities in annual income, household wealth, and educational attainment. The number of police shootings of civilians has dropped dramatically, while a police officer involved in a high-profile shooting incident was recently convicted by a multiracial jury. And despite the ongoing concerns about climate change, the president is prepared to report that, for the tenth consecutive year, the country continues to meet its annual net-zero emissions policies. After a challenging year, she allows herself to breathe a sigh of relief. She thanks the Speaker of the House and acknowledges her vice president behind her.

"Members of Congress," the president says, "The state of our union is strong."

If it seems absurd to imagine women holding the positions of president, vice president, and Speaker of the House, and the majority of the Supreme Court all at the same time, remember that this is precisely how America has operated, with white men in those positions for more than two hundred years. The first woman vice president only took office in 2021. The first woman Speaker of the House took control of the gavel in 2007. And the first woman on the Supreme Court began serving in 1981. For two hundred years before that time, every president, vice president, Speaker of the House, Senate majority leader, and member of the Supreme Court was a white man, even though white men today make up less than a third of the nation's population. The real absurdity is not the possibility of empowering women and people of color; it is perpetuating an unfair and unsustainable two-hundred-year oligarchy for a powerful minority.

The choice we face now is between fear and love. Fear encourages a scarcity mentality that excludes those most easily marginalized. Love teaches an abundance mentality that embraces the vulnerable along with everyone else. For those of us who are fortunate enough to live in the richest country in the world, a country that has never lived up to its promise of "justice for all," we have a duty to embrace love and treat all those on our soil with dignity and respect.

In my most hopeful dreams for America's future, I see a loving, diverse, inclusive, and equitable nation striving to make real the promises of the republic. But in my most discouraging nightmares of the future, I see a dangerous, divided land, rife with fear and violence. Neither of these outcomes is guaranteed. The future of America is not inscribed in stone. It is, instead, what we choose to make it. It is our actions today that will define the world we live in tomorrow.

I've watched the world change for the better and the worse during my life. I graduated from college at a time when a concrete wall still separated East and West Berlin and Black South Africa was ruled by a white racist apartheid regime. And when I took my first job after college, the very thought of gay marriage or a Black president was only a distant fantasy for wide-eyed optimists. On the other hand, even during my most pessimistic college moments during the Reagan administration, I never imagined that America would elect an incompetent game show host as president or that he would incite a racist white mob to attack the Capitol.

If there's one thing I've learned as a Black man in America, it is that time does not heal all wounds. I've seen how the unhealed wounds of slavery, segregation, racism, and white supremacy still continue to divide our country, and I know that this pattern will persist unless we change. It is for this reason that Dr. King warned that "time itself is neutral; it can be used either destructively or constructively." King cautioned us in 1963 to avoid the "strangely irrational notion that there is something in the very flow of time that will inevitably cure all ills."

Despite the enormous racial strides we've made since Dr. King's time, America remains just as broken as it was all those years ago. Every day that our pain lingers unaddressed, every day the psychic wounds of war fester unhealed, every day we deceive ourselves to believe that future generations will peacefully resolve the tension, we continue drifting toward dissolution. The changing complexion of America does not ensure a welcoming multicultural and multiracial future. It threatens as much as it inspires.

This has brought on our new cold civil war—a daily series of conflicts and confrontations, big and small, between competing interests and individuals struggling to win control of the future. If a cold war is a state of political hostility between countries without direct warfare, then a cold civil war is a state of hostility between people of one nation without direct combat. Unlike the Cold War of the twentieth century, this cold civil war is not a battle between superpowers but rather a clash among the people of one nation. And unlike the US Civil War of the nineteenth century, it is not a crusade of horses and canons and gunfire but a proxy war of policymakers and citizens acting as satellites in a larger struggle. What connects this cold civil war to America's bloodiest war is that it is still a war about skin color. And this is the sad reality of modern America. More than a century and a half after Confederate General Robert E. Lee surrendered to Union Commander Ulysses S. Grant at Appomattox Courthouse in Virginia, the thorny issue of racism and white supremacy in America has yet to be resolved.

Now we've reached a critical juncture, testing whether we will continue to repeat the mistakes of the past or move forward into a bright new future. As I've tried to document in the previous two sections of this book, every approach we have tried in the past has failed to stop our intermittent racial crises, and the most common current proposals under discussion will likely fail as well. That's because most of the approaches are not designed to resolve America's fundamental race problem. They are designed only to respond to the crisis of the moment. Which is why I believe there is still a way out.

The lessons from the past teach us that we will not solve America's race problem in one presidential administration. The way forward will require a long-term national commitment beyond the lifetime of any of us alive today. It will require Americans of all races to work both separately and together. And it will require a reaffirmation of the founding principles of our nation.

As I indicated at the beginning, there is no panacea or magic elixir to solve racism in America. However, I still believe we can move in the right direction if we each take responsibility with constructive steps toward healing and progress. These, again, are the steps: First, white America must atone for a legacy of racism and slavery that still persists today. Second, Black America must hold the dominant political parties and our own leaders accountable to the needs of our community without exception. Third, America, as a country, must embrace a new approach to racial equality that is based on equal outcomes and not just equal access.

Now that we know the challenges, let us begin with atonement.

10

ATONEMENT

Tony was still unconscious when I arrived at Houston Methodist Sugar Land Hospital on a winter Monday afternoon. His heart, lungs, and kidneys had all failed, and although he was only sixty-three years old, the doctors told us he had virtually no chance of survival. He had been in critical condition for nearly a week, and the medical staff asked my mother if she was ready to remove him from life support. She asked for more time, called the pastor of her church to visit the hospital, and consulted with me and my sister. The next day, after hours of prayer, she reluctantly agreed to take a small first step—to remove him from a dialysis machine. Less than an hour later, Tony passed away. The retired Army sergeant had served his country in South Korea and Germany, worked as a correctional officer in a Texas prison, and trained boxers at a local gym, but this was a fight he could not win.

At the same time, more than 1,600 miles away, Calvin Bell started feeling sick in his apartment in New York City. He took a cab to the emergency room at Allen Hospital, a small three-story brick-and-glass building that resembled a suburban office complex. The hospital sat in a tranquil setting, at the northernmost point of the island of Manhattan, where a large creek merges with the Harlem River. There he was diagnosed with double pneumonia, a condition that could have been fatal for others, but as a healthy twenty-nine-year-old and a former master gunnery sergeant in the Harlem Youth Marines, he was, by all accounts, a fighter who was expected to recover. Calvin returned home to rest, but barely two weeks later, he passed out and was rushed to St. John's Medical Center in the Bronx. He died the same day. An autopsy revealed the cause of death as complications from coronavirus.

We buried Tony on the exact same day that Calvin passed away. Our immediate family gathered for a small private service in the hot Texas sun at Houston National Cemetery. Because of newly implemented COVID restrictions, we were not able to hold a funeral, and no outsiders were permitted to attend Tony's burial. I wore plastic gloves and kept six feet away from the cemetery staff as they lowered Tony's remains into the grave. The brief ceremony lacked all the pomp and circumstance I remembered from the day when my father, William Boykin, had been buried at the Abraham Lincoln National Cemetery in Elwood, Illinois, just a few years earlier. This time, there was no motorcade to a committal shelter, no seated ceremony, no folding of the flag, no gun salute, no military formality. Just a box being placed deep into the ground.

Far away from Houston, on that same day that Calvin passed away, a successful lawyer named George Valentine was admitted to a hospital in the nation's capital. While the city remained largely shut down, George was considered an "essential worker," and he had continued coming into the office during the height of the pandemic. It was that same dedicated work ethic, along with his colorful personality, that had helped George move his way up from Oakwood University in Alabama to Harvard Law School to become deputy director of the Office of Legal Counsel for DC Mayor Muriel Bowser. But just two days after he entered the hospital, as Mayor Bowser was preparing for her Friday-morning coronavirus briefing, she learned the devastating news: George Valentine had died from coronavirus.

Tony Parker, Calvin Bell, and George Valentine were three Black men who died just days apart at the height of America's first wave in the global coronavirus pandemic. Tony was my stepfather in Houston. Calvin was the brother of a close friend in New York. George was an old friend from Washington, DC. On March 25, 2020, their stories intersected as George entered the hospital; Calvin took his last breath; and Tony settled into his final resting place.

By the middle of spring, it became abundantly clear that Black and brown and Indigenous people would be the primary victims of the novel coronavirus. In St. Louis, Missouri, an eighty-six-year-old woman named Velma Moody, the sister of Representative Maxine Waters, passed away on May 1 at a nursing home just a mile away from the hospital where I was born. She, like every single St. Louisan who died from COVID-19 in the early days of the pandemic, was Black, the *St. Louis Post-Dispatch* reported in April 2020. That same month, a study from the Centers for Disease Control and Prevention stated that more than 80 percent of hospitalized COVID patients in Georgia were Black. In Louisiana, 70 percent of the people who died from coronavirus in the first month were Black, according to *The Times-Picayune*. And in Chicago, Illinois, 70 percent of COVID-related deaths that first month were Black, according to an analysis from Chicago Public Radio station WBEZ. From city to city, Black people were overrepresented in the daily death toll, and the racial disparities convinced some white Americans that the pandemic was no longer a serious concern. It was almost precisely at that point, as America came to terms with the demographics of the pandemic, that the nation's tolerance for public safety restrictions began to dissipate. Black and brown lives had become collateral damage, mere casualties to be sacrificed at the altar of the economy. Politicians began demanding an end to the lockdown, governors announced plans to reopen, and the president of the United States defied the recommendations of his own task force in calling for his supporters to "liberate" states that followed his own administration's guidelines. By June, there was a sharp increase in the number of hospital beds in Montgomery, Alabama, with critically ill COVID patients, 90 percent of whom were Black, according to Jackson Hospital pulmonologist

William Saliski. But when given a chance to take action to stop the spread of the virus, four of the five white city council members voted against a simple mask ordinance, while all three Black council members who were present supported it.

The haste to reopen businesses belied the oft-repeated cliché that "all lives matter," and yet the loss of hundreds of thousands of Americans would not shame the conservative apostles of this fiction. What may have been a mere inconvenience for anxious politicians was an end-of-life tragedy for an untold number of Black Americans. And despite the president's slander that the virus "affects virtually nobody," each passing week brought more sad news of death in the African American community.

For every new number added to the daily death toll, there was a buddy, a relative, or coworker who lost a friend, a family member, or a colleague. But as the weeks passed, large parts of the country simply became tired of hearing about those stories and tired of hearing about the pandemic. Encouraged by the selfish and insensitive leadership from the White House, Americans began venturing back outside, confident in the belief that only a few tens of thousands—then, later, hundreds of thousands—would die. And as stories of the ailing and confined victims appeared in the news, more Americans also grew confident that large numbers of the hospitalized and eulogized would not be white. By the end of spring, when more than one hundred thousand Americans had perished, the president flew to Tulsa, Oklahoma, to hold the world's first large indoor event since the beginning of the pandemic. Among those who attended the mask-optional event was a prominent Black business executive and former Republican presidential candidate. Despite our political disagreements—I had debated him on television before—I found him to be a likable person. But just over five weeks after he attended the Tulsa rally, seventy-four-year-old Herman Cain died of coronavirus.

For the Black community, Cain's death was met with mixed emotions. Some blamed him and other Black Republicans for the folly of attending an indoor rally in the middle of a pandemic without a mask. Others were more sympathetic to the thought of yet another Black life lost to the virus and noted how the pandemic's disproportionate impact on people of color had changed the public's response to it. But Cain's death also underscored a tragic year of loss for Black America. Just two weeks before he died, two civil rights legends— eighty-year-old Representative John Lewis and ninety-five-year-old Reverend C. T. Vivian—passed away on the same day. And just one month after Cain's death, forty-three-year-old actor Chadwick Boseman, who starred as the inspiring superhero in the film *Black Panther*, also passed away.

By election week in November, more than a thousand Americans a day were dying from the virus, and the number of new cases soared to record highs unimaginable during the terror of the spring lockdown. But, as many of us knew all along, the suffering had never been evenly distributed. A *Washington Post* analysis in November found that Black Americans were 37 percent more likely to die than whites, while other research indicated they were more likely to be employed as "essential workers" in jobs where they could not work remotely.

It did not matter that even the president, himself, had been hospitalized with the virus. He was fortunate to be airlifted at taxpayer expense to an elite military facility where he was given access to the nation's top doctors and the most advanced therapy. Nor did it matter that he, the first lady, the White House chief of staff, the press secretary, and numerous aides and advisers had all tested positive. They collectively decided to pretend it wasn't happening. Shockingly, even the president's top adviser on the pandemic, Dr. Scott Atlas, discouraged Americans from using protective masks and urged supporters to "rise up" against new public health restrictions in Michigan, knowing full well that the threat of insurrection endangered the life of the state's governor, who had recently been targeted in a kidnapping and murder plot.

Taking their cues from the top, whole parts of the country resolved to move on. Governors ignored federal guidelines and flung open the doors of their states to business. Conspiracy theorists posted widely distributed misinformation on social media that downplayed the severity of the crisis. Even hospitalized patients, dying of the very disease they ridiculed, reportedly crept into their death beds in denial. During the lockdown in the spring of 2020, journalists and commentators began using the term "COVID fatigue." But by the end of the year, the persistent attempt to diminish the pandemic, long after the lockdowns had ended, was more than just fatigue. It was denial. Millions of Americans decided they no longer wanted to hear about it, so they chose to pretend it did not exist.

America confronted the coronavirus pandemic in much the same way it dealt with the chronic disease of racism. Our limited attention span could not sustain the commitment necessary to overcome the incessant American desire to forget our uncomfortable past. This is why the nation quickly tried to move beyond the "racial reckoning" of 2020. It was in our DNA to forget. From time to time in our history, a spike in cases or a regional outbreak would prompt focused public attention. But then, after a few days, a few weeks, or, in some cases, a few months, the country's patience would wear thin and the nation simply moved on to other things.

This pattern has repeated numerous times since the twentieth century. Sparked by some flagrant new outrage, Black America would force the nation to think about the uncomfortable topic it most often avoided. For a few days or weeks, the country would be thrown into a compelling national debate or a "conversation on race." Top Black scholars and commentators would be solicited to speak on television news programs, at corporate conferences and college campuses. Academic reports and blue-ribbon commissions would issue dire warnings. "The treatment of the Negro is America's greatest and most conspicuous scandal," Nobel Prize–winning economist Gunnar

Myrdal wrote in his 1944 tome, *An American Dilemma: The Negro Problem and Modern Democracy*. "The United States is approaching a new crisis in race relations," the Moynihan Report observed in 1965. "Our nation is moving toward two societies, one black, one white—separate and unequal," the Kerner Commission warned in 1968. "America is still struggling with the impact of past policies, practices, and attitudes based on racial differences," Clinton's race initiative observed in 1998.

Each time, the reports would propose earnest recommendations to heal the wounds that divide us. Each time, politicians and pastors would deliver eloquent speeches and sermons about racial unity and vow to do better in the future. And each time, the moment would end. We would gradually drift back to our favorite television shows and sports teams and travel plans and office drama and all the other day-to-day activities that typically consume our time.

The earliest experience I remember with this evanescent wokeness was in 1984, in the same year I made my first trip to New York City with my college track team. That October, NYPD officers burst into the apartment of a sixty-six-year-old Black woman named Eleanor Bumpurs. She had a history of mental illness and was being forcibly evicted from her apartment in a Bronx public housing project because she was four months behind on her monthly rent of $98.65. When she refused to leave and pulled out a kitchen knife, police officer Stephen Sullivan blasted her with two fatal bullets from a twelve-gauge single-barrel shotgun.

Then, two months later, just days before Christmas, a thirty-seven-year-old white man boarded a downtown Number 2 train at the 14th Street Station in Manhattan and shot four Black teenagers with an illegal .38 caliber handgun. The shooter, Bernhard Goetz, claimed he was acting in self-defense, but he admitted that he shot one of the victims, eighteen-year-old Darrell Cabey, a second time after their initial interaction. "You seem to be all right," Goetz told Cabey. "Here's another." That second shot severed Cabey's spinal cord and left him paralyzed, yet a New York criminal court jury acquitted Goetz on charges of attempted murder and first-degree assault and only convicted him on a minor gun-possession charge.

Year after year, there came a new outrage, a new short-lived period of public alarm and another failure to follow through with substantive change. It did not matter if a Democrat or a Republican sat in the mayor's office, the governor's mansion, or the White House. It did not matter if the nation's political leaders were Black or white. Nor, unfortunately, did it matter if the police chiefs or the officers in many of these incidents were Black, Hispanic, or white. Black lives were routinely devalued everywhere, and episodes of outrage and consciousness began happening with greater frequency as the years passed.

It happened in 1985, when police dropped a bomb on a residential building occupied by members of a Black organization called MOVE and destroyed sixty-one homes in a West Philadelphia neighborhood. It happened in 1989 when officials wrongly accused and convicted five Black and brown teenagers of a rape in New York City's Central Park. It happened in 1991 when police were caught on camera beating unarmed motorist Rodney King in Los Angeles. It happened in 1997 when officers sodomized a young Haitian immigrant named Abner Louima in New York. It happened in 1999 when police fired forty-one shots at unarmed Guinean immigrant Amadou Diallo in New York. It happened in 2006 when the same police department fired fifty shots at a car in Queens and killed Sean Bell the morning before his wedding. It happened in 2012 when an overzealous neighborhood watchman racially profiled seventeen-year-old Trayvon Martin in Sanford, Florida, and killed him. It happened in 2014 when police in Ferguson, Missouri, killed eighteen-year-old Michael Brown and again when officers in Cleveland, Ohio, killed twelve-year-old Tamir Rice. In happened in 2015 when Sandra Bland died in police custody in Waller County, Texas, and Freddie Gray was killed in police custody in Baltimore, and, most notoriously, when a twenty-one-year-old white supremacist killed nine African Americans during a Bible study at the Emanuel A.M.E. Church in Charleston, South Carolina. It happened in 2016 when police killed Philando Castile during a traffic stop in Minnesota while his partner and his four-year-old daughter watched in horror. It happened in 2017, when tiki-torch–bearing white supremacists marched through the streets of Charlottesville. And it happened again and again until 2020, when Breonna Taylor was shot and killed by officers in Louisville and unarmed George Floyd was slowly and publicly executed in broad daylight by Minneapolis police officers.

At various points of crisis, when all other options had been exhausted, the nation would consume itself with yet another "reckoning" on race. Pontificating politicians would proclaim that this is not who we are as a nation, but in the eyes of many Black Americans, this was exactly who we were. It is who we have been since the beginning. The obligatory moments of racial reconciliation were the exception, not the rule. When white America observed us going about our lives without expressions of visible rage, we were simply wearing Paul Laurence Dunbar's mask that "grins and lies."

In many progressive spaces, it has become almost an article of faith that America's original sin was slavery. I do not entirely disagree with this analysis, but I wonder if it oversimplifies a larger truth. I suspect that racism, or, more specifically, white supremacy, was the nation's original sin. This is not to negate Ibram X. Kendi's myth-busting research that racist policies preceded racist ideas. Rather, I suggest a broader observation that those racist policies were more expansive than the institution of slavery.

The European colonizers who settled in America did not invent the social construct of race, and they were not the first to hold racist beliefs, but the practice of white supremacy has been a primary feature of colonized America since its inception. From the removal and genocidal extermination of Indigenous people, one can trace a direct line to the importation, enslavement, and segregation of African

Americans, the exclusion of Chinese immigrants, the internment of Japanese Americans, and the construction of an impractical wall on the southern border to keep out Latin Americans.

But as the nation grew and evolved, the federal government that authorized many of these racist policies maintained an uneven record of atonement for the atrocities committed in its name. The Civil Liberties Act of 1988, for example, formally apologized to Japanese Americans who had been incarcerated in internment camps from 1942 to 1945 and compensated more than sixty thousand survivors and their heirs with monetary reparations. One year after Congress passed that law, US Representative John Conyers of Michigan introduced a similar but far more modest bill simply to establish a commission to study and develop reparations proposals for African Americans. The bill went nowhere. He introduced it again in the next legislative session. Again, it went nowhere. He tried a third time in the following session. It, too, failed to win passage. Congressman Conyers continued to introduce his reparations bill in every legislative session between 1989 and 2017, when he left office. The bill never passed. It did not pass when Democrats controlled Congress or when Republicans held power. Nor did it pass when the first Black president took office, nor at any point during his terms.

In roughly the same period of time from when the Civil Liberties Act was first passed by the House of Representatives in the summer of 1987 to the last time Conyers introduced his own reparations bill in 2017, I worked for Democratic candidates for president, served in a Democratic White House, and advocated for Democratic policies as a strategist on cable television. My beliefs on race, civil rights, and social policy were almost always more progressive than the candidates I supported, and I convinced myself the party would gradually evolve over time. But after decades of waiting for substantive racial progress, I grew impatient not only with the resistance of my country, but with the timidity of my party. In my youth, I believed the country that twice elected Ronald Reagan was not quite ready to accept my radical indictment of centuries of American white supremacy and Western imperialism. As I grew older, I started to appreciate exactly why that indictment was so critical. Try as it may, America will never fully embrace the future until it comes to terms with its past.

This is a responsibility specifically and exclusively for white America.

Back in 2015, on the 150th anniversary of Juneteenth, *New York Times* columnist Timothy Egan wrote a provocative piece urging President Obama to apologize for slavery. "The first Black man to live in the White House, long hesitant about doing anything bold on the color divide, could make one of the most simple and dramatic moves of his presidency: apologize for the land of the free being, at one time, the largest slaveholding nation on earth." There was, of course, a seductive and poetic symmetry in the well-intentioned proposal for a Black head of state to lead the nation in apologizing for slavery. But with all due respect, it was not Barack Obama's place to do so. American slavery was a white institution created by white people for the benefit of white people. It was George Washington, not Barack Obama, who held more than three hundred kidnapped Black people in captivity and literally took the teeth from some of the enslaved people on his Mount Vernon plantation. No words are strong enough to communicate the countless crimes of slavery, and no Black person should ever bear the burden to apologize for this evil. Even today, the inherited wealth of white America rests on the bloody, buried plunder of Black bodies.

Egan's argument misses this critical point. Atonement is an act of personal responsibility for white people and white people alone. It must be performed both individually and collectively as a community. And it cannot be delegated to outside representatives.

The concept of making amends for the past is something that most of us were taught in our childhood. If you did something to hurt your brother or your sister, you should apologize. If you took something that belonged to them, you should give it back. It was basic human ethics. But what do you do when someone won't apologize? How do you respond when they won't return what was taken? And what if someone else committed the offense long before the beneficiary was even born? If your father stole a bicycle from my father when they were children, isn't he still obligated to return it, no matter how much time has passed? And if you're still riding that bicycle that was taken from my family, don't you bear responsibility as well?

It was not until my adulthood that I realized that the answers to the vexing questions of race in America could have been resolved with elementary school logic. They could have, but they weren't because a substantial percentage of white American adults would not bind themselves to the basic rules of decorum that they expected from schoolchildren. It was easier for many white adults to deny their privilege than to discard it, and they calculated that it was safer to maintain the status quo than to eliminate it. But this calculation was based on the mistaken belief that disrupting the imbalanced social order posed more of a threat than maintaining it. The truth is that preserving an inequitable status quo to benefit white people actually sustains the conditions for Black and brown hostility and ensures more conflict to follow. Just as dangerously, it also deprives white America of its own opportunity, responsibility, and necessity to atone and make peace with its past.

I started thinking about these ideas around the time I worked for President Clinton and attended church regularly for the first time in my adult life. As a child in St. Louis, I had always enjoyed church, but I had fallen out of the habit in the busy years of high school, college, and law school. Once I settled into my new life in Washington, DC, I was eager to find an inspiring and welcoming place of worship, and my best friend introduced me to his church. Admittedly, the most appealing idea about the church was its proximity to my apartment building near Malcolm X Park. The church was just across the street from me. The major drawback was the faith. I was a lifelong Baptist, and the church was Catholic. I knew very little about Catholicism at the time. I remembered that my younger sister wore a plaid-skirt uniform every day to her Catholic elementary school, and our family would sometimes buy takeout fish and spaghetti at the school's Friday fish fry. Later in life, I attended Catholic mass with a college roommate once or twice, but I found the service dull and monotonous. Because of these experiences, I was never intrigued by Catholicism until I discovered St. Augustine's Catholic Church in Washington, DC.

With a mostly Black congregation, a multiracial gospel choir, and three Black priests, St. Augustine's fascinated me. Compared to the Baptist churches I knew in St. Louis, the services were brief and the attire was compassionately casual. I learned the liturgy, sang the hymns, and discovered new dimensions to my own faith. And, for the first time in my life, I received Holy Communion, a ritual that did not exist in my hometown church. When the parishioners in my aisle at St. Augustine's stood up, I meekly followed them to the altar and mimicked their actions. My best friend had to explain to me the concept of transubstantiation, afterward. But the most unusual observance in the church was the practice of confession. I had seen the sliding doors of the confession booths on television shows and in movies, but I did not understand why this seemingly antiquated performative ritual was necessary in the modern world. That's when my friend told me of the seven sacraments in the Roman Catholic Church and listed them off from memory. One of them was the sacrament of penance, and the concept taught me an important lesson about forgiveness.

I had always believed in forgiveness, but that belief mostly focused on the healing of the victim. Until I learned about the sacrament of penance, it had never occurred to me that there might be some orderly process to be taken for the perpetrator to seek relief as well. One of those steps was the act of confession, and it helped me to understand that there could be no absolution without contrition and no contrition without confession.

When I tried to apply the concept to modern life, I understood why atonement was such a critical component for America's absolution from its "original sin." The nation would never move beyond its racial division until it confessed its sins, expressed sincere contrition, and took steps to mend its ways. But the notion of contrition contradicted the myth of "American exceptionalism," that the framers of this country were uniquely wise and that they created an ideal form of government and a land of opportunity unlike any other. Leaders on the left and the right have embraced various forms of this myth. Ronald Reagan spoke of America as a "shining city on a hill," while Barack Obama argued that "in no other country on earth, is my story even possible."

Shortly before Obama accepted his party's nomination for president in the summer of 2008, the US House of Representatives passed a nonbinding resolution by a voice vote that apologized for slavery. The Senate passed a similar symbolic resolution the following year. Most Americans, including most African Americans, probably never heard of either resolution. There was no South African–style Truth and Reconciliation Commission. There were no months of public hearings to document the racist policies the federal government implemented for centuries in America. The votes were historic and unprecedented, but they were only resolutions, each passed with no names attached to the votes. At the dawn of the new Obama era, the resolutions felt like hopeful progress to those who knew about them, but reexamined years later, they were more symbolic than substantive, a continuation of the effort to avoid a deeper and still unwanted conversation.

The compromises that Massachusetts senator Charles Sumner condemned at the end of the Civil War had continued long after Robert E. Lee's surrender. The Supreme Court's *Plessy v. Ferguson* compromise established a kinder, gentler rebranding of racism under the legal doctrine of "separate but equal" in 1896. Even the Supreme Court's historic 1954 *Brown v. Board of Education* decision was followed a year later by a less prominent compromise that allowed white school districts time to desegregate "with all deliberate speed." And when the country finally enacted substantive change with the Civil Rights Act of 1964, the Voting Rights Act of 1965, and the Fair Housing Act of 1968, cynical white political leaders then spent the next half century devising new methods to undermine those laws and perpetuate their privilege through criminal justice policies that fueled mass incarceration of Black people, economic policies that cut off funding for Black communities, and voter suppression policies that disenfranchised Black people.

Throughout centuries of American history, at various intervals when Black people demanded justice, white leaders responded, instead, with a tenuous, negotiated peace. It was precisely for that reason that Dr. King, in his 1963 "Letter from a Birmingham Jail," expressed his frustration with "the white moderate, who is more devoted to 'order' than to justice; who prefers a negative peace which is the absence of tension to a positive peace which is the presence of justice."

This was the cry of the movement for Black Lives Matter—"No justice! No peace." It was a simple request. You could not expect all Black Americans to continue to go about their business quietly and peacefully while they witnessed their brothers and sisters murdered with impunity at the hands of the state. When the well-mannered "respectable Negroes" took to the picket lines to protest the latest injustice, it was often politely applauded in liberal circles and quickly forgotten in the course of political inaction. It was only when the "ill-mannered" and "impolite" Black people rose up that the rest of America finally paid attention and recognized the tenacity and ferocity of Black rage.

I saw this in the summer of 2020 as I covered protests throughout New York City. The disorderly protests that defied police instructions, that violated curfews, that shut down buildings and blocked vehicular traffic quickly gained media attention. But the more civil, respectable protests that followed a predesignated, police-approved parade route would rarely awaken the media's consciousness, absent a celebrity participant. The ruling class had few qualms about respectable civil actions. Such protests served as a useful safety valve to allow the disempowered to blow off steam without threatening the existing social structure. The destruction of property and the violation of rules, on the other hand, would set a dangerous precedent that had to be quashed with "law and order." Those protests—some of which were infiltrated by disguised white supremacists hoping to provoke a race war—and demands for revolutionary action were portrayed as un-American by the very same people who worshipped the guerrilla warriors and revolutionary fighters who founded America.

Reprimanding Black protesters for their misbehavior provided a convenient deflection from white guilt. White America was more willing to criminalize Black outrage against state violence than to eliminate the initial violence itself. This approach recentered white victimhood by shifting the public debate away from the suffering of Black people to a conversation on the loss of white property. It was also a transparent power play for innocence, and it reminded me of a controversial article I had read years ago.

It was 1988, in the early days of the presidential campaign between Bush and Dukakis, and frustrated Democrats could not understand how the incumbent president had weathered so many scandals and controversies. Black conservative writer Shelby Steele offered an explanation in a piece called "I'm Black, You're White, Who's Innocent?" in *Harper's Magazine*. "I'm convinced that the secret of Reagan's 'teflon' coating, his personal popularity apart from his policies and actions, has been his ability to offer mainstream America a vision of itself as innocent and entitled (unlike Jimmy Carter, who seemed to offer only guilt and obligation)," Steele wrote.

Needless to say, as a Democrat I profoundly disagreed with Steele's analysis of Carter, and much of the rest of his essay, for that matter. But I could not disagree with his analysis of Reagan. If there was one thing that the Hollywood actor-turned president did well, it was to make white people feel good about themselves. After they had absorbed the shocks of the civil rights movement, the feminist movement, the LGBTQ movement, the Watergate scandal, and the failed Vietnam War, Reagan offered ordinary white Americans absolution from their guilt. Under his leadership, they could feel proud of themselves again and did not have to apologize for racism, sexism, homophobia, public corruption, xenophobia, or American imperialism. It was the same mentality that led Senate Majority Leader Mitch McConnell to dismiss Black calls for reparations. "We tried to deal with our original sin of slavery by fighting a Civil War, by passing landmark civil rights legislation, elected an African American president," McConnell said. "I don't think we should be trying to figure out how to compensate for it." The Civil War, the Civil Rights Act, and the election of President Obama were all significant milestones in American history, but they did absolutely nothing to compensate Black people for hundreds of years of slavery and segregation. The election of one Black president cannot serve as reparations for forty-three million African Americans. The claim is especially insulting because the majority of white voters did not support President Obama in either of his two elections. They did, however, support his successor, who spent four years trying to undermine almost everything Obama accomplished.

From Reagan to Trump, the most successful white Republican politicians understood at least one important principle—white people don't want to feel guilty about the past. In fact, the denial of racism and white supremacy in the twenty-first century flows directly from the unwillingness to accept guilt from the legacy of the past centuries. As a result, some white Americans have become more likely to identify Black people as racist than to accept that truth about themselves or their white counterparts. In fact, I have been called "racist" repeatedly by white critics on social media any time I simply mention race or point out a factual racial disparity. But the same critics rarely, if ever, chastise the racist actions of white political leaders that actually damage Black communities.

Not long after the November 2020 election, I found myself back in Texas for a few weeks visiting my mom. I had spent three months living with her after she lost her husband during the coronavirus lockdown in the spring, and this was my first visit back in nearly six months. One Friday morning, as I read the *New York Times*, I was alarmed to discover that the federal Justice Department had executed yet another inmate overnight. After almost two decades with no federal executions, suddenly they were being scheduled with startling frequency. I had been a lifelong opponent of the death penalty. It's racially discriminatory; it's an ineffective deterrent; it's not cost-effective; and, most important, I believe it's morally wrong. I had not followed the issue closely in recent years, but whenever I read about a new execution, I would make a point to express my opposition publicly once again to capital punishment. I was also accustomed to being criticized for this opinion.

I learned long ago that friends and family members, Republicans and Democrats, and people of all races supported capital punishment, and they were not shy about telling me they disagreed with my view, especially when it came to difficult cases. When white supremacist Dylann Roof was sentenced to death in 2017 for the Charleston church massacre, I condemned the decision. "Dylann Roof is an unrepentant racist murderer who deserves to spend the rest of his life in prison," I wrote on Twitter. But, I added, "I remain opposed to the death penalty." And when white supremacist Daniel Lewis Lee was executed by the Trump administration in the summer of 2020, I spoke out again. "For the record, I continue to remain 100 percent opposed to capital punishment in all circumstances," I tweeted. "Even for murderers with Nazi tattoos. Even for white racists who shoot up churches. Even in the event of my own death. Abolish the death penalty." So, when I tweeted about the execution of a Black inmate in November 2020, I expected to generate the same sort of polite mixed response that I had gotten in the past. But I was seriously mistaken.

"Orlando Hall was executed last night," I wrote. "Hall was a Black man convicted by an all-white jury. He is the eighth person executed this year by the Trump administration. There were no federal executions under Pres. Obama, and Biden plans to end them as well." That was the tweet. Four sentences. All statements of fact taken directly from the *New York Times* article I attached. I could not fit all my points within Twitter's 280-character limit, so I even abbreviated the word "president" in my tweet, even though I generally hate title abbreviations. Then, something happened. That tweet quickly became the most criticized statement I had ever posted on Twitter. More than fourteen thousand people commented. "You are a disgrace," one person responded to me. "Good riddance," said many others. You left out the part about how he kidnapped, raped, and murdered a sixteen-year-old Black girl, many critics added. You're defending a rapist and a pedophile, dozens chimed in.

I made the mistake of telling my mom about the controversy that I had unintentionally generated, and she urged me to post another tweet to explain and contextualize what I meant. I resisted. After years of public exposure, I had learned not to engage these types of rabid detractors, and I felt that responding would only embolden them. But my mom persisted, warning me that I was endangering my life after she saw some of the more violent threats directed at me. Finally, I reluctantly agreed to post a follow-up tweet to clarify my views. "My previous tweet expressed no opinion on the facts of this case, but for the record, I remain opposed to the death penalty under all circumstances—no matter the crime, the victim or the perpetrator. Period."

Just as I suspected, it only made matters worse. Thousands more tweets came flooding in to castigate me. Soon, the attacks spilled over to my other social media pages. Dozens of people who didn't follow me started posting disturbing comments on unrelated posts. I reported many of them and deleted the rest. Quite a few others went to the trouble of finding my contact information on my website and sent threatening emails. They called me every dirty name you could imagine. All because I expressed an unpopular opinion—mercy.

The personal threats I received shocked me, but the bloodthirsty demands for vengeance against Orlando Hall worried me even more. Clearly, the crime for which he was convicted was horrific. An innocent Black girl, Lisa Rene, lost her life in a senseless murder, and I grieve for her family and loved ones. Yet, I still believe that a modern, civilized society should deploy other nonlethal mechanisms to avenge the victims and punish the guilty. In the context of capital cases, life in prison, itself, already punishes the convicted with a permanent deprivation of liberty. But it was always easier to build a consensus against the death penalty in the cases where the facts were murky, the crime was questionable, the process was flawed, or the accused was sympathetic. That was never my approach. It seems to me the hard cases are the ones that really test us as a people, and what I learned from my experience questioning the execution of Orlando Hall deeply troubled me about our nation.

As I scrolled through the profiles of the people who posted the most vicious attacks against me, I noticed a clear trend. Many were self-described Christians. Others proudly boasted that "All lives matter." A lot of them were Trump supporters. But nearly all of them were white, an unusual demographic selection for a commentator whose social media audience skews disproportionately Black. Many of the death penalty supporters who lectured me against ignoring the pain and suffering of a young Black female murder victim were the same people who casually justified the Louisville Police Department's killing of Breonna Taylor in her own home. They were the same people who called themselves "pro-life." And, I discovered, they were the same people who believed that killing a Black person in response to the murder of a Black person made them, in their minds, civil rights heroes, and made me a racist.

Aside from the death threats, what was most exasperating during this discussion was the gaslighting commentary that diminished the significance of racism in the criminal justice system and in every other sphere of life for African Americans. It was part of an unmistakable pattern from recent decades. White leaders have devoted prodigious energy to the task of convincing themselves that the social, economic, and legal mechanisms they created that disproportionately impact Black people are not racist because these mechanisms are supposedly race-neutral in their construction. This has been a clever distraction. Policymakers clearly understand that any so-called race-neutral policy or law can be designed or implemented in a race-specific manner. They also know that any purported race-neutral law that freezes in place an existing racist status quo effectively serves a racist purpose. But this rhetorical pretense is designed to force us to debate the presence or absence of racism in every instance. This is a trap that should be avoided.

As author Toni Morrison explained in a 1975 speech,

> The very serious function of racism . . . is distraction. It keeps you from doing your work. It keeps you explaining over and over again, your reason for being. Somebody says you have no language, and so you spend twenty years proving that you do. Somebody says your head isn't shaped properly, so you have scientists working on the fact that it is. Somebody says that you have no art, so you dredge that up. Somebody says that you have no kingdoms, and so you dredge that up. None of that is necessary. There will always be one more thing.

This is also the larger problem for America. These fruitless racial conversations not only trap Black people, they trap white people as well. We squander our time and energy when we engage in these counterproductive debates. We all know that racism exists, and we all know that white Americans benefit from it. Even the white Americans who most adamantly deny the existence of racism against Black people, surely understand this, rendering our debates a performance designed to divert our attention from the need to dismantle white supremacy. Black feminist writer Audre Lorde described it as "an old and primary tool of all oppressors to keep the oppressed occupied with the master's concerns."

It's time to stop the deflection. White Americans must understand that the process of atonement—the statement of confession, the expression of contrition, the performance of a service for restoration, and the request for absolution—is not merely to mend the victim; it is to heal the soul of the perpetrator. "At the root of the American Negro problem," James Baldwin wrote, "is the necessity of the American white man to find a way of living with the Negro in order to be able to live with himself."

11

ACCOUNTABILITY

I was watching television one afternoon in my grandmother's family room, riveted by the theater happening in front of me. It was not a soap opera that stole my attention, although I imagined my grandmother was watching one on the TV in her bedroom. It was October 1991, and I was watching a congressional hearing.

I was a third-year law student, visiting St. Louis for a few days to see my family. One of my law professors, Charles Ogletree, was on television. He had only a supporting role that day, but I was excited to see him. He sat behind a distinguished-looking law professor from Oklahoma, whom I had recently come to know from the news. The law professor stood up, raised her right hand, and swore an oath to tell the truth. At that moment, I did not have a positive opinion about the person who administered the oath. He was a senator from Delaware named Joe Biden, and all I knew about him at the time was that one of my coworkers in the Dukakis campaign had been responsible for making an "attack video" that forced him out of the 1988 presidential race. Biden was the chair of the Senate Judiciary Committee that presided over the hearing that day, and he took his seat between Senator Ted Kennedy on his left and Senator Strom Thurmond on his right. Every person on the committee was a white man.

The law professor began reading her written testimony. "Mr. Chairman, Senator Thurmond, members of the committee. My name is Anita F. Hill."

Professor Hill described how she had once worked for Clarence Thomas, who had recently been nominated to the US Supreme Court. She described her working relationship with him as "positive" in the early days and said Thomas "respected my work" and "trusted my judgment." After a few months, she said, Thomas asked her to go out socially. She declined several times, and that's when their relationship began to change. In lurid detail, Professor Hill described a disturbing pattern of behavior that she had observed. "After a brief discussion of work, he would turn the conversation to a discussion of sexual matters," she said. His conversations were "very vivid," she told the committee, and she explained them in detail.

At some point as I was watching the hearing, I heard the familiar shuffle of slippers coming closer to the family room. Whenever I stayed at my grandmother's house, she would typically spend most of her time in her bedroom, and every now and then she would walk out to the kitchen or the laundry room. Sometimes she would walk all the way to the family room and stand there for a minute and make small talk. She had been married two or three times, and she operated with the fluidity of someone who knew exactly how to read the patience of a man. But on this particular day she seemed to completely misread my thoughts.

She shuffled into the kitchen, looked into the refrigerator for nothing in particular, and yelled a question into the family room. "Still watching the hearing, huh?" It was obvious that I was, so I shot back a one-word answer. "Yep," I said, figuring she would retreat to her bedroom after a moment. But she did not. Instead, she walked through the small dining room and to the edge of the family room, where I was seated. She stood for a second as if she wanted to get something off her chest. I didn't look up or pay attention and kept watching the hearing.

Then she said something I will never forget: "I wish that woman would stop lying about that man."

I was stunned. I turned to face her. "Why would you assume she's lying?" I asked.

From my vantage point, Clarence Thomas was the one who had the vested interest in lying. He needed to protect his career against allegations of sexual harassment. Anita Hill, on the other hand, had nothing to gain. She knew she would be vilified by Thomas's supporters for coming forward, and there was no guarantee that the testimony of a thirty-five-year-old Black woman would have any impact on a group of older white male senators.

My grandmother did not see it that way. Born and raised in segregated St. Louis during the early days of the Great Migration, she had been taught gender roles that centered the "strong Black man" as the defender of the Black community. Although she was a working woman and the primary breadwinner in at least one of her marriages, she still seemed to support the idea that the Black woman's job was to support the Black man, not only in her own relationship with him but in the community at large. Her support for Thomas was an unexpected expression of what author Kate Manne might call "himpathy," which she described in the *Washington Post* in 2018 as "the inappropriate and disproportionate sympathy powerful men often enjoy in cases of sexual assault, intimate partner violence, homicide and other misogynistic behavior." I supported the concept of Black unity, but I did not subscribe to the view of unquestioning loyalty to Black public figures or of a heteronormative *intraracial* hierarchy that prioritized cishet Black men above all others. What made this scenario even more troubling is that the Black man she was defending had a questionable record of defending other Black people, and every indication suggested that he would act against the interests of Black people if confirmed to the Supreme Court. So here we were in an act of role reversal, in which I was the Black man defending the Black woman, and my grandmother was the Black woman defending the Black man.

The very next year, however, when my grandmother attended my law school graduation ceremony, she did not extend the same deference to me. While I sat with my classmates for the ceremony, my grandmother confronted my boyfriend seated with my family and told him that she did not approve of my "lifestyle" and insisted that he give his mother's telephone number to her so she could have a woman-to-woman conversation about our relationship. When I heard what happened, I confronted my grandmother, we argued again, but she did not budge. It appeared that her values were rooted not so much in deference to Black men but rather in support of the institution of the Black family that she felt was somehow threatened by the recognition of my personal agency.

What concerned me about the conversation with my grandmother, and the conversations I would have with other African Americans in the 1990s, was that we often reflexively defended prominent Black men, even if they had questionable commitments to the Black community. Clarence Thomas, for example, started off as a radical Black nationalist and a cofounder of the Black Student Union at Holy Cross College, which adopted a militant manifesto declaring that "the Black man does not want or need the white woman." But by 1987, Thomas had evolved into a Black conservative who divorced his Black wife and married a white woman. By the time he was nominated to the Supreme Court in 1991, he had already expressed his opposition to affirmative action and demonstrated his hostility to civil rights laws as the chair of the Equal Employment Opportunity Commission under President Reagan. Given Thomas's history, it was tragically foreseeable that the man George H. W. Bush chose to replace Thurgood Marshall on the Supreme Court would one day cast the deciding vote to invalidate a key provision of the Voting Rights Act.

I felt a similar sense of disappointment when many of my African American friends and family members cheered the acquittal of O. J. Simpson in his celebrated 1995 murder trial. Their excitement was not based in their belief that O. J. was innocent; many of them thought he was guilty. They were excited simply because a Black man had beaten the white man at his own game. The fact that he had beaten the system with an articulate Black lawyer made the acquittal even more impactful. White men had been raping and killing Black women since the days of slavery, and O. J.'s acquittal felt like a vindication for many people in the Black community. I understood the mentality, but I did not agree with the celebration. I had no special insight into O. J.'s innocence or guilt, but I had no reason to celebrate O. J. Simpson, the man. In my opinion, he had abandoned the Black community years before as he tried to whitewash himself with his career and personal life, and he only reluctantly returned to us when he needed our help to spring him from jail.

Time and time again, we would support prominent Black men, even when they had turned their backs on others in our own community. I saw the same trend with Bill Cosby, who had, inarguably, contributed more positive images of Black culture than almost anyone for at least three decades. Cosby had created TV shows with Black actors, donated to Black colleges, and supported Black causes in a way that earned him his rightful place as a hero in the pantheon of Black celebrities. But how could that history overcome the horrifying allegations that he had drugged and raped Black women? Like Clarence Thomas, Bill Cosby seemed to have become more conservative over the years, and, like Thomas, he cloaked his conservatism in language that invoked the best interest of the Black community. The incarcerated "are not political criminals," Cosby said in his famous 2004 "pound cake" speech. His remarks were delivered in the same venue where Bill Clinton had staged his "Sister Soulja" moment in 1992 and where George W. Bush delivered his "soft bigotry" speech in 2000. In each instance, they spoke at the NAACP's annual convention, and in each instance, they saw an opportunity to reach an audience that might be receptive to their messages.

I am not sure if Clinton, Bush, and Cosby knew this consciously, but at some level, each man must have understood a fundamental contradiction about African Americans. Despite the reputation that we are overwhelmingly liberal, the truth is more complicated. In reality, I have found that Black people tend to be politically progressive but socially conservative. You can hear the paradoxical overtones in Black churches, beauty salons, barbershops, and fraternal organizations, where we fiercely defend radical visions of equality and social reorganization but still traffic in the conservative Christian politics of respectability.

In the research for my first book in the 1990s, I came across another example of the paradox. I discovered in multiple public opinion surveys that Black people were as supportive or more supportive than white people of equal rights for LGBTQ Americans, despite the stereotype of Black homophobia. But there was a catch. On one major issue, Black Americans were far less supportive of LGBTQ equality than white Americans—the issue of same-sex marriage. When it came to notions of social justice and discrimination, we got it. But when it came to our vision of morality, we didn't.

In numerous other examples, Black people could not be pigeonholed into simplistic categories. We could rap along to the lyrics of NWA's "Fuck Tha Police" but still complain when the cops failed to show up in our neighborhoods. We could complain about harsh prison sentences but still support the death penalty. We could denounce Republican attacks on welfare and still shame people in our own communities for living in the projects. So, it was not surprising that Bill Cosby might find support for his message at the NAACP. It was, after all, not substantially different from the same judgmental message I had heard at a number of progressive Black churches throughout the 1990s.

Cosby's 2004 speech imagined a scenario in which a Black person was shot in the head simply for stealing a piece of pound cake. "Then we all run out and are outraged," Cosby complained. But "what the hell was he doing with the pound cake in his hand?" It was a troubling statement, posed in the form of humor. The idea that police officers might be justified in killing a Black person simply because he or she stole a piece of pound cake was inherently problematic and contributed to the view that state violence should be used to resolve deep-seated American socioeconomic problems that Cosby, himself, had been warning about for years. Cosby's twenty-first-century respectability politics blamed Black people for our own condition without holding white America accountable for their failure to dismantle a racially discriminatory criminal justice system. "We cannot blame white people," Cosby said in that speech. It was a message he would not apply to himself. Years later, when Cosby was convicted of rape, his first instinct was to blame white people. "This has been the most racist and sexist trial in the history of the United States," Cosby's publicist announced, without a hint of irony.

Cosby's "racism" defense exposed a fracture within the Black community. I've encountered quite a few African Americans who think Cosby may be guilty but don't care because he's Bill Cosby, and just as many others who don't want to know if he's guilty because, again, he's Bill Cosby. Still others are absolutely certain he's innocent if for no other reason than because, as I said before, he's Bill Cosby. A similar community fracture could be seen after broadcast journalist Gayle King's famous 2019 interview with R&B star R. Kelly. Some attacked her for bringing down a successful Black man, while others focused on Kelly's long history of questionable behavior.

Black unity does not oblige us to deliver our unconditional support to all prominent or successful African Americans, especially when they do wrong or harm our community. Nor should our pride be reserved to center or elevate cisgender heterosexual Black men above all others. Instead, meaningful Black accountability requires an egalitarian willingness to embrace the most vulnerable among us and to address sexism, misogyny, patriarchy, xenophobia, homophobia, and transphobia within our own communities. As law professor Kimberlé Crenshaw wrote in her groundbreaking 1989 article on intersectionality, "If any real efforts are to be made to free Black people of the constraints and conditions that characterize racial subordination, then theories and strategies purporting to reflect the Black community's needs must include an analysis of sexism and patriarchy."

I thought about what Crenshaw called the "conceptual limita-
tions of the single-issue analyses" when I participated in the Million
Man March in 1995. I joined with Black AIDS Institute founder
Phill Wilson, former Cambridge (Massachusetts) mayor Kenneth
Reeves, Reverend Rainey Cheeks, Dr. Dennis Holmes, Dr. Maurice
Franklin, Steve Walker, Gary Daffin, and hundreds of other Black
gay men and a handful of Black women and allies. We marched
through the streets of Washington, DC, chanting, "We're Black!
We're gay! We wouldn't have it any other way!" Even my heterosexual former law professor Derrick Bell spoke at our rally as an ally.
It was a difficult decision to participate because the march was organized by Minister Louis Farrakhan, the controversial leader of the
Nation of Islam, who had a disturbing history of sexism, homophobia, and anti-Semitism. Still, I felt that our presence in an openly gay
contingent that day sent an unsolicited but powerful and positive
message of inclusion. Ten years later, in the summer of 2005, Minister Farrakhan called me up one day to talk about another march.
At the time, I was the board president of the National Black Justice
Coalition, and he was preparing a tenth-anniversary march to com-
memorate the first event. But this time, he wanted to recruit Black
LGBTQ participants to join.

Needless to say, I was shocked. I had only met Farrakhan once
before, and I never expected him to reach out to me, an openly gay
man. Still, I followed up on his phone call, and my colleagues Donna
Payne, Alexander Robinson, and I met with Minister Farrakhan at a
hotel conference room in Washington, DC. We had a contentious
meeting. Farrakhan remained calm, but his deputy—a homophobic
pastor named Reverend Willie Wilson, the organizer of the march—
launched into a bizarre tirade attacking the Black LGBTQ community. At one point, Wilson pulled out a candy G-string from a bag
and hurled it on the table and ranted nonsensically about Black lesbian women allegedly using these edibles to lure young Black girls
into homosexuality. I stared at him in stunned disbelief, struggling

to wrap my head around the surrealism of the experience in which I had found myself.

When the theatrics ended, Farrakhan still insisted that he wanted LGBTQ people at his march and asked me to speak at the event. I had little interest in doing so, and our organization suggested a list of other Black speakers. I had been a Black gay activist for several years at this point, and I was ready to retire from activism and return to politics. But several people in the community encouraged me to accept the offer and use the platform to educate the participants. That never happened. At the last minute, Reverend Wilson pulled the plug on my participation and refused to allow me to speak on stage. Minister Farrakhan was nowhere to be found.

The entire ordeal wiped me out, and it hastened my transition from activism back to politics. But even in failure, it reminded me why it was so important that we hold our Black leaders accountable. Minister Farrakhan had made important contributions to inspire Black people in America, yet his words and his actions still hurt other Black people. For years, he had practiced the same single-issue analysis that Professor Crenshaw warned against, and the effect was to harm his own people who did not fit into his vision of Black patriarchy. It served as a stark contrast to the principle articulated by Dr. King that "injustice anywhere is a threat to justice everywhere."

My purpose in raising these examples is not to assess blame but rather to address our own capacity and willingness to hold our community leaders accountable. To be clear, accountability does not necessarily require eternal condemnation. After all, Black people have a long history of forgiveness. I lived in Washington, DC, when the Black community forgave former mayor Marion Barry after he was convicted and released from prison and then reelected him to the same office. But accountability does require a willingness to investigate troubling credible allegations, all with the same presumption of innocence to which any other American is entitled. Most important, if those allegations prove true, accountability requires sincere repentance and atonement from the responsible party. Finally, accountability demands that we practice a prefigurative politics that is inclusive of the most vulnerable people in our communities.

But why is accountability important for African Americans in a discussion about a four-hundred-year history of white supremacy and systemic racism? Doesn't that put the onus on Black people?

First, if we don't practice accountability, we will likely repeat the tragic mistakes of the past. We've seen how politicians of both parties have failed our communities when we tied our fortunes too closely to theirs. We can't continue to do this without reward. Lack of accountability will allow charismatic leaders to beguile us again and again, only to wake up four years, eight years, or ten or twenty years later with no substantive progress.

Second, if we don't practice the politics of inclusion for the most marginalized people in our own communities, it is more difficult to demand that non-Black communities include us. Accountability requires us to represent the interests of those who are most vulnerable, not just those who are most presentable.

Third, when I talk about accountability, I'm not proposing a new iteration of Black respectability politics or the adjustment of Black behavior to satisfy the white gaze. Nor am I suggesting any sort of false equivalence between white atonement and Black accountability. What I am arguing is that we can't let anyone take advantage of our community and exploit us, either from the inside or the outside. Whether it's Clarence Thomas denouncing his confirmation hearings as "a high-tech lynching for uppity Blacks," Donald Trump asking us "What the hell do you have to lose?" or Lil Wayne hawking Trump's two-page "Platinum Plan" for Black America, we have to be sophisticated consumers of the messages and messengers that surround us. This holds true for people who are Black and those who are not, for those we love and those we despise.

In his 2021 book, *The Devil You Know: A Black Power Manifesto*, Charles Blow makes a provocative case for African Americans to return to the South, which many families fled in the twentieth century. Blow notes that Hispanics will become the majority populations of Nevada, Arizona, New Mexico, and Texas and the largest racial group in California in the next thirty years, and he argues that African Americans could create our own regional power base by targeting nine specific Southern states in a strategy that he calls "reverse migration." I think it's a clever, workable approach to self-empowerment; Blow persuasively argues that Black people could use his plan to elect senators and governors to wield real political power. But even if we implement Blow's blueprint, we still must hold our elected officials accountable, and we haven't always done this. Even in our Black congressional districts, we have sometimes continued to reelect long-standing incumbents long after they've served their utility to the community.

One of the most difficult challenges that African Americans faced in the Obama presidency was holding a Black president accountable. Many of us were so elated to have one of our own in the White House that we often gave him a pass when we shouldn't have. I would sometimes jokingly tell my friends that it seemed the only thing that President Obama could do to lose Black support would be to divorce First Lady Michelle Obama and marry a white woman. That may exaggerate the truth a bit, but many of us were reluctant to speak critically about a Black leader who, even if he wasn't doing everything we wanted him to do, was doing no worse than all the white presidents before him.

I had trouble with this myself. I disagreed with President Obama on a number of issues—his drone policy, capital punishment, reparations, legalizing marijuana, a public option for the Affordable Care Act, negotiating with Republicans on budgets, and, of course, on gay marriage (before he "evolved"). When I spoke out about these issues on social media or on television, I was criticized for bringing down a strong Black man, despite the fact that I clearly supported the president and unapologetically voted for him twice. It was as if any weakness that a Black person exposed in a Black leader's armor would somehow give ammunition to white people to attack him. This concerned me for two reasons. First, exposing the weakness could actually help our Black leaders by preparing them for critiques that, surely, we weren't the only ones to notice. Second, as Black people, we have to learn to critique and question *any* leader, even those whom we support. That doesn't mean we have to be rude, dismissive, or disrespectful. It does mean we have to hold one another accountable.

Of course, accountability also means that Black people should hold white leaders accountable. On the surface, this sounds easy and obvious. Black Americans rarely hold back in criticizing white people in positions of power when they do wrong. But we do sometimes create exceptions for people we support. Bill Clinton provides a perfect example of this—not because of the adulterous affair that got him impeached but because of his compromises on the crime bill and welfare reform and policies that had a harmful impact on Black people.

One of the lessons we have to learn is how to be critical of the people we support. Political accountability doesn't mean we stop voting or withdraw from the democratic process. In fact, we have to vote more, not less. But we can't just vote in presidential elections once every four years. We have to vote in congressional midterm elections every two years, and in local races for governor, state representative, mayor, city council, school board, judge, and district attorney. We must understand that electoral politics alone is not enough to change America and also use our economic power, our personal power, our moral power, and the power to protest in the streets. And to do all that, we must be informed participants in our democracy.

We must also remind the people we elect that we put them in office and demand that they serve our needs. This was true for Bill Clinton. I worked in his administration and voted for him twice because I believed he was the best available option, but I also understand that he was far from perfect and deserved criticism, scrutiny, and pressure on issues where he failed us. The same held true for Virginia's Democratic governor Ralph Northam, who confessed in 2019 to having worn blackface in the past. We can't speak with moral clarity against racism in the Republican Party if we don't speak about it in the Democratic Party.

The problem is that Republicans have not shown themselves to be as principled. They were quick to call for Northam to resign in Virginia but just as quick to excuse Alabama's Republican governor Kay Ivey when she admitted to wearing blackface. They have learned to use the language of racism almost exclusively as a cudgel to attack Black people and Democrats but not to examine the Republican Party's own disturbingly racist behavior. For this reason, many Black Democrats refuse to practice "unilateral disarmament" in the nation's political battles. If they hold Democrats accountable, they want assurances that Republicans will do the same in their party. This is understandable but misguided. Once you start excusing racism in your own party, it makes it difficult to challenge it in another. Opposition to racism must transcend the tribalism of partisan political identification.

This is not the shallow both-siderism that pretends that Republicans and Democrats are the same. They are not. "We have been studying Washington politics and Congress for more than 40 years," political scientists Thomas Mann and Norman Ornstein wrote in 2012. "We have criticized both parties when we believed it was warranted. Today, however, we have no choice but to acknowledge that the core of the problem lies with the Republican Party." Even recognizing the unique dysfunctionality of the modern Republican Party, Black Americans must still hold both parties accountable. Although the outright racism of the Republican Party is in no way comparable to the racial timidity that too often marks the Democratic Party, neither major party—nor any other party—should ever escape accountability. The long history of outright racism in the Democratic

Party from 1828 to 1964 and in the Republican Party from 1964 to the present should remind us that no party can be fully trusted forever. Parties are not static institutions that are resistant to outside forces. They comprise humans, and in this country, those humans have repeatedly shown themselves willing to sacrifice the persistent demands of Black people for justice to pursue the predictable pleas of white people for peace.

It is also for this reason that I believe that some Black people should join the Republican Party. I say this fully aware that it may be too late to salvage the Republican brand, and Black conservatives might be better off joining or starting a new nonracist political party. But for too long, the absence of credible Black voices in the GOP has allowed the party to ignore the concerns of the African American community. To be clear, I am a lifelong Democrat who has no intention of ever becoming a Republican. My great-great grandfather, John H. Dickerson, was the chairman of the 1912 Florida State Republican Convention. He would likely be ashamed of how his party has transitioned. I do not trust today's modern Republican Party, and I believe it to be fundamentally racist to its core. But I know that not every Republican shares these racist beliefs. The problem is that the Black people who have identified with the Republican Party in recent years are exactly the wrong people to change it. They are the people who enabled and excused the racism of Donald Trump and failed to speak up about the racism of the party's elected officials from the local school board to the exalted halls of Congress.

In a chilling appearance on the PBS show *Frontline* in 2016, Omarosa Manigault Newman, the Trump campaign's director of African American outreach, described Trump's election as "the ultimate revenge," in which he would become the most powerful man in the universe. "Every critic, every detractor will have to bow down to President Trump," she boasted. I'm not even sure Omarosa was ever a Republican. I don't recall meeting her in the 1990s, but I'm told she worked with me in the Clinton White House. By the time she left the

Trump White House in 2017, she finally admitted that Trump was, in fact, a "racist," just as the rest of us knew all along. Her willingness to play along with Trump's dangerous politics, however, reflected the shameful and transactional opportunism of the Black Republicans who supported him and continue to support the GOP.

The problem was not limited to Trump staff members, as was sadly demonstrated by Black Republican senator Tim Scott of South Carolina. "Woke supremacy is as bad as white supremacy," Scott told Fox News in March of 2021. "We need to take that seriously," he said. Scott's remarks came in response to comments made by MSNBC host Joy Reid, who said that the sole Black Republican in the Senate stood behind his white counterparts at a press conference as part of an effort to provide "the patina of diversity" to the Republican campaign against raising the minimum wage. No one was violently dragged from their home and lynched because of Reid's gentle political critique, but Scott claimed to be so offended that he actually likened her mild rebuke to the worst evils of "white supremacy." White supremacy remains a very real threat in America. We saw it from the deadly protests in Charlottesville to the deadly insurrection at the US Capitol. But "woke supremacy" is not a thing. Scott's new terminology ranks along with the overused conservative complaints about "cancel culture," according to *Washington Post* columnist Jonathan Capehart. "The purpose of both phrases is to shield folks from criticism when they are called out for their actions or their deeply ignorant musings that peddle in racism, xenophobia, or misogyny," Capehart writes.

Tim Scott's remarks were also reminiscent of Black Republican Ben Carson, who complained in 2013 that "Obamacare is really, I think, the worst thing that has happened in this nation since slavery." In Carson's twisted vision of American history, providing health care to millions of Americans like myself was worse than the lynchings, voter suppression, assassinations, church bombings, police shootings, and mass-incarceration policies that had hurt and killed Black people since the end of the Civil War.

Years ago, a Black friend from law school revealed to me that he was thinking of becoming a Republican, not because he agreed with the party, but because, he said, "the line is shorter" than in the Democratic Party for ambitious young Black people who want to rise to the top in politics. When I say we need Black Republicans, I don't mean Black Republicans like the ones I've just mentioned. Instead, I'm thinking of a line that I once heard in a speech from openly gay Representative Barney Frank. The problem with these gay Republicans, Frank said, is that they spend all their time selling the idea of the Republican Party to gay people instead of selling the idea of gay people to the Republican Party. This, too, is the problem with so many of today's Black Republicans. Instead of trying to convince Black people to support Republicans, they should start spending their time convincing Republicans to support Black people.

This is why I believe that when Black people gain access to power, we should not be afraid to use it to advance our community's interests, and we should not be concerned when white people inevitably accuse us of being biased for doing so. This holds true for Black Republicans in Congress as well as a Black Democratic president in the White House.

Years ago, when I was deeply involved in the diversity campaign at Harvard Law School, I remember learning that Black businessman Reginald F. Lewis, the CEO of TLC Beatrice, planned to make a significant financial contribution to the school. I suggested to the Black Law Students Association that we ask him to use his leverage to extract a promise for greater faculty diversity. I don't know if the message ever reached Lewis, but I do know that the campus diversity controversy was national news at that time. I also know that there was no immediate change in the diversity of the faculty around the time of Lewis's gift. That would come years later. The year after I graduated, however, there was one change on campus. The building where I had once been photographed chasing the dean of the law school across the campus during my first diversity protest now had a new name. It was the Reginald F. Lewis International Law Center. It was, I believe, the only building on campus named after an African American, and it was an impressive accomplishment for the Black Harvard graduate. But for me, it did not feel sufficient. I'll never know for sure if Lewis understood what we were doing, but his generous gift seemed like a missed opportunity to use Black power to hold a traditionally white institution accountable.

Many years later, when I was working as a commentator for the business network CNBC, I appeared on a show talking about the controversial Troubled Asset Relief Program, known colloquially as "the bank bailout" that bolstered America's financial institutions during the economic crisis of 2008 and 2009. I made what I thought was an uncontroversial statement that the banking system would have collapsed without government's support. Not long after the show, while I was riding home that night, I received a call on my cell phone from an unfamiliar phone number. I answered. It was Jamie Dimon, the CEO of JPMorgan Chase Bank.

I have never met Jamie Dimon and have never given him my phone number. As far as I know, we've never even been in the same circle. I know nothing about the man. But he found my number and called me up to yell at me for implying that his bank was insufficiently capitalized. I explained to him that my analysis was the same one that President Obama's economic adviser Larry Summers had made. "Larry doesn't know what he's talking about either," Dimon shot back. We talked for a few minutes, he hung up, and I never spoke to him again.

I don't know if Jamie Dimon was trying to intimidate me or educate me. I was never a business reporter, so his tirade had little impact on my subsequent commentary. But it did teach me something about the way that entitled white men exercise their power. It was the way George W. Bush and Donald Trump each lost the national popular vote but governed like they had a mandate from God and the American people. It was the way Senate *Minority* Leader Mitch

McConnell demanded a power-sharing agreement with his Democratic counterpart to protect the racist-tainted filibuster immediately after the Republican Party lost control of the US Senate in January 2021. And it was that way that hundreds of angry white people stormed the United States Capitol and demanded that members of Congress overturn a free and fair democratic election after their candidate lost by seven million votes.

If white men, who are only 29 percent of the nation's population but have controlled more than 90 percent of the nation's power for four hundred years, can act with such entitlement and privilege, then Black people, after everything we have suffered through at the hands of this nation, should feel no shame in demanding justice for our own community and holding anyone and everyone accountable along the way. That includes the white media executives, like CBS CEO Les Moonves, who knowingly enabled a racist president when he quipped about Trump, "It may not be good for America, but it's damn good for CBS." This is also why I refused repeated requests from Fox News producers to appear on that network after host Bill O'Reilly cut off my mic in the middle of an October 2015 debate because he didn't like my answer about Black Lives Matter.

As long as white men remain disproportionately overrepresented in positions of power in America, Black people have every right to hold those white men accountable who call themselves allies. And as long as all white people continue to hold white privilege, then we should insist that they use it for good—to eradicate white privilege itself. It is partly for this reason that Michael Eric Dyson argued in 2015 that Hillary Clinton had the potential to do more for Black people than President Obama did. Secretary Clinton could deliver "a presidency built on racial transparency and honesty, one that doesn't lecture Black people about what they should do to get themselves together, but instead thrives on principled engagement with Black suffering," Dyson wrote in *The New Republic*.

I know from personal experience that accountability works. I've been held accountable when I've done wrong in my life. This public and personal accountability has led me to reconsider my own actions, apologize, make amends, and be a better person. I've also watched it work with other people. And perhaps no example is better than my own grandmother. Years after she defended Clarence Thomas and accused Anita Hill of lying, my grandmother took her own step forward. Inspired by the example of younger women in government, my eighty-year-old grandmother ran for office and was elected to the city council of Berkeley, Missouri, a St. Louis County suburb next to Ferguson. And years after we argued about my sexual orientation, my grandmother surprised me again. When I published my first book and visited St. Louis on a book tour, she showed up at the bookstore with several members of her Baptist church. They sat quietly in the front rows as I spoke, and after the event was over, they approached me. I asked them why they came, and they told me that my grandmother, unbeknownst to me, printed up invitations to the book signing, handed them out at her traditional Black church, and asked the church announcer to read the invitation in the announcements the Sunday before I came to town. All this from a religious Black grandmother in the 1990s for a book that was indiscreetly titled *One More River to Cross: Black and Gay in America.*

I learned from those experiences that when we have the courage to be open and honest about who we are and what we believe, people may not always accept us, but they will respect us more. I learned another important lesson as well. There are no shortcuts on the road to justice. Only when we hold each other accountable will we reach our ultimate goal—equality.

12

EQUALITY

I t was well after midnight, and I was in desperate need of sleep. It was almost exactly one year since the day I returned home from Mexico and struggled with that mysterious illness in January 2020. In the subsequent twelve months, every country in the world had been impacted by the spread of the coronavirus. America had erupted into racial conflict. The economy was limping hesitantly into the new year. Nearly four hundred thousand Americans had died from COVID-related complications. And the nation was still gripped by the news of a brazen and unprecedented presidential attempt to overturn the election from two months earlier.

I was tired. Nearly every day there was a shocking news alert waking me up in the morning or interrupting my dinner. I had yet to recover from the first week of November, when I survived an entire week of all-nighters, sitting on my couch flipping between CNN and MSNBC, waiting for projections and election results in obscure counties that I had never visited. For two months, I had paid close attention to electoral college news, manual recounts, court challenges, state certification deadlines, and even county canvassing board meetings, none of which I'd ever bothered to follow in any previous election I'd covered.

This, I told myself, will be my last sleepless night. I waited nervously for an official projection from the results in Georgia, unwilling to accept the confident prediction of the *New York Times* election needle that seemed to defy historical precedent.

In my mind, I knew it was possible. But deep in my heart, I still feared the worst. With a Black population of 33 percent and an empowered Black community in its capital city, Georgia had real potential to elect Democratic senators, but it hadn't happened in nearly two decades, as the state trended Republican along with the rest of the South. Even in its Democratic years, Georgia had always been conservative. It was the state where I had once warily eyed old white customers that I served at the Gap clothing store in the Cumberland Mall in Smyrna. It was the state where my family had once lived down the street from former segregationist governor Lester Maddox in Marietta. And it was the only state where I had ever seen a Ku Klux Klan rally in person.

I remained glued to the television, still waiting, until CNN anchor Chris Cuomo walked across the studio and made the announcement: "CNN will now project that Democrat Raphael Warnock is elected to the US Senate."

I jumped out of my seat. A Black man, who served as the pastor of Dr. King's Ebenezer Baptist Church in Atlanta, had become the first African American Democrat from the South to be elected to the US Senate. He would become only the eleventh Black person in all of American history to serve in the Senate, and all but two of those senators had served in my lifetime. I rejoiced. It was the work of Black women like Stacey Abrams and Natasha Rothwell and many others who had helped turned Georgia blue in the presidential election, and now it was clear that it was not a fluke. If the results in the other Georgia Senate runoff race held up that day, Georgia would become the only state in the Deep South with two Democratic senators—one a fifty-one-year-old Black man and the other a thirty-three-year-old Jewish man. As social media commentators bluntly described it, in the span of two months, the state of Georgia voted for a Black, a Jew, a woman, and a Catholic. All in the land of the old Confederacy.

This will be a historic day, I told myself. Now I can finally turn off the television and go to sleep. It was just after two in the morning on January 6, 2021, and I had no idea what was about to happen next.

I woke up in the morning with a smile on my face. I checked my phone to see if the other Senate race had been called yet and then turned on the news again to see what I had missed overnight. The second runoff looked promising. At any moment, Jon Ossoff was poised to become the youngest member of the United States Senate.

Later that day, Congress met to certify the electoral college results from November. I caught glimpses of the news as I walked past the television in my living room, but I had little interest in watching Republicans make fools of themselves in a futile effort in service of Donald Trump's delusions. I laughed when I noticed that his protest rally only merited a small mute "picture-in-picture" box on the lower corner of the cable news screen. The spectacle was so outrageous that I couldn't believe anyone was still dumb enough to have faith in this well-known con artist. Two more weeks, and he's gone. I ate lunch, took a break and walked to the gym.

The first news alert interrupted Beyonce's *Homecoming* album on my headphones. I stared at the words on my phone with incredulity for a moment. Then I opened the TV app and watched the news as I worked out. This can't be real, I thought. It looked like hundreds of people were trying to break into the US Capitol building. That was impossible, my brain said to my eyes. I lived in Washington for years, and I knew the building was well-guarded and secure. I turned to another channel and the images were even more dramatic. It left me transfixed, sitting on the workout machine, unintentionally preventing anyone else from using the equipment for several minutes. Finally, I forced myself up, gathered my belongings from the locker room, and ran back home to catch the news. Like millions of other Americans, I would spend the rest of the day in horror as I watched a bloody, violent, and deadly mob of domestic terrorists attempt a coup d'état on live national television.

Like so many other Black people, I had always known this type of mob violence was possible. It had happened many times before in history. In the angry faces of the people storming the Capitol, I could see the images of those who assassinated Dr. King in 1968, who bombed four Black girls in Birmingham in 1963, who lynched Emmett Till in 1955, who massacred Blacks in Tulsa in 1921, who burned down East St. Louis in 1917, who overthrew the government of Wilmington in 1898, and who fled the union in 1861. In my view, the Capitol insurrectionists were the spiritual descendants of the very people who lynched thousands of African Americans when federal troops withdrew from the South.

They could not accept the idea that their white racist president had been defeated, that the former vice president to America's first Black president had received a record eighty-one million votes, that a Black and South Asian woman had been elected vice president, and that a Black man had just been elected as a senator from the state of Georgia. This was the darkening America that they had long feared. It represented a diminution of their power and privilege that could not go unchecked, and incited by their leader, they launched one more desperate sprint in the race against time to stop it. "If you don't fight like hell," Donald Trump told them that day, "you won't have a country anymore."

I imagine every American president has held racist beliefs at some point, but Donald Trump was the first president in our country's history to willingly stoke a dangerous race war solely for his personal political benefit. His followers were so emboldened by their president and so blinded by their privilege that they attacked their own country in broad daylight, on live television, in what was supposed to be a heavily guarded federal government building. They did so, knowing full well that their white skin, and the white cause for which they fought, would protect them from bullets and tear gas and night sticks that had been deployed against the peaceful Black Lives Matter protesters outside the White House only seven months earlier.

By the end of the attack, after five people had been killed and numerous others injured, after police officers had been beaten and assaulted by "law and order" Trump supporters, after terrorists erected gallows and a noose outside the Capitol, after members of Congress who espoused "American exceptionalism" had been forced to flee from their seats and evacuate the House and Senate chambers, 147 Republicans in the United States Congress still cast their votes that night to overturn the results of the November 2020 election.

Republicans had already determined years earlier that they could not win elections if too many people voted. That was why they concocted voter fraud conspiracy theories, passed restrictive voter ID laws, reduced the number of polling locations, and cut the number of early-voting days. The Pennsylvania Republican House Speaker Mike Turzai flagrantly admitted before the 2012 presidential election that his state's new voter ID law would "allow Governor Romney to win the state." Texas Republican Governor Rick Perry signed a law in 2015 that allowed registered voters to present a concealed handgun license as identification to vote but not a valid student ID from one of the state's own universities. And a federal appeals court in 2016 found that North Carolina's Republican voter law was used to "target African Americans with almost surgical precision."

Donald Trump, who would later become the first and only president to lose the popular vote twice, recognized the problem for his party long before the November 2020 election. As Democratic and Republican states geared up to expand mail voting in the midst of the deadly 2020 coronavirus pandemic, Trump complained that easy access to absentee voting would ruin GOP chances to keep the White House. "If you'd ever agreed to it, you'd never have a Republican elected in this country again," he grumbled.

When Trump's reelection campaign failed, the party of white racial resentment could see the sands of time slipping through the hourglass more clearly than ever. They had lost the popular vote in the presidential elections of 1992, 1996, 2000, 2008, 2012, 2016, and 2020, and they had little hope of winning in the future without drastic change. Losing Georgia's Senate seats was the last straw, and Georgia Republicans responded by passing legislation to restrict absentee voting; to limit early voting on Sundays, when Black churches coordinate "Souls to the Polls" campaigns; and to prohibit volunteers from providing water, snacks, or chairs for voters waiting in long lines. Republican legislators followed suit in dozens of other states, as well. If they couldn't win their race against time with numerical superiority against the emerging majority, they could still rely on voter restrictions, gerrymandering, conservative judicial decisions, and a Constitution written by fifty-five white men in 1787 to ensure decades of white rule long into the twenty-first century.

Republicans had been "preparing for this moment for years," Ari Berman explained in *Mother Jones* in 2021. Although Joe Biden won the most votes of any candidate in history, "fifty Republican senators will be able to thwart most of his legislative agenda, even though Democratic senators represent forty-one million more Americans," Berman wrote. And any action that a Democratic president or Congress might take could be reviewed by a hostile Supreme Court, "even though a majority of those justices were appointed by Republican presidents who came to office after losing the popular vote."

In the midst of this ongoing power grab, Donald Trump became the first president in American history to be impeached twice. But not long afterward, the same whispers of compromise that plagued the country in 1776 and 1820 and 1850 and 1877 could be heard again. Once again, they tried to prioritize peace over justice in the name of unity. "It's time to move on," said Republican Ted Cruz. Trump's actions were "not great," Republican Nikki Haley admitted, but "give the man a break." Republicans in the Senate did just that, and forty-three of the fifty GOP senators refused to convict him in the second impeachment trial. The belated and self-serving post-insurrection Republican calls for unity also demonstrated the way that many white Americans instinctively cling to the performance of innocence. But the nation could not unify by erasing its history. "The president of the United States committed an act of incitement of insurrection," Speaker Nancy Pelosi responded. But it did not matter. On May 28, Senate Republicans brazenly blocked a bipartisan commission to investigate the January 6th insurrection.

America had reached yet another crossroad, forcing us to choose what type of country we hope to become. It was a choice illustrated in the image of a man walking inside the US Capitol, as he came upon the portraits of Southern slave owner John C. Calhoun on the left and Northern abolitionist Charles Sumner on the right and approached a bust of the "Southern strategy" president, Richard Nixon. In antebellum America, Calhoun represented the nation's immoral embrace of slavery. In the Reconstruction era, Sumner represented the failure of early white liberals to follow through on their commitment to newly freed African Americans. In the post–civil rights era, Nixon represented the willingness of the Party of Lincoln to exploit Black pain for white political benefit. But here was this man named Kevin Seefried, from President-elect Joe Biden's home state of Delaware, carrying a Confederate flag, and implicitly asking the country if we would continue repeating the mistakes of the past or finally learn from them and change.

It was the first time in American history that the Confederate flag had flown in the United States Capitol—it was yet another battle in our never-ending civil war.

Years ago, Dr. Martin Luther King Jr. posed a question for America in the title of a book. It was called, *Where Do We Go from Here: Chaos or Community?* It was a question uniquely suited for the country after the passage of two historic laws—the Civil Rights Act of 1964 and the Voting Rights Act of 1965, but it also feels appropriate for the changing America of the twenty-first century. Will America choose the chaos represented by the insurrection in Washington on

Wednesday, January 6 or the community represented by the election held in Georgia on Tuesday, January 5?

In King's book, and in a speech he gave about it in Atlanta, he took stock of what the civil rights movement had accomplished in recent years and what was left to do. "We still have a long, long way to go before we reach the promised land of freedom," King acknowledged. Harkening back to the three-fifths compromise in the original US Constitution, King wrote that this "strange formula" declared that "the Negro was 60 percent of a person." But he noticed that another "curious formula" had also emerged. This one, he said, declared that a Black American was only "50 percent of a person," he wrote in his book.

"Of the good things in life, the Negro has approximately one half those of whites. Of the bad things of life, he has twice those of whites. Thus, half of all Negroes live in substandard housing. And Negroes have half the income of whites. When we turn to the negative experiences of life, the Negro has a double share: There are twice as many unemployed; the rate of infant mortality among Negroes is double that of whites; and there are twice as many Negroes dying in Vietnam as whites in proportion to their size in the population," King said in Atlanta.

African Americans understand these racial disparities even today. During the 2020 economic crisis, we were reminded of the old adage that we are "the last hired and first fired." And during the coronavirus pandemic, we remembered the old Negro proverb, "When white America catches a cold, Black America gets pneumonia." All these years after Dr. King wrote that book and delivered that speech, one thing has not changed. The "curious formula" of racial inequality still exists. Black Americans remain behind white Americans on nearly every socioeconomic indicator. For the average Black American, this racial disparity begins even before birth and continues well after death.

Before a child is born, Black women are less likely to receive prenatal care in the first trimester of their pregnancy.

At the point of birth, Black babies are twice as likely to die when delivered by white doctors instead of by Black doctors.

Even after birth, Black children are more than twice as likely as white children to die before their first birthday.

By the time they arrive in preschool, Black students are nearly four times more likely than white students to be suspended.

Throughout grade school, junior high, and high school, Black students remain nearly four times as likely as white students to receive out-of-school suspensions.

During those high school years, Black teens are less likely than white teens to find employment, even though white families often have more economic resources to support their children than black families.

Black students are also increasingly more likely to attempt suicide in high school.

When the time comes to cross the stage to receive a diploma at commencement, Black students are less likely than white students to graduate.

For those not in school, Black youth are five times more likely than white youth to be incarcerated.

For those who go to college, Black students are more likely to enroll in overcrowded and underfunded open-access colleges.

After starting college, Black students are less likely than whites to receive a bachelor's degree.

And among all students who score above average on standardized tests, Black and brown students are less likely to attend a selective college.

Back in the workforce, Black students graduate with thousands of dollars more in student loans, on average, than their white peers.

More than a decade out of college, Black women graduates are less likely to have paid off a significant portion of their student loans than white men.

And for households with a bachelor's degree or higher, the typical white family is sitting on nearly $400,000 of net worth, compared to $68,000 for college-educated Black households, according to the think tank Demos.

But the average Black *college graduate* still earns less than the average white *high school dropout*.

Black applicants with no criminal record are less likely to be hired for jobs than white applicants with prior felony criminal convictions.

Perhaps that explains why the Black unemployment rate has stubbornly remained higher than the white unemployment rate for the past five decades.

Blacks are also less likely than whites to own a home and more likely to incur higher debt when they do purchase one.

Black borrowers are more likely to pay a higher amount to purchase homes or refinance mortgages.

Black homeowners are also less likely than whites to achieve this milestone before the age of thirty-five.

As a result of these inequities, the median net worth of Black Bostonians was just $8 in 2017, compared to $247,500 for white Bostonians, according to a report in the *Boston Globe*. Yes, you read that correctly. "That was no typo," the *Boston Globe* headline explained. The median net worth of Black Bostonians was $8. Not $800. Not $8,000. Just $8.

Black and Latinx households are also nearly twice as likely as white households to lack access to indoor plumbing.

And Blacks are more likely than whites to suffer from asthma, diabetes, HIV/AIDS, and heart disease, according to the Kaiser Family Foundation.

In Ferguson, Missouri, researchers found Blacks were more than 3.5 times as likely as whites to be pulled over by police officers at traffic stops.

In New York City, 87 percent of the nearly seven hundred thousand people who were detained by police during the height of the stop-and-frisk policy were Black or Latino, and 88 percent of them were innocent.

Black people are incarcerated in state prisons at more than five times the rate of whites, according to the Sentencing Project.

And prosecutors are more likely to seek, and juries are more likely to deliver, the death penalty for the murder of whites than for the murder of Blacks.

As we age, more than half of Black Americans will not be able to maintain our standard of living in retirement, while most whites will, according to a 2018 study from the Center for Retirement Research.

Even after we die, Black families are less likely to receive an inheritance to pass onto the next generation.

When there is an inheritance, the average amount for Black families is less than a third of the average for white families, according to researchers at Brandeis University.

From cradle to grave—from childhood to adulthood to retirement, and, ultimately, to death—white Americans benefit from structural societal advantages and Black Americans do not.

What explains the persistent racial disparities in America well into the twenty-first century? The answer by now should be self-evident. America has never resolved the issue of racism and white supremacy. White America has never atoned for the country's original sin of racism, and America's government has never followed through on any commitment to make African Americans whole.

For centuries, the nation's leaders have tried to compromise with half-measures, symbolism, and cyclical moments of feigned reconciliation, each time kicking the smoldering can down the road for another generation to clean up. Now, after hundreds of years of ignoring the simmering fires, the country has finally run out of time.

As America has become Blacker and browner, the combination of fearful whites, angry and newly empowered Blacks, and the racial antagonism coming from what was once the Party of Lincoln has created ideal conditions for conflict, from the daily microaggressions broadcast on social media to the deadly insurrection at the Capitol.

Even when Trump had left office, after spending his last year implicitly demonizing Asian Americans by referring to COVID as the "China virus" or "Kung Flu," America continued to suffer the consequences of his corrosive rhetoric. In one dramatic example, a young white man in Georgia killed six Asian women at three different Atlanta-area massage parlors, and even he claimed his actions were not racially motivated.

But the people who are most angry do not necessarily fit our convenient stereotypes. This is why the list of suspects arrested after the Capitol insurrection included a cross section of America. A doctor. A real estate broker. An Olympic gold medalist. The son of a Brooklyn judge. A former US Marine. An occupational therapist. The CEO of a marketing company. An off-duty police officer. A county commissioner. A mayoral candidate. A former Army veteran. A member of the West Virginia House of Delegates. The lead singer for a heavy metal band. And a retired Air Force lieutenant colonel. They are our neighbors, our colleagues, our classmates, the woman seated next to you on your flight and the man standing behind you in the grocery store.

The people who want to disenfranchise millions of Black voters and install an unaccountable racist cult leader will easily blend into the crowd. "They will not come clothed in brown, and swastikas, or bearing chest heavy with gleaming crosses," the poet Pat Parker warned in her 1978 poem, "Where Will You Be?" "The time and need for ruses are over," she wrote. As we should have learned from the examples of Los Angeles Clippers owner Donald Sterling, Las Vegas casino magnate Sheldon Adelson, and the infamous gun-toting couple who threatened protesters outside their St. Louis mansion, there are no income cutoffs for racism.

This helps us understand why white rage has found its voice in official acts by those in positions of authority—gerrymandering congressional districts to dilute Black power, voter suppression to discourage Black votes, felony disenfranchisement to reduce Black voting numbers, census rigging to undercount Black and brown communities, and stacking the courts with judicial appointments to undermine the decisions of future Black and brown majorities. Conservative elected officials also began a desperate race to stop other social changes taking place in America. In Mississippi, Governor Tate Reeves signed a law banning transgender students from participating in girls' and women's sporting events. It was one of seventy-three bills pending in early 2021 that directly targeted transgender people, according to the advocacy group Human Rights Campaign. And when President Biden selected Interior Secretary Deb Haaland to become America's first Native American cabinet secretary, she too became a target of conservatives.

As millions of white Americans continue to resist any attempt to build a more inclusive nation, a new danger arises with Black America as well. The failure to resolve centuries-old racial inequities, especially in criminal justice policy, creates the conditions for conflict. "Those who make peaceful revolution impossible," President John F. Kennedy warned in 1962, "will make violent revolution inevitable." This is the reality that threatens to heat America's cold civil war once again to the boiling point of a full-on conflict.

But there is a way out of our burning race crisis.

The crisis will not be resolved by symbolic gestures of inclusion or by taking down Confederate monuments that should never have been erected. It won't be resolved by placing our faith in any particular politician or political party. Nor will it end with well-intentioned economic reform that reduces class-based income inequality while freezing racial imbalances in place.

If we accept the premise of our founding that all Americans are created equal, then we must conclude that persistent inequalities among racial groups—in employment, wealth, health, education, housing, crime, incarceration, life expectancy, success, and achievement—exist solely because of racial barriers and not because of racial differences in talent or capacity. "When you truly believe that the racial groups are equal," Ibram X. Kendi writes in *Stamped from the Beginning*, "then you also believe that racial disparities must be the result of racial discrimination." To accept America's enduring racial imbalance as the natural order of things is, itself, a form of racism. Thus, the new goal of our society must be to eradicate these racial disparities.

We can only eliminate these inequities if we act purposely to do so. This will require a race-based, historically informed, results-oriented fundamental restructuring of the nation's existing policies to make equality the goal. That means we cannot simply enact new laws and adopt new policies to make life marginally better for African Americans. Instead, we must make Black lives equal with white lives. And we have to maintain these new standards in place indefinitely until the goals are achieved.

This new society cannot be colorblind. It must be color conscious in order to observe, understand, and eliminate glaring and persistent disparities in racial and ethnic groups. In every instance and in every industry where we find inequities, we must ask ourselves difficult questions about the obstacles and barriers that contribute to these differences and then take decisive action to eliminate the disparities. It will not be easy, but neither is the alternative of permanent racial unrest.

It cannot be sufficient to lower Black unemployment or to increase Black household income as long as Black unemployment remains significantly higher than white unemployment and Black household incomes pale in comparison to white incomes. The goal, in every example, must be to put Black and white people in relatively equal positions.

To understand this further, consider the history of Black economic inequality. The Black unemployment rate has never been anywhere near as low as the white unemployment rate at any time since the Labor Department began collecting that data in the 1970s. To put this in perspective, the highest white unemployment rate ever recorded was 9.7 percent in 1982. In that same month, the Black unemployment rate was more than twice as high, at 20.9 percent. In fact, the Federal Reserve estimates the normal unemployment rate for the US economy as between 3.75 percent and 4.50 percent. The white unemployment rate has reached this target in every decade since the 1950s. Yet, in the entire history of Federal Reserve data, the Black unemployment rate has never reached this "normal" level. Even when the Black unemployment rate dropped to a record low of 5.2 percent in 2019, it still remained nearly 53 percent higher than the white unemployment rate at 3.4 percent. This is one of the clearest indicators that structural racial economic inequality has persisted for decades and that it is unlikely to be resolved without race-specific economic remedies.

Similar patterns appear in other areas of social policy. After eight states and the District of Columbia legalized marijuana from 2012 to 2018, the Drug Policy Alliance studied the effects on arrests. Not surprisingly, the number of marijuana arrests dropped in each jurisdiction, but what did not disappear were the racial disparities in enforcement. In Colorado, for example, in the first years after legalization, marijuana arrests for white people dropped by 51 percent, but only decreased by 25 percent for Black people. And in Washington, DC, even after legalization, a Black person was still eleven times more likely than a white person to be arrested for public consumption of marijuana.

Other well-intentioned progressive policies have also failed to resolve long-term racial inequalities, at the same time that those policies largely succeeded in their primary objectives. The juvenile justice movement, for example, has successfully pushed to reduce the number of young people who are incarcerated. Between 2003 and 2013, the rate of youth committed to juvenile facilities after an adjudication of delinquency fell by 47 percent, according to the Sentencing Project. Every state in the union witnessed a drop in its commitment rate. Despite what the group calls a "remarkable achievement," it points out that the racial disparities in the system did not improve during those years. In fact, the racial gap between Black and white youth in secure commitment actually increased by 15 percent.

Examples can be found again and again throughout American history. Popular race-neutral policies for a forty-hour workweek, the minimum wage, Medicare, Medicaid, Social Security, unemployment insurance, affordable housing, and public assistance contributed to the reduction of poverty, disease, homelessness, and unemployment in twentieth-century America. What those policies did not accomplish, however, was to eliminate the racial disparities between Blacks and whites in any of these areas. In fact, in many instances, progressive economic policies were accompanied by the perpetuation of racial exclusion.

When President Lincoln signed the Homestead Act in 1862, the post–Civil War United States government gave away 246 million acres of land—roughly the size of California, Florida, New York, Illinois, and Ohio combined—to more than a million mostly white families, at the same time it refused to provide the proverbial "forty acres and a mule" to nearly four million former Black slaves.

When Samuel Gompers and the American Federation of Labor advocated for workers' rights in the early 1900s, the group clarified that it "does not necessarily proclaim that the social barriers which exist between the whites and the Blacks could be or should be obliterated."

When President Franklin Roosevelt signed the Wagner Act in 1935, he gave workers the right to organize but also allowed labor unions to discriminate against African Americans. When he signed the Social Security Act of 1935, the law excluded agricultural and domestic workers, two groups in which African Americans were disproportionately represented. And when he signed the Servicemen's Readjustment Act—often referred to as "the G.I. Bill"—the government gave returning World War II veterans assistance to go to college or buy a home, but it still allowed racist state officials to discriminate against Black veterans.

Later, when President Truman signed the Hill-Burton Act in 1946, he enabled the construction of thousands of new hospitals in underserved communities but at the same time provided grants to racially segregated facilities. Throughout the nineteenth and twentieth centuries, when the US government was giving away land and money almost exclusively to white people, neither party centered its political platform on complaints about welfare and dependency. That would come later, and the historical inconsistency suggested to me that America might be a socialist worker's paradise were it not for the presence of Black people. Even if there had been no racial bias, the history of progressive legislation revealed little evidence that ambitious race-neutral policies could ever eliminate persistent race-specific disparities.

This is a fundamental challenge facing progressives in the twenty-first century. It is perfectly appropriate to pursue social justice policies and economic policies that make life fairer for everyone. But until we address the lingering racial inequality in America, these policies will not depose the existing racial hierarchy. A rising tide may lift all boats, but it will not turn a canoe into a cruise ship. For Black Americans, we have survived for centuries in the functional equivalent of canoes while white America has sailed relatively smoothly, even in sometimes stormy weather, in the comparative comfort of a cruise ship.

When lawmakers have chosen to address racial disparities directly with race-specific policies, they have often faced resistance, from the Freedman's Bureau during Reconstruction to the debate over reparations and racial equity today. But there need be no inconsistency in embracing broad and inclusive economic policies while also adopting race-specific policies to eradicate persistent disparities.

All of this will require some discomfort, but as Ibram X. Kendi explains in *How to Be an Antiracist*, "The only remedy to racist discrimination is antiracist discrimination," and "the only remedy to past discrimination is present discrimination." We can no longer pretend that treating everyone equally will magically lead to equality as long as one group in society continues to benefit from hundreds of years of racial entitlement denied to all others.

President Lyndon Johnson delivered this message to the graduates of Howard University at the commencement exercises in 1965: "You do not take a person who, for years, has been hobbled by chains and liberate him, bring him up to the starting line of a race and then say, 'you are free to compete with all the others,' and still justly believe that you have been completely fair."

When I speak of equality, I understand that, for many, the term "equity" better explains the principle I am articulating. But I have chosen to embrace the term "equality" because it is the language of our founding document. The equality I speak of is an equality of outcomes, not just opportunities. Equality cannot continue to serve as a convenient excuse to avoid distinctions between racist discrimination and antiracist discrimination. It cannot simply be the act of treating everyone equally today and ignoring the inequality of yesterday. And it cannot be a subterfuge to perpetuate long-standing racial privilege. In short, equality can no longer remain an unattainable ideal; it must become the actual result.

I am under no illusion that the current white majority in America, goaded by desperate demagogues who exploit white racial resentment, will voluntarily surrender what it perceives to be its dominant birthright. "Power concedes nothing without a demand," Frederick Douglass observed in 1857. But he also understood that "the limits of tyrants are prescribed by the endurance of those whom they oppress."

For centuries, white America has been able to cling to power while safe in the knowledge that Black America remained powerless to challenge it. Yet now, as the information age has exposed irrational fears and beliefs of the past, an emerging multiracial and intergenerational coalition has begun to dismantle outdated shibboleths from our old way of life. The tired, racist messaging that focused on crime, welfare, socialism, atheism, and political radicalism has lost its ferocity for a new generation that finds itself more endangered by police brutality, income inequality, unfettered capitalism, white evangelicalism, and political incrementalism.

What's happening in America right now is not "cancel culture"; it's accountability. People who have long been privileged because of their race, their gender, their sexual orientation, their occupation, their religion, their economic status, or their political party are suddenly finding themselves challenged by people who previously had no major platform from which they could object. White people are being held accountable for their daily casual racism. Men are being held accountable for their sexual misconduct in the workplace. Cisgender straight people are being held accountable for their homophobia and transphobia. Police officers are being held accountable for their brutality. Christians are being held accountable for their failure to live up to their principles. The wealthy are being held accountable for their failure to contribute their fair share to the nation. And Republicans are being held accountable for perpetuating an antidemocratic system of government that distorts the will of the new emerging majority of the American people. In their complaints about "cancel culture" and the alleged deprivation of their freedom, many of the people in privileged positions refuse to acknowledge the first fundamental rule of freedom—that freedom of speech does not mean freedom from consequences of your speech.

But this is a debate that Republicans now relish. After spending the 2020 campaign warning the country about "radical Democrats" and "socialism," they discovered that the Democrats' economic proposals were actually quite popular. A Politico/Morning Consult poll in March 2021 found that 75 percent of Americans approved of the Democrats' American Rescue Plan to respond to pressures wrought by the COVID pandemic. The law provided direct payment of $1,400, expanded unemployment assistance, and a new monthly child tax credit. As it turns out, Bill Clinton was wrong when he declared "the era of big government is over." As I had long believed,

Americans have never fully opposed government support. Instead, they opposed other people, whom they considered undeserving, getting government support. The new economic reality poses a challenge for the GOP. Republicans haven't bothered to develop any serious new economic policies to respond to America's needs, and so they have little choice but to divert our attention to divisive social issues. They would rather complain about a handful of Dr. Seuss's books being removed by his estate or about the degendering of Mr. Potato Head because these issues contribute to their false narrative about an oppressive "cancel culture" that victimizes cisgender heterosexual white men, who currently control nearly every lever of power in America.

Years ago, I came across a passage in the writings of John Boswell that forced me to consider what my law professor Derrick Bell called "the permanence of racism." Boswell quoted German author Moritz Goldstein to explain the difficulty of convincing people to abandon their prejudices: "We can easily reduce our detractors to absurdity and show them their hostility is groundless. But what does this prove? That their hatred is real. When every slander has been rebutted, every misconception cleared up, every false opinion about us overcome, intolerance itself will remain finally irrefutable." I am not at all convinced that the changing demographics of America will reduce or eliminate racism and prejudice in this country. But I do believe we have an opportunity to create change if we use this time wisely.

We have reached the point where the clichéd threats of the past no longer command electoral majorities or frighten oppressed minorities. Only under these conditions, when white interests finally recognize a threat to the dominant social structure of ignoring the pleas of Black and brown voices, will the powerful even consider concessions. As Derrick Bell argued in his "interest convergence" theory, "the interest of Blacks in achieving racial equality will be accommodated only when it converges with the interests of whites." But Black liberation need not be dependent on white acceptance, as Charles Blow argues.

And now we find ourselves facing two distinct choices. Will we accept another temporary truce to cease the fire between the warring factions of the nation and restore the existing world order, or will we finally negotiate a new treaty that commits America to its founding goal of equality?

We cannot simply relax and expect that the passage of time and the diversification of the nation will inevitably eliminate the problems of racism in America. Indeed, there is every reason to believe that these changes will exacerbate racial tension in the years to come for those who most fear the change. But we have a duty to create the change we seek in the world, to live it, to be it. As civil rights icon John Lewis reminded us, we have "a moral obligation" to go out and seek justice for all and to "get in good trouble" to build what Dr. King called "the beloved community."

This work will not be easy. But I find inspiration in the poetry of three Black women. The first, Audre Lorde, reminds me, "When I dare to be powerful, to use my strength in the service of my vision, then it becomes less and less important whether I am afraid." The second, June Jordan, tells us, "We are the ones we have been waiting for." The third, Amanda Gorman, shares this truth: "There is always light, if only we're brave enough to see it. If only we're brave enough to be it."

AUTHOR'S NOTE

Much of my understanding of race in America is shaped by my personal experience as a Black gay man and by my nontraditional path from St. Louis to Harlem by way of politics, journalism, law, academia, and, ultimately, media. These experiences have taken me from the White House to American University to the National Black Justice Coalition to a Showtime reality TV series to BET, CNN, and the Institute for Research in African-American Studies at Columbia University.

Additionally, a number of important books have influenced the ideas in this book. These include *Notes of a Native Son* and *The Fire Next Time* by James Baldwin, *The New Jim Crow: Mass Incarceration in the Age of Colorblindness* by Michelle Alexander, *Stamped from the Beginning: The Definitive History of Racist Ideas in America* and *How to Be an Antiracist* by Ibram X. Kendi, *White Rage: The Unspoken Truth of Our Racial Divide* by Carol Anderson, *Caste: The Origins of Our Discontents* by Isabel Wilkerson, *A Promised Land* by Barack Obama, *The Loneliness of the Black Republican* by Leah Wright Rigueur, *Between the World and Me* and *We Were Eight Years in Power* by Ta-Nehisi Coates, *Sister Outsider* by Audre Lorde, *Brother to Brother: New Writings by Black Gay Men*, edited by Essex Hemphill and conceived by Joseph Beam, and *Home Girls: A Black Feminist Anthology*, edited by Barbara Smith.

The writings and speeches of Malcolm X and Dr. Martin Luther King Jr. were my earliest life influences, along with the books *The Autobiography of Malcolm X: As Told to Alex Haley* and *The Mis-Education of the Negro* by Carter G. Woodson. At Dartmouth College, I won an award that enabled me to buy a copy of the comprehensive 1,500-page book *The Negro Almanac: A Reference Work on the Afro-American*, which I still proudly use. At Harvard Law School, I was influenced by my professors Derrick Bell, Charles Ogletree, Randall Kennedy, Chris Edley, William Rubenstein, Frank Michelman, and Laurence Tribe. It was also there that I was introduced to two hugely influential legal writings. The first was *Brown v. Board of Education and the Interest-Convergence Dilemma* by Derrick Bell. The second was *Demarginalizing the Intersection of Race and Sex: A Black Feminist Critique of Antidiscrimination Doctrine, Feminist Theory and Antiracist Politics* by Kimberlé Crenshaw.

I've also been influenced by the work of Reverend Jesse Jackson, whom I first met as a college student at Dartmouth in January 1984, when he was on his way to a presidential primary debate. He came to Harvard Law School to support our protest movement in 1990. He led our delegation to Zimbabwe in 1997. He sat for a public forum with me at Columbia University in 2016. And he even cornered me in January 2019 in Representative Maxine Waters's office to talk about the importance of recognizing the four-hundred-year anniversary of slavery in America.

Over the years, I've also learned from watching and reading Bree Newsome, Nikole Hannah Jones, Jamil Smith, Jelani Cobb, Michael Eric Dyson, Cornel West, Donna Brazile, Paul Butler, Charles Blow, Rashad Robinson, Clay Cane, Dorian Warren, Malcolm Kenyatta, Jasmyne Cannick, Mandy Carter, Phill Wilson, George M. Johnson, Darnell Moore, Ravi Perry, James Jones, Jemele Hill, Reverend Al Sharpton, Jericho Brown, Tarell Alvin McCraney, Hari Ziyad, Symone Sanders, and Samuel Sinyangwe, and from my media colleagues Joy-Ann Reid, Tiffany Cross, Eugene Scott, Abby Phillip,

Michael Harriot, Don Lemon, Aisha Mills, Jonathan Capehart, Zerlina Maxwell, Bakari Sellers, and Angela Rye.

Finally, the only pleasure reading I had time to do while writing this book was Robert Jones Jr.'s beautiful novel *The Prophets*; choosing to read it was one of the best decisions I ever made.

ACKNOWLEDGMENTS

In the fall of 2018, one of my former students from Columbia University reached out to me with a question. He wanted to know if I had followed up on an idea that I had mentioned in the classroom that I might write a book based on the themes we discussed in the course he took. Although I wanted to write that book, I was overwhelmed at the time with the day-to-day grind of keeping up with Donald Trump for my job as a CNN political commentator. Nevertheless, my former student persisted, offering his help and volunteering to serve as a research assistant if I did pursue my idea. I took him up on that offer, and over the course of the next year, we'd meet nearly every week, researching issues, bouncing off ideas, and developing themes—many of which would eventually find their way into this book. My first acknowledgment is to that former student, Andrew Wang, for his time, dedication, and commitment to this project.

Of course, I also must thank the Institute for Research in African-American Studies at Columbia University, which gave me the opportunity to develop the syllabi for the courses I taught on race and politics, and especially to Shawn Mendoza and Sharon Harris. The young students of all colors who took my classes also deserve credit for challenging me to think more broadly on a number of issues.

Before I began this book, I also had a brief but fortuitous conversation with historian Douglas Brinkley that encouraged me to write. During a break in a TV segment on CNN one day, he asked what projects I was working on. When I mentioned that I was struggling to find time to write a new book, he reminded me that my life would not be defined by "one more TV appearance" but by the body of work that I left behind.

Many others contributed to my ability to complete this book, but a few deserve special recognition. I have to thank my agent, Jane Dystel, for believing in me; my editor, Brandon Proia, for his patience; and my publisher, Clive Priddle, for understanding the importance of this project. Thanks also to Andre Bell, Logan Carrington, and Tony Pinder for sharing your stories with me.

I especially want to thank my friends, Neil Stanley, Flo McAfee, and Nathan Hale Williams, for repeatedly encouraging me to write this book. Thanks to my mom for opening her Texas home to me for nearly four months in 2020, while I was writing and quarantining. Thanks to my TV-scriptwriting partner, Jarrett Hill, who patiently allowed me time to write while we were developing a screenplay. And thanks to my close friends and family— Jeremy Graves, Lorin Brown, Michael Adams, Dr. Maurice Franklin, Kyeng Beeman, James Grooms, Ted Winn, Cheryl Jones, Mike Ramsey, Cameron Jones, Jardin Douglas, Brandon Adams, Keith Dickerson, Robert Dickerson, Reginald Dickerson, Lori Newberry, Hulon Bahar, Julian Roberson, Will Reese, Rochelle Teague, Allen Orr, Krystal Adams, Maiysha Simpson, and Corece, all of whom made this book possible with their love and support.

Credit: Ricky Day

Keith Boykin is a CNN political commentator, *New York Times*–bestselling author, and a former White House aide to President Bill Clinton. Boykin has taught at the Institute for Research in African-American Studies at Columbia University in New York and at American University in Washington, DC. He is a cofounder and first board president of the National Black Justice Coalition. He was a cohost of the BET Network's talk show *My Two Cents* and starred on the Showtime reality television series *American Candidate*. A graduate of Dartmouth College and Harvard Law School, Boykin is a Lambda Literary Award–winning author, and *Race Against Time* is his fifth book. He lives in New York City.